July 3[...]

Dear Elizabeth and Newton —
In celebration of your
fortieth anniversary.
    Love, Sharon and Phil

Netsuke

Netsuke

Fantasy

and Reality

in Japanese

Miniature

Sculpture

JOE EARLE

mfa PUBLICATIONS

a division of the Museum of Fine Arts, *Boston*

MFA PUBLICATIONS *a division of*

the Museum of Fine Arts, Boston

465 Huntington Avenue

Boston, Massachusetts 02115

ISBN 0-87846-622-3

Library of Congress Control Number:

2001088637

Edited by Melanie Drogin

Design and composition by
Lucinda Hitchcock

Typesetting by Frances Presti-Fazio

Printed and bound at

Henry N. Sawyer Company, Inc.,

Charlestown, Massachusetts

For a complete listing of MFA Publications, please contact the publisher at the
above address, or call 617 369 4367.

Available through D.A.P. /

Distributed Art Publishers

155 Sixth Avenue, 2nd floor

New York, NY 10013

TEL. 212 627 1999 FAX 212 627 9484

First edition

Printed in the United States of America

OPPOSITE PAGE: DETAIL,
EAGLE CLUTCHING A MONKEY, CAT. 220;
OVERLEAF: *CHOKARŌ SENNIN*, CAT. 7,
SEATED TIGER, CAT. 256,
THE SUMO BOUT BETWEEN KAWAZU
SABURŌ AND MATANO GORŌ, CAT. 163

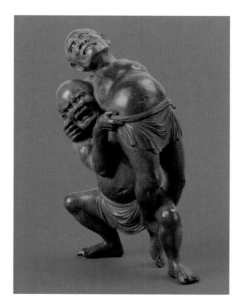

CONTENTS

Director's Foreword

NETSUKE, ENORMOUSLY POPULAR AMONG WESTERN AND, MORE recently, Japanese collectors, have nevertheless received comparatively little attention from art historians and curators. At the Museum of Fine Arts, over the past two years, we have undertaken a systematic re-evaluation of our collection of netsuke – a previously neglected aspect of our immensely rich Japanese holdings. *Netsuke: Fantasy and Reality in Japanese Miniature Sculpture* is one of the largest exhibitions of netsuke ever organized in this country and the quality of objects displayed is unprecedented. Our own finest examples of this miniature art form are displayed alongside masterpieces from private holdings, and we hope that, as a result, interest in our collection as well as in the genre itself will be rekindled among scholars and the general public alike.

One of the tasks of a great museum is to encourage new ways of seeing and thinking, and the present exhibition and catalogue aim to stimulate a significant shift in the world of netsuke studies. Since their introduction to the West, netsuke have become part of a self-contained tradition of collecting, allied to a style of informal scholarship that has seen little need for reference to wider aspects of Japanese or East Asian culture. However, two recent exhibitions held in the United States and Germany attempted, for the first time, to set netsuke firmly in their original cultural context. *Netsuke: Fantasy and Reality* builds on these initiatives, and presents interpretations that can be based on the systematic study of extant netsuke, of contemporary or near-contemporary Japanese documents, and on recent fieldwork in Japan itself.

I would like to express my deep appreciation to Dr. Joseph Kurstin and the other private collectors who, through their generous loans to this exhibition, have shared with the public their passion for these remarkable sculptures. The Museum is also extremely grateful to Joe Earle, formerly Keeper of the Far Eastern Department at London's Victoria and Albert Museum, our guest curator and author of the present catalogue. His innovative approach to the study of netsuke brings new insights to these exquisite objects, making them all the more fascinating and compelling.

Malcolm Rogers
ANN AND GRAHAM GUND DIRECTOR

Netsuke at the Museum of Fine Arts
BOSTON

Anne Nishimura Morse
CURATOR, JAPANESE ART, DEPARTMENT OF THE ART OF ASIA, OCEANIA, AND AFRICA

with Ann B. Simonds

BY 1880, JUST FOUR YEARS AFTER OPENING ITS DOORS, THE MUSEUM OF Fine Arts was acclaimed for the Japanese art it then had on display – embroideries, lacquers, and ivories (*netsuke*) – for it included "the finest examples of every department of Japanese art at its best period and would find a welcome place in any European museum." *The American Architect and Building News* felt confident that these decorative arts would "do much to give prestige to the museum." Since that time the collection of Japanese art at the Museum has indeed attained international recognition. However, since the early twentieth century its reputation has rested primarily in the unrivaled strength of its holdings of paintings, sculptures, and prints, and in the unique role played by its early curators and collectors in the interpretation of Japanese art history. Unlike many of their European and American contemporaries, these men self-consciously strove to acquire works consistent with mid-nineteenth-century Japanese tastes. For these men more "popular" art forms like netsuke, which had previously been seen at the center of the collection, might be placed on view in the galleries, but were not objects for serious study.

In 1877, Edward Sylvester Morse (1838–1925) traveled to Japan, where he assumed a position as a professor of zoology. Morse, who became interested in ceramics and later sold his collection of over five thousand objects to the Museum, trained under the antiquarian Ninagawa Noritane. Through this introduction, Morse came to prefer understated tea-ceremony wares rather than the exquisite porcelains favored in the West. Similarly, Ernest Francisco Fenollosa (1853–1908), professor of philosophy in Tokyo and a member of the Imperial Art Commission, sought

instruction in painting connoisseurship from members of the Kanō school – formerly the hereditary painters to the military rulers. As a consequence, Fenollosa came to elevate the works of the established schools of aristocratic art, and voiced his disdain for *ukiyo-e* by the "plebeian" artists, then so widely admired in Europe. William Sturgis Bigelow (1850–1926), the scion of a wealthy Boston family who followed Morse to Japan and became a patron of the arts there, purchased thousands of Japanese paintings of the types preferred by Fenollosa and Japanese collectors. Nevertheless, he also purchased Japanese art of the type so appreciated by Westerners – more than 50,000 *ukiyo-e* prints and about 625 netsuke, some of which he gave to the Museum in 1911 and others he bequeathed in 1926.

In the early decades of the Meiji era (1868–1912), when the three Boston collectors were in residence in Japan, few Japanese were actively forming netsuke collections (one notable exception was the head of Mitsubishi, Iwasaki Yanosuke (1851–1908)). The Tokyo National Museum would not acquire any significant works until the bequest

of the Gō collection in 1942. Dealers in Yokohama, such as Wakamatsuya, Deaken Brothers & Company, and E. Amsden, and others in Tokyo, such as Handaya in the Ginza, offered "ivory carvings and all other kinds of curios," but they were primarily for the Western market. Although Bigelow must have acquired at least two-thirds of his netsuke in Japan from 1882 through 1889, his interest in the art form actually was developed earlier during his post-graduate years in Europe. Traveling to Vienna in 1876 and then to Paris in order to study bacteriology with Louis Pasteur, Bigelow soon discovered the delights of netsuke. The miniature sculptures had become increasingly popular in Europe since the Japanese govern-ment had presented a small number of works at the international exposition in Paris in 1867, and approximately forty at the exposition in Vienna in 1873. French dealers – Siegfried Bing and Philippe and August Sichel, for example – also tried to satisfy the growing fashion for "things Japanese" through offerings of woodblock prints, printed books (*ehon*) and decorative arts, netsuke among them. Bigelow himself is known to have frequented

A L'Empire Chinois, a Parisian shop on the Rue Vivienne, which not only offered tea and "chinoisseries" but also the Japanese works then so in demand.

Immediately upon his return from Europe in 1879, Bigelow shared his newly acquired netsuke with the Boston public by placing over 177 on loan to the Museum for exhibition. A similar loan was made in 1890 of the netsuke he acquired in Japan. By the first years of the twentieth century, the Museum had devoted a large glass case in its galleries to these netsuke. Archival photographs reveal an interest in nineteenth-century *okimono*, but works included in the current exhibition – *Eagle Clutching a Monkey* by Rantei II of Kyoto (cat. 220), *Sleeping Shōjō* by Ichiun of Nagoya (cat. 108), the Iwami school *Centipede on a Taro Leaf* by Seiyōdō Bunshō (cat. 182), and *Hare and Biwa* by Okatomo of Kyoto (cat. 260) – also are displayed on the shelves.

In 1914, following the first complete cataloging of the Bigelow gift, the Museum produced a gallery book devoted to netsuke. Part of a then innovative program created by the Museum at the suggestion of Okakura Kakuzō, the former Curator of the Department of Chinese and Japanese Art, these guides were not intended necessarily to provide "instruction about the objects shown, but to dispose to their enjoyment." The Museum felt that it was important to explore the art of Asia in the initial volumes "since it most needs interpretation to our public." By 1915 the netsuke catalogue had been rewritten to include sixty pages with descriptions of every object shown; Japanese characters were provided for all terms. Repeated editions followed, and the 1923 version noted, "When something more is known of the great variety of subjects the carvings portray, drawn from the life and legends of old Japan, their study becomes a delight."

Following the Bigelow loans and gifts to the Museum, a small number of collectors continued to add to the Museum's holdings of netsuke, which now have come to number over 1300 examples ranging in date from the late seventeenth to the late nineteenth century. Contributors have included the Boston physician Charles Goddard Weld, who left the Museum over thirty *kagamibuta* (turned

ivory or wood disks fitted with metal plates) in 1911, and the trustee and benefactor Denman Waldo Ross, who donated six netsuke in 1917. In that same year, Lydia S. Hays of Pittsburgh willed thirty-four netsuke to the Museum. Among these were the stained boxwood *Frog on a Taro Leaf* by Shimizu Tomiharu (cat. 187) and *Baku King* by the mid- to late-nineteenth-century artist Gyokumin (cat. 90). Writing to John Ellerton Lodge, who was then Assistant Curator in the Department of Chinese and Japanese Art at the Museum, Hays stated that she had been forming her collection "to express the beliefs, miths[sic] and folklore of the Japanese . . . and to secure the best workmanship that comes to [her] notice." However, the most significant additions to the collection were made shortly after the Second World War by Ernest Goodrich Stillman (1884–1949).

Ernest Goodrich Stillman, an epidemiologist of respiratory diseases at Rockefeller Hospital in New York, was also the director of many companies, including a small publishing house, Duffield & Green. He became fascinated by netsuke following a pre-college trip to Japan, and developed an extensive collection which he kept together with Nō masks and prints in his home. In 1924, Stillman edited a translation of *Netsuke*, the authoritative volume by the German scholar Albert Brockhaus. Unable to reproduce the illustrations of the original, Stillman used photographs of works from his own collection – pieces such as the late-eighteenth-century *Ijin with Drum* by Hōgen Higuchi Shūgetsu of Osaka and Edo (cat. 27), the late-eighteenth- or early-nineteenth-century *Broom* (cat. 176), the mid-nineteenth-century *Ashinaga Hugging a Tree Trunk* (cat. 28), and the boxwood *Mushrooms* (cat. 179) by an unidentified mid-nineteenth-century artist. An extremely private person, whose many contributions to his alma mater, Harvard College, and to his community were made anonymously, Stillman wrote a most unassuming letter of inquiry to the Museum in 1946. Addressing his letter to the Curator of the Japanese Collection, Stillman mentioned, "As I have a few Japanese mementos which I am bequeathing to the Boston Museum of Fine Arts I thought you might like to glance at them." By the beginning of 1947, Stillman had donated 582 netsuke to the Museum; a similar gift of 628 objects was made to the Peabody Museum in Salem that year.

For many years the Museum's netsuke, displayed in their original early-twentieth-century exhibition case, were some of the objects most beloved by members of the public. However, with the closing of the Japanese galleries in the late 1970s for a renovation intended to provide a more "up-to-date" presentation, the netsuke were taken off view. A small selection was returned to display in 1997, though without individual labeling. Thus, the current exhibition provides the Museum with an exciting opportunity to reexamine its netsuke. Not only has guest curator Joe Earle selected some of the finest pieces from the collection, but he has also approached these fascinating objects with the inquiry of a scholar of Japanese art and culture. Referring to a vast array of Edo period encyclopedias, painting commentaries and manuals, illustrated books from the Museum's extensive collection, and other original sources in Japanese, Earle has explored the rich visual context for the creation of netsuke and has increased our knowledge and appreciation of these fabulous objects – for which collectors and curators alike can be most grateful.

Netsuke: FANTASY AND REALITY IN JAPANESE MINIATURE SCULPTURE

Joe Earle

The Origins and Functions of Netsuke

THE TERM *NETSUKE*, AS UNDERSTOOD TODAY BOTH INSIDE AND OUTSIDE Japan, most often refers to a miniature sculpture, not more than about six inches in its largest dimension and usually nearer to two or three, that is carved from wood or ivory and drilled with a passage allowing it to be threaded on a cord. Netsuke are generally believed to have been first used in Japan toward the end of the sixteenth century or the beginning of the seventeenth century, when it became fashionable to carry everyday necessities in a number of small containers suspended from the waist, including cloth and leather purses, *inrō* (tiered medicine containers), and pouches for tobacco. These containers were suspended by silk cords. At first, the cords were tied to a ring that passed around the *obi* or sash, but in time the ring was replaced by the *kara*, a smaller, thicker ring that did not pass around the o*bi*. Instead, the cords were tied together through the hole in the center of the *kara;* the *kara* then was drawn up between the *obi* and the wearer's body until it emerged above the *obi*. The *kara* was worn either just above or tucked into the folds of the *obi*, serving as a toggle that prevented the cords from slipping down and the suspended containers from falling to the ground. Toward the middle of the seventeenth century, these simple *kara* evolved into a buttonlike shape with two *himotōshi*, connecting holes through which the silk cords could be passed, drilled unobtrusively in one side only (see fig. 1). Such simple proto-netsuke began to be replaced by imported Chinese ivory carvings, and during the last quarter of the seventeenth century Japanese craftsmen started to make figure netsuke, at first mainly in ivory but later often in wood and other materials as well. The earliest Japanese netsuke were carved in Osaka and Kyoto (the Imperial capital), but in the late eighteenth century the production of netsuke began in Edo (the shogun's capital) as well as in several regional centers. During the nineteenth century, carvers proliferated and enormous numbers of netsuke were turned out, until the gradual abandonment of traditional dress (at least for everyday male wear) during the 1860s and 1870s eliminated the need for netsuke, which continued to be made for export and for specialized Japanese collectors.

Although postwar scholars have tended to stress the practical origins and nature of netsuke, as outlined above, a study of the written, pictorial, and material evidence suggests that this emphasis may be misplaced. It would be easy to create a narrative in which the practical need for, and use of, toggles in ancient cultures (African, European, and mainland Asian) leads inexorably through time and space to their adoption in early modern Japan. Such an approach is temptingly fashionable, since it favors the propaganda of the "Silk Road," according to which Japan has been presented on occasion as a pioneer of globalism. However, this model fails to take account of the fact that netsuke were never, strictly speaking, necessary or practical: they should be viewed primarily as fashion accessories and cultural artifacts, rather than as mere mechanical toggles that somehow were transmuted into "works of art," as most conventional accounts would have it.

The existence of netsuke is invariably ascribed to the fact that traditional Japanese dress has no pockets. Other cultures, however, also lack pockets in their dress but have failed to develop toggles, and the containers used by the Japanese could have been secured just as (if not more) safely by passing the cords around (instead of just behind) the *obi* and finishing them in a knot, which could have been hidden behind the *obi*. The very existence of the ring device described earlier (which seems to have been in occasional use as late as 1690) demonstrates that other solutions to the problem were tried out before, or concurrently with, the earliest toggles, and some early screens show suspended containers without any sort of toggle or similar device at all.

Above all, conventional accounts fail to take note of the importance of netsuke as fashion accessories. In paintings, our only early source of evidence about the appearance of netsuke prototypes, even the early rings and buttons are depicted as white objects. Thus, they presumably were fashioned not from mundane, workaday wood, but from ivory, a rare, expensive, and exotic imported material (a written source indicates that, by 1686, they also were made from copper). Like other accessories worn and used in the Momoyama (1573–1615) and early Edo (1615–1868) periods, such as Christian rosaries or tobacco pipes, *kara* marked their users as culturally sensitive men of the world (even at this early stage, women do not seem to have worn netsuke or the earlier prototypes), aware of the customs and products of distant lands. A little later, small branches of coral were favored as netsuke for the same reason, as were materials such as quartz and imported hardwoods. If the practical function of proto-netsuke was ambiguous at best, this is truer still of the figure netsuke that seem to have developed from the 1680s. As we have seen, the earliest were Chinese objects of a kind depicted in volume seven of *Sōken kishō,* a key netsuke text published in Osaka in 1781. The compiler of *Sōken kishō,* Inaba Tsūryū, notes that such carvings did not "hang" in their country of origin, but served instead as seals, sword hilts, hat decorations, and the like. Some of these objects had to be drilled with holes before they could be used as netsuke in Japan, where (as Inaba stresses) they were admired above all for their *ki,* "strangeness." Perhaps significant is the fact that Inaba was unaware of Chinese toggles, simple carvings of ivory or wood which are sometimes similar in subject matter to early Japanese figure netsuke, including *sennin, shishi,* horned dragons, Tekkai Sensei, and Kō Sensei. Inaba's ignorance of them may be due to the fact that they were fashionable in northern China rather than in the lower Yangzi River region, the area from which most trade with Japan was conducted. Bigger ivory carvings from that part of China, by contrast, seem to have been a significant source of ideas for the first carvers of figure netsuke, and may even account for the large size of some old pieces, while "strangeness" or otherness, as we shall see, was one of the keynotes of all early netsuke.

It is significant that the presumed date of the earliest Japanese figure netsuke, around 1700 or a little earlier, coincides with the growth in popularity of dolls in Japan. Although of ancient origin, so-called "traditional" Japanese *ningyō* dolls actually reached something like their modern form in the middle of the Edo period, as did the widespread popularity of the custom – previously restricted to elite circles – of displaying large arrays of court dolls on the Girls' Festival (third day of the third month) and of samurai dolls at the Boys'

Festival (fifth day of the fifth month). Such dolls were, of course, clothed, but they were also painted, as were netsuke by many of the artists described in *Sōken kishō,* although few of them have survived. At a more sophisticated level, the priest-sculptor Shimizu Ryūkei, who was born in 1659 and still active in 1732, took time off after the death of his master, Tankei, to produce figurines instead of Buddhist images. Ryūkei's masterpiece in this genre was an extraordinary series of one hundred miniature carvings, mostly about 2½ in. (6 cm) high, representing different types of people walking the streets of Kyoto. Twentieth-century historians have tried to account for the existence of these unexpected rarities by describing Ryūkei as "eccentric," but his figurines are in fact significant as attributed examples of a more widespread production of Kyoto artisans. *Saga ningyō,* for example, thought to have originated in the middle of the seventeenth century, depict subjects that are also very popular in netsuke, such as Hotei with *karako* (Chinese children) or children holding dogs or birds. In the case of netsuke, by the eighteenth century the children would often be replaced by Chinese or Dutch figures whose garments are adorned with the same wave-crest motifs seen on the Saga dolls. *Kamo ningyō,* carved from willow at Kyoto's Kamo Shrine, are on the same scale as Ryūkei's creations, and their smiling expressions are strongly reminiscent of some late-eighteenth- and early-nineteenth-century figure netsuke, while *karakuri ningyō,* automated (rather than static) human and other figures of every size, from miniature to larger-than-life, certainly played a very important part in the popular urban culture of the middle and later eighteenth and nineteenth centuries. Furthermore, while it has long been understood that netsuke were often produced as a sideline by artisans who were employed principally as carvers of Buddhist images, there is also evidence that some netsuke carvers were better known for their dolls. A shopping guide published in 1824, about a century after the date of Ryūkei's figurines, lists Hara Shūgetsu (Shūgetsu II), familiar to Western collectors as a carver of figure netsuke, as a master maker of dolls for the Girls' Festival. Writing around the same time, Matsura Seizan (1760–1841), a learned daimyō (regional lord) whose account of his lost collection of dress accessories is a valuable source of information about the consumption and appreciation of netsuke, uses the term *ningyō* (doll) in his detailed discussion of one of his treasures, a standing peasant woman: "When you looked at this *ningyō* from underneath, you could just see her private parts between her thighs."

Matsura could remember around forty-five of his netsuke, and this quantity reveals to us just how rarely an individual netsuke might have been worn during its owner's life. Furthermore, Matsura's very clear and specific recollection of many pieces suggests that he must have been in the regular habit of looking at and handling (as opposed to wearing) them. Many of the miniature sculptures presented in this catalogue show signs of wear on the outer surfaces that cannot be attributed to long periods of time hanging at their owners' *obi*, but which are due, more likely, to years (or perhaps decades) of loving appreciation of their tactile qualities. It might be imagined,

although there is no pictorial or written testimony to support this, that they sometimes served also as paper weights or simply as desk ornaments (executive toys, if you will), much as smaller jades apparently were used in China. In 1778, at the very time at which some of the most highly regarded netsuke – Kyoto animal figurines – were being carved, the *Shikigusa*, a collection of essays, noted that "*inrō* have lost their function and are only popular trifles." Perhaps the same was already true of many figure netsuke as well. In any event, such evidence as we have suggests that, until about 1800 or even later, both figure netsuke in particular and *katabori* netsuke in general (those carved in the round, including both figures and other subjects) were outnumbered by other types, such as *kagami* or *kagamibuta* netsuke (a durable, turned ivory or wood disk fitted with a metal plate), seals, small natural dried gourds, pieces of coral, and so on. While all (or nearly all) early *katabori* netsuke are drilled with *himotōshi* holes, the very fact that these are nearly always shaped and positioned in such a way that they not only allow the carving to hang naturally, but also interfere as little as possible with the design, implies that it was as important for netsuke to be appreciated in private (off their cords) as in public (on their cords).

During the first half of the nineteenth century, ivory *katabori* netsuke were carved in Edo in enormous numbers. These netsuke grew more and more elaborate and, to modern eyes, of less aesthetic significance (few examples are included in this catalogue). They were also increasingly impractical, with a host of intricate and protruding details that could easily break off in use. It may be this trend, rather than (as is often suggested) the destruction wrought by the great earthquake of 1855, that made the *kagamibuta netsuke* an even more popular alternative toggle at the end of the Edo period, while some later netsuke perhaps came to be appreciated simply as homely curios. If this hypothesis is correct, it is possible that netsuke had become little more than collectors' items even before the arrival of large numbers of foreign tourists eager to buy them as intricate, portable souvenirs. It would be only a slight exaggeration, then, to turn conventional wisdom on its head and suggest that sculptural netsuke, rather than being developed from functional toggles into works of art, originated, and continued to be appreciated, as cultural artifacts that could also be put to the service of a physical need. The functional aspects of netsuke that are regarded as masterpieces by today's collectors – compactness, avoidance of easily breakable protrusions – were perhaps appreciated even in the Edo period as much for their creative as for their practical significance.

The Singularity of Early Netsuke

Contemporary American and European netsuke-lovers are apt to lament that their treasured carvings have received scant attention from mainstream academic historians of Japanese art. It is true that, to some extent, netsuke have suffered much like other applied arts of the Edo period, such as lacquer and metalwork, which often have been neglected in the academy (if not in the marketplace) in favor of prints, paintings, and other artifacts. In the case of netsuke, it is perhaps their very oddness that has contributed most to this lack of scholarly regard. The strongly China-centered focus of many of the early carvings, discussed below, runs contrary to conventional ideas about the emergence of a uniquely Japanese style of *chōnin bunka* ("townspeople's culture"), and with it, a uniquely Japanese style of decoration, in the late seventeenth and early eighteenth centuries. These anonymous figurines are apparently "popular" in some sense, yet they are made from an alien, nontraditional material not seen much in Japanese art before the seventeenth century. The very idea of creating figures in ivory owes much to the ivory carving industry that sprang up in coastal regions of China (partly stimulated by Western demand for Christian religious images) toward the end of the sixteenth century. Furthermore, the subjects of early netsuke tend to be rather obscure continental deities and other beings that do not fit comfortably into any predefined social or cultural category.

Sōken kishō (1781), the important netsuke text mentioned earlier, includes a much-quoted list of netsuke artists that is headed by a detailed biography of Yoshimura Shūzan (d. 1777), a resident of Osaka. Shūzan never signed his work, but he is known widely even today as the presumed author of a number of powerful, unsigned netsuke of mythical humans, semihumans, and deities, carved in lightweight cypress wood and with traces of color. In addition to having more of his designs reproduced than any other artist featured in *Sōken kishō*, Shūzan received the singular accolade of a short essay by his son Shūkei, which goes further than the brief entries on most of the other carvers listed. This little biography mentions that Shūzan took many of his netsuke motifs from Chinese illustrated books such as *Shanhaijing* (The Book of Hills and Seas) and the *Liexian zhuan* (Classified Accounts of Deities). The latter work, of uncertain origin, is thought to have been compiled during the Eastern Han Dynasty (25–220). The original text contained seventy accounts of *xian* or *xianren* (in Japanese, *sen* or *sennin*), perfected human beings who transcend everyday life and seek freedom by taking leave of their bodies or dwelling in the depths of rivers. The book was augmented in later dynasties, and an illustrated version, *Liexian quanzhuan* (Complete Stories of Immortals), was published in 1600. Featuring no fewer than 497 deities, it was reissued without significant alteration in Kyoto in 1650 under the title *Yūshō ressen zenden* (Complete Illustrated Stories of Immortals), the first of many Japanese *sennin*-related titles that would be immensely influential for early netsuke. The other work referred to by Shūkei, *Shanhaijing,* is even earlier than *Liexian zhuan,* parts of it dating back to China's Warring States period (4th–3rd century BC). This work attempts to give a comprehensive account of Chinese geography and folklore, providing details, region by region, of rivers, mountains, roads, peoples, products, medicines, and, most importantly for netsuke history, fabulous creatures. An illustrated version appeared during the late Ming Dynasty (1368–1644), a boom time for picture books of every kind, and numerous ephemeral versions, in a variety of different formats, were published during the following Qing Dynasty (1644–1912).

Although Shūkei does not mention Japanese (as opposed to Chinese) encyclopedias as an influence on his father's work, the visual evidence suggests that such publications were another important source of subject matter for early carvers. Works such as *Kinmō zui* (an encyclopedia published in 1666) include prototypes, the majority of Chinese origin, for many of the most popular netsuke subjects, among them *oni* (demons), *sennin*, both Asian and European foreigners, *konron* (people of color), Tartar archers, *ashinaga* (long legs) and *tenaga* (long arms), fabulous beasts such as *kirin* and *baku,* long-haired dogs, and different types of dragons. Among later encyclopedias, the much-cited *Wakan sansai zue* (Illustrated Japanese-Chinese Encyclopedia of the Three Powers), published by the Osaka-based physician and scholar Terashima Ryōan in 1716, is perhaps the most famous of all reference works published during the first half of the Edo period.

Shūkei's biography of his father, Yoshimura Shūzan, fails to mention one exceptionally significant fact: in his own time, Shūzan was best known not as a netsuke carver but as a painter, and especially as the illustrator of a number of volumes of reproductions of earlier Japanese and Chinese paintings. The internal evidence of *Sōken kishō* suggests, in fact, that it was associated with a very close-knit group of painters working in the great commercial center of Osaka. The reproductions of Shūzan's own works by his grandson Shūnan include some of the subjects encountered most frequently in early netsuke: Kan'u with his halberd, Shōki the Demon Queller, and Tekkai Sensei, as well as a few outlandish creatures such as the tentatively identified God of Mount Shitsugozan and the rain dragon. But most of the pictures in *Sōken kishō* are by Tachibana Kunio, another Osaka artist, whose master Tachibana Morikuni (1679–1748), like Shūzan, was a prolific book illustrator. Morikuni's published works include a pictorial encyclopedia of things Chinese, *Morokoshi kinmō zui,* as well as a wealth of other volumes depicting scenes from Japanese and Chinese history and legend.

As numerous examples in this catalogue demonstrate, illustrations by Shūzan and Mitsukuni (as well as those of another Osaka-born artist, Ōoka Shunboku [1680–1763], who produced very similar books) strongly influenced the designs of contemporary netsuke as well as those produced in the half century or so after the artists' deaths. Those by Shūzan in particular are replete with images of fabulous Chinese beasts – *kirin, hakutaku, shishi,* and the like – while Morikuni's pictures offered an exceptionally rich selection of scenes from Japanese and Chinese myth and legend. Both artists, Shūzan and Morikuni, had trained in the studios of the Kanō dynasty of official academic painters. Morikuni was a pupil of Tanzan, himself a pupil of no less a painter than Kanō Tan'yū, one of the greatest artists of the seventeenth century, but Morikuni's habit of publishing Kanō pictures in book form is said to have enraged the Kanō school, which forced Tanzan to disown him. Shūzan was the pupil of another Kanō artist, Mitsunobu. In studying the painters associated with *Sōken kishō,* as well as the illustrated books and encyclopedias that appear to have influenced early netsuke, a picture emerges of a group of intellectuals and artists based

in Osaka (where some of the earliest signed netsuke certainly were carved). These artists possessed an educating, popularizing instinct and a strong interest in things un-Japanese: imaginary Chinese beings, faraway places, and real and imaginary foreigners, a class of subject matter that has been subsumed in this catalogue under the single title *ijin* ("people of difference"). As one of the first applied art forms to be influenced decisively by illustrated books (and a very particular class of illustrated book), figure netsuke, from their earliest years, stood somewhat outside the mainstream of traditional craft production. They were "popular" items, to be sure, but not in the conventional sense. Theirs was a kind of learned popularity that appealed, we may speculate, to the escapist instincts of a small segment of the Osaka elite whose dangerous, even subversive, curiosity about the world beyond Japan was sublimated into small, inconspicuous artifacts.

Netsuke and the Printed Page

The picture books mentioned in the previous section were not designed primarily with the netsuke carver in mind, although Ōoka Shunboku designed three volumes of patterns for *ranma,* the decorative openwork transoms seen in Edo period interiors, which could have been used by other carvers. Works like Yoshimura Shūzan's *Wakan meihitsu zuhō* (An Illustrated Treasury of Japanese and Chinese Painting), or the anonymous *Ehon shoshin hashiradate* (An Illustrated Primer for Beginners), were intended to offer instructive

examples to aspiring painters. This was precisely why they were occasionally resented, as we have seen, by the academics for revealing secrets and thereby depriving them of gainful employment. Without these books, familiar Edo period motifs such as Tekkai Sennin would never have achieved wide currency. Tekkai had been known in Japan since the fourteenth century, when a painting of him by the Chinese artist Yan Hui was imported, but such ancient treasures remained largely inaccessible in the storehouses of Zen temples, while sixteenth- and seventeenth-century versions by the Kanō masters were hardly any easier to study and copy.

The evidence of examples in this catalogue demonstrates that these books, or perhaps copies of selected pages from them, also were used by netsuke carvers. In a few cases, the connection between printed image and carved miniature seems very close, but still more striking is the fact that the medium of the original – monochrome woodblock prints – had a profound influence on the appearance of early netsuke. The strong black lines on white paper translated naturally to ivory carving with heavy staining, and the need to turn these images into practical netsuke inspired ingenious efforts to simplify their overall forms. It is sometimes possible even to propose a change in design source for a particular subject, as with the three carvings of Kan'u in this catalogue: the first two were likely based on Chinese carvings, while the third is a close adaptation of a printed page by Morikuni. In other cases, such as the duck by Masanao of Kyoto or the boar carvings that conclude this catalogue, we can even try to identify the dividing line between the visible prototype and hidden elements, only necessary in a three-dimensional treatment, that were the product of the carver's imagination.

These early illustrated manuals were followed closely by others that were targeted directly at craftsmen. One of the most famous late-eighteenth-century examples is Kitao Masayoshi's *Shoshoku ekagami* (A Pictorial Reference Book for All Crafts, 1794), with its spreads of animals (fig. 2) or different poses for Shōki the Demon Queller (fig. 3).

Although not specifically intended for use by netsuke carvers (designs from the book also are seen in lacquer, for example), the publication of *Shoshoku ekagami* may point to the moment in history when *katabori* netsuke production really took off, attracting less skilled artisans who needed a ready source of designs. It is perhaps significant that many of its illustrations are of zodiac animals, so important in middle- and later-period netsuke. The myriad of tiny vignettes in Hokusai's vast series of *Manga*, published from 1814, were another source of incidental inspiration. However, later books such as *Banshoku zukō* (Pictures and Designs for All Crafts, 1835) by Hokusai's follower Katsushika Taitō, or Ichiryūsai Hiroshige's *Shoshoku gatsū* (Designs for All Crafts, 1864), are much more prescriptive, effectively offering detailed blueprints, sometimes with front, back, and side views, which enabled even the most uncreative carvers to produce passable carvings. Such netsuke have been excluded, however, from the present selection.

Netsuke from 1781 to the Twentieth Century

The year 1781, when *Sōken kishō* was published, coincidentally may mark something of a watershed in netsuke history. Although the vast majority of the carvers listed therein were residents of Osaka and Kyoto, a few lived in Edo and other regional centers, such as Nagoya; the reputation of Tomotada (a Kyoto artist) had reached Edo, to the extent that large numbers of fake Tomotadas were already in circulation. Perhaps one of the reasons for the publication of volume seven of *Sōken kishō*

was to tap into a pool of aspiring but igno-rant collectors, eager to buy a guide to a newly fashionable art form that was no longer the preserve of an informed elite. It seems to have been around this time, or perhaps a little earlier, that some of the netsuke most highly regarded by today's collectors began to appear on the market. The animal carvings of the Kyoto artists Masanao, Tomotada, Okatomo, and their immediate successors certainly took netsuke to a new level, exploiting real or imagined practical requirements to create a type of precise, detailed, and compact sculpture that is perhaps without equal anywhere in the world. For this reason, they are represented quite disproportionately here.

As the introductory notes and individual entries indicate, netsuke in the classic "Kyoto" style, aside from their unique sculptural qualities, also may seem truer to life than the carvings of the early and mid-eighteenth century; hence the "Fantasy and Reality" of our title. This development owes something to contemporary developments in painting, but we should be wary of claiming that it has much to do with direct observation of nature. Most of the animals, after all, are still imaginary: dragons, *kirin*, and *shishi* literally so, while eighteenth-century artists had limited access to goats or tigers (Kyoto carvings of the latter are based closely on traditional Kanō models). At the same time, there is no denying the very marked contrast between, for example, "traditional" netsuke of foreigners and the more naturalistic figurines by Masanao, even if these, too, perhaps were based on a printed source, this time Dutch rather than Japanese.

The Kyoto carvers also may have been the first to introduce a narrative element into their work. While the earlier figures of Shōki with an *oni* are essentially static and iconic, the groups of I no Hayata killing the *Nue* and Nitta no Shirō slaying a boar depict a moment in a violent sequence of events, and succeed in doing so without losing sight of the sculptural compactness for which Kyoto netsuke are celebrated. Influenced by the boom in illustrated historical romances in the early years of the nineteenth century, carvers based in Edo exploited the narrative potential of netsuke to the limit, producing a mass of very detailed ivory carvings that are not held in high esteem today. Many of them seem to deny the very nature of the material from which they are made, unlike Kyoto animals, the curving sides of which are not only sculpturally satisfying, but also follow the natural line of the elephant tusk. To modern eyes, the most successful early Edo netsuke are those which stay closer to Osaka and Kyoto prototypes, especially the figures by Shūgetsu (who apparently moved from Osaka to Edo and then back again), Gesshō, and their successors.

Regional carvers such as Toyomasa of Tanba Province, Masanao of Ise Province (not represented here), Otoman of Chikuzen Province, or Tametaka and Tadayoshi of the city of Nagoya were perhaps more inventive than their Edo-based contemporaries in adapting the Kyoto manner and developing a vast range of new models. Toyomasa, in particular, added his own brand of naturalism, tinged with a humorous tendency toward grotesque exaggeration and unexpected reversal of relative sizes. In the remote province of Iwami, the absence of printed design sources may account for the appearance of a relatively limited number of unusual subjects, including centipedes, frogs squatting on taro leaves, and snails. In Osaka, the birthplace of netsuke, the trend during the nineteenth century is toward ever greater refinement, as seen in the work of Mitsuhiro and especially Masatsugu, whose exquisitely finished miniatures were destined mainly for the burgeoning global market. Masaka, another Osaka artist, was more receptive to artistic developments outside the world of netsuke, his oversize *okimono* (larger, nonfunctional carvings) combining elements from early Buddhist statuary as well as from classical Western sculpture. At the same time that Masatsugu was at the height of his powers, netsuke carving in Edo (soon to be renamed Tokyo) was at something of a crossroads. The "eccentric" Kokusai succeeded in reclaiming something of the subversive, otherworldly character of the earliest netsuke, and a good deal of his output was intended for Japanese buyers, while Tōkoku followed Masatsugu down the internationalist route, creating highly finished carvings that used a combination of costly materials to appeal to the Western taste for the mysterious and exotic. Of the few twentieth-century carvers whose work is featured in this catalogue, Sōsui and Gyokusō, both of Tokyo, revived the Edo narrative style in a new form, renouncing all pretense of functionalism and concentrating instead on virtuoso miniature carving, while Shōun of Kyoto faithfully maintained the high finish and hypernaturalism seen in some of Masatsugu's marine subjects.

A Note on the Catalogue

The vast majority of netsuke are, inevitably, copies of (or variations on) other netsuke. Even the earliest pieces were not, in the main, original sculptures springing unaided from the imaginations of their carvers, but were creative, three-dimensional reworkings of a vast inherited corpus of exotic imagery spanning a huge geographical area and a chronological range of more than two millennia. In order to stress this aspect of netsuke history and to stay close to the roots of Edo period miniature carving, the emphasis in this catalogue is on early pieces. This is, therefore, probably one of the first major netsuke catalogues in which over half of the items date from before the early nineteenth century. It is also biased heavily in favor of the western cities of Osaka and Kyoto, with fewer pieces from the eastern city of Edo. As a consequence of the stress on Osaka and Kyoto, there are only a few of the detailed, story-telling, mostly nineteenth-century netsuke that were such favorites with some of the early collectors and curators. It seems that these early connoisseurs may have believed, as noted by Anne Morse in her introduction to this catalogue, that the true delight of netsuke lay in the "great variety of subjects the carvings portray, drawn from the life and legends of old Japan."

To illustrate issues of design origin and sculptural treatment, the present catalogue is organized not into geographical areas, chronological periods, or "schools," but into six sections covering different categories of subject matter. These are preceded by an introductory grouping of four sets showing netsuke in combination with a variety of other items worn at the waist. A special effort has been made not only to give a detailed description of each piece, but also to identify subject matter correctly, particularly by trying to use both words and images from sources such as encyclopedias and picture books that might also have been available to the carvers themselves. This sometimes has led to surprising results, with regard to both identification and nomenclature. In addition, some of the pieces are shown alongside reproductions of Edo period graphic sources, drawn mainly from the extensive holdings of the Museum of Fine Arts, Boston. The purpose of this method of presentation, however, is not to treat netsuke as a kind of encyclopedic window on the Japanese past. The aim instead has been to show how the finest carvers were able to use a received body of imagery to create miniature sculptures of unparalleled beauty and power. In this act of almost magical transmutation, the true delight of netsuke surely lies.

Netsuke

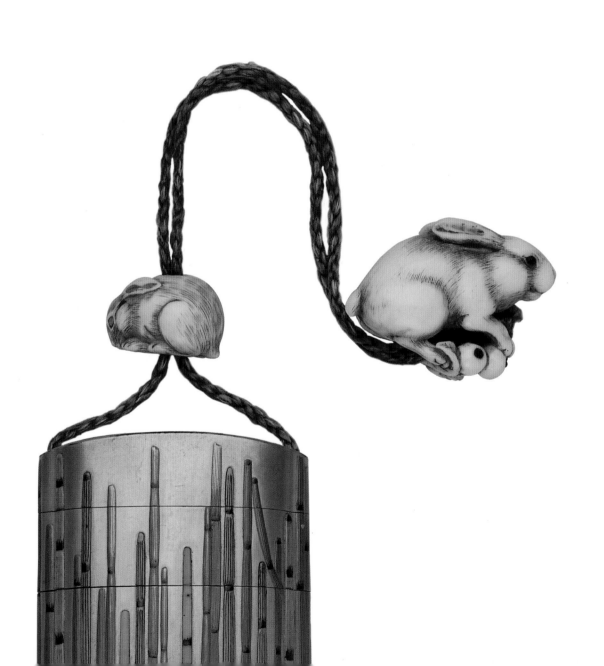

Netsuke in Use

THIS SELECTION OF FOUR SETS SHOWS SOME OF THE OBJECTS THAT WERE worn at the waist in conjunction with netsuke during and just after the Edo period. Although contemporary museum displays in both Japan and the West most often feature netsuke in combination with *inrō* (tiered medicine containers), the available literary and pictorial evidence suggests that during the Edo period, they were used just as often (if not more often) to support other items from the *obi*, such as tobacco pouches, pipecases, or money purses. Sometimes several different items were worn at the same time and supported by a single netsuke, but during the eighteenth century the *inrō* and the *kinchaku,* or purse, came to be separated. The usual custom was for the *inrō* to be be worn at the right and the other items at the left.

The writings of Matsura Seizan (see page 20) offer striking evidence of the importance that was attached to creating appropriate ensembles of netsuke, *inrō*, pipecases, tobacco pouches, and purses with a consistent decorative scheme or symbolic program. Toward the end of the nineteenth century, however, when large numbers of such items were sold to Western collectors, so many ensembles were broken up for commercial reasons that it is often difficult to illustrate this important aspect of the art of the netsuke. Of the four sets shown here, the first is a twentieth-century recreation of a traditional ensemble, but the second may well have been assembled in Edo period Japan. The remaining two both include netsuke of the type known as *kagami* or *kagamibuta*, consisting of a metal plate let into a flat, cup-shaped piece of another material, typically wood or ivory. The decoration of their metal components, at least, is linked by the theme of *Sangokushi*, a popular romance chronicling the heroic deeds of some of China's greatest heroes.

1 | *INRŌ* (medicine case), **NETSUKE** (toggle), **AND** *OJIME* (tightening bead)

The *inrō* in this set, decorated with a large sperm whale emerging from the waves, is made up of four interlocking compartments, each of which could be used to store a different medicine, with a fitted lid covering the uppermost compartment. Each side of the *inrō* is pierced by a *himotōshi* (cord channel) through which a woven silk cord is passed; the cord is then finished beneath the *inrō* in an elaborate knot. The upper ends of the cord emerge from the cord channels and are passed through the *ojime* (tightening bead or cord cinch), which ensures that the compartments of the *inrō* are held together securely. The long section of cord would have passed behind the *obi*, a wide belt or sash (not shown here), and then through another *himotōshi* in the netsuke (toggle), in the form of a whale, which hung against the top edge of the sash and prevented the whole assemblage from falling down.

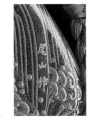

Whaling became an important industry in Japan during the eighteenth and nineteenth centuries, and incidentally helped bring about some of the earliest direct contacts between the peoples of Japan and New England: Nakahama (John) Manjirō (1827–1898), a whaler from Shikoku, the smallest of Japan's main islands, was blown off course, picked up by an American ship and brought to New Bedford in the early 1840s. Nothing is known of Oyama, whose signature is seen on only a small number of *inrō* (often with decoration of sea creatures) that are generally agreed to be of twentieth-century date.

THE *INRŌ* BY OYAMA (20TH CENTURY); THE NETSUKE
AND *OJIME* ALSO PROBABLY 20TH CENTURY
THE NETSUKE IN IVORY WITH EYES INLAID IN HORN;
THE *INRŌ* IN WOOD OR PAPER WITH DECORATION IN
BLACK, SILVER, GOLD, AND COLORED LACQUER;
THE *OJIME* IN POLISHED *UMIMATSU*
INRŌ: H. 3⁵⁄₁₆ IN. (8.5 CM); NETSUKE: L. 2¹³⁄₁₆ IN. (7.1 CM)
THE *INRŌ* SIGNED WITH SMALL, GOLD LACQUER
CHARACTERS IN THE WAVES ON THE BASE: *OYAMA SAKU*
(MADE BY OYAMA); THE OTHER PARTS UNSIGNED
PRIVATE COLLECTION

This set may well have put been together during the Edo period, although it is also possible that the combination of hare motifs was assembled by an American collector before the set was acquired by the Museum of Fine Arts. It consists of components made in each of Japan's two most important cities during the Edo period: Kyoto or Keishi, the location of the Imperial Palace and the traditional center of political power; and Edo, the capital of the shogun, which was the world's largest city at the end of the eighteenth century. The *inrō* is signed by a member of the Kajikawa dynasty of lacquer artists who were active in Edo beginning in the seventeenth century. Its design of hares with *tokusa* (scouring rushes) alludes to the very ancient traditional belief that hares live on the moon, using the rushes to polish the moon's face and maintain its pristine brilliance. The netsuke of a hare and *biwa* fruit (see also cat. 260) is signed *Okatori*, the name of one of several artists active in late-eighteenth-century and early-nineteenth-century Kyoto who are especially celebrated today for their animal carvings in ivory. The unusually large *ojime*, in the form of a crouching hare, is another example of Kyoto work, and is signed with a cursive monogram known as a *kaō*. When used without an accompanying signature, such *kaō* are often difficult or impossible to identify. Both the *ojime* and the netsuke bear the marks of prolonged but careful use. The lost collection of Matsura Seizan (1760–1841), Lord of Hirado (see page 20), seems to have included a similar set with an ivory netsuke of a hare and a black lacquer *inrō* with tokusa in "green lacquer;" unfortunately Matsura could not remember anything about the *ojime*.

THE *INRŌ* BY KAJIKAWA BUNRYŪSAI (EARLY 19TH CENTURY); THE NETSUKE BY OKATORI OF KYOTO (LATE 18TH–EARLY 19TH CENTURY); THE *OJIME* LATE 18TH–EARLY 19TH CENTURY

THE NETSUKE IN IVORY WITH EYES INLAID IN DARK HORN; THE *INRŌ* IN WOOD OR PAPER WITH DECORATION IN STAINED AND UNSTAINED IVORY AND SHELL ON A GOLD AND BLACK LACQUER GROUND; THE *OJIME* IN IVORY WITH EYES INLAID IN CORAL

INRŌ: H. 3⅛ IN. (7.9 CM); NETSUKE: H. 1³⁄₁₆ IN. (3 CM) THE *INRŌ* SIGNED WITH GOLD LACQUER CHARACTERS ON THE BASE: *KAJIKAWA BUNRYŪSAI*, WITH A RED *KAŌ*; THE NETSUKE SIGNED WITH INCISED AND STAINED CHARACTERS ON A RECTANGULAR RESERVE ON THE HARE'S LEFT HAUNCH: *OKATORI;* THE *OJIME* SIGNED UNDERNEATH WITH AN INCISED AND STAINED *KAŌ* MUSEUM OF FINE ARTS, BOSTON 27.180

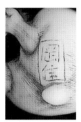

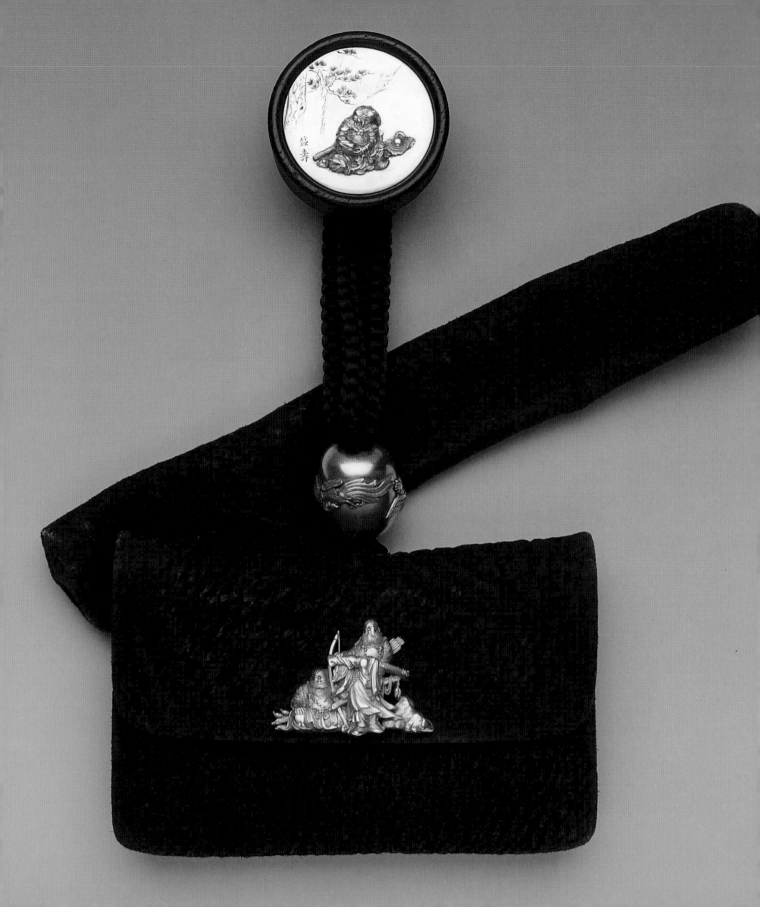

3 | *DŌRAN* (tobacco pouch), ***KISERU-ZUTSU*** (pipe case), ***KAGAMI*** **NETSUKE** (toggle), **AND** *OJIME* (tightening bead)

Although made toward the end of the nineteenth century, this remarkable set is not very different from the assemblages worn from the late eighteenth century onward, after it became the custom to take one's own smoking equipment to social gatherings. The nonmetallic components are made from *harasha*, a type of dyed leather originally imported from Holland or Persia (from which the name *harasha* is derived). The metal components bear the signatures of some of the most skilled traditional metalworkers of the Meiji period; two of them (Teikan and Moritoshi) were scions of a celebrated school of craftsmen based in the Mito domain, which, beginning in the seventeenth century, was the seat of one of the three branches of the ruling Tokugawa family. During the late Edo period, scholars in the service of the Mito Tokugawa played a leading part in the intense national debate about Japan's future development in the face of growing encroachment by the Western powers. These scholars advocated both military preparedness and adherence to the ideals of the Chinese political and philosophical system known to us as Confucianism, in particular *chū* (in Chinese, *zhong*), loyalty. Accordingly, many examples of later Mito metalwork are decorated with motifs from China's heroic past, especially the events of the third century AD as related in *Sangokushi* (in Chinese, *Sanguozhi*) and other works that were much translated and immensely popular in Japan during the Edo period. The two Chinese dignitaries depicted on the tobacco pouch are Kan'u (see also cat. 39) and Chōhi (in Chinese, Guanyu and Zhangfei), two of the three heroes whose oath of fraternal loyalty forms the background to the plot of *Sangokushi*. On the *kagami* plate, the seated warrior cradling a baby in his arms is Chōun (in Chinese, Zhao Yun), who rescued the infant son of the third hero, Gentoku (in Chinese, Xuande), from a battle with their archenemy Sōsō (in Chinese, Caocao).

THE *KANAGU* (POUCH CLASP) OF THE *DŌRAN* BY ŌKAWA TEIKAN OF TOKYO (1828–ABOUT 1900); THE *KAGAMI* NETSUKE BY UNNO MORITOSHI OF TOKYO (1835–1896); THE *OJIME* BY FUKUI KAZUTOSHI (1835–1903)

THE *DŌRAN* AND *KISERU-ZUTSU* OF *HARASHA* (DYED LEATHER); THE *KANAGU*, THE PLATE OF THE *KAGAMI* NETSUKE, AND THE *OJIME* ALL OF GOLD AND SILVER GILT; THE BOWL OF THE *KAGAMI* NETSUKE OF HARDWOOD

DŌRAN: W. 5 IN. (12.7 CM); NETSUKE: D. 1¹³⁄₁₆ IN. (4.6 CM)

THE *KANAGU* SIGNED WITH CHISELED CHARACTERS ON THE REVERSE: *TŌBŪ OTONASHIGAWA NO ATARI NI OITE MOTOME NI ŌJITE TEIKAN SEI* (MADE BY TEIKAN TO SPECIAL REQUEST BY THE OTONASHI RIVER IN EASTERN MUSASHI [TOKYO]); THE *KAGAMI* NETSUKE SIGNED ON THE FACE: *MORITOSHI;* THE *OJIME* SIGNED ON THE SIDE: *KAZUTOSHI*

MUSEUM OF FINE ARTS, BOSTON 11.24750

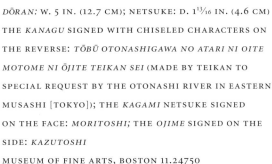

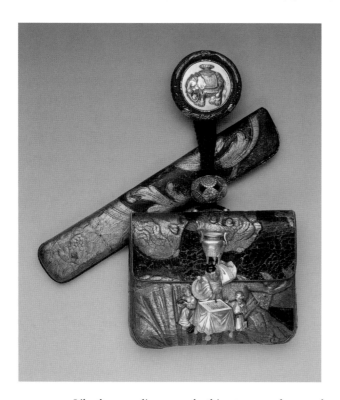

Like the preceding example, this set was made toward
the end of the nineteenth century and incorporates
a *kagami* netsuke. Despite the very high quality of the
metal components, only the *kagami* plate is signed,
in *hiragana* syllables instead of the *kanji* usually employed
for signatures on metalwork. Nevertheless, it is likely
that these components are the work of members of the
Mito school, and that the *kanagu* depicts an unidentified
episode from *Sangokushi* (see preceding entry). The
standing figure holding a tripod above his head is likely
one of the three heroes Kan'u, Chōhi, and Gentoku,
and the text that he writes is an incomplete, fairly standard
paragraph of Chinese cosmological theory: "Since
the beginning of time heaven has depended on earth and
earth on heaven . . . the waters of the rivers come down
from heaven of their own accord, and Mount Tai already
has produced the Kunlun Range . . ." The nonmetallic

components are formed from embossed and lacquered
leather, a material mentioned by Inaba Tsūryū in *Sōken
kishō*, published in 1781 (see page 19), and the tobacco
pouch is decorated with a European design of a Dutch
man and woman, which is only visible in full when the
flap is opened and the pouch is laid flat. This may be an
instance of the recycling of earlier material, but bearing in
mind the surprising popularity of "Japanese leather"
during the Victorian period (the Irish aesthete and writer
Oscar Wilde decorated an entire ceiling in his London
house with it), it is also possible that eighteenth-century
leather was copied toward the end of the nineteenth
century.

THE *KAGAMI* NETSUKE BY MITSUYOSHI (LATE
19TH CENTURY); THE OTHER METAL PARTS LATE 19TH
CENTURY; THE LEATHER POSSIBLY 18TH CENTURY
THE *DŌRAN* AND *KISERU-ZUTSU* OF *YODOYAKAWA*
(EMBOSSED AND LACQUERED LEATHER); THE *KANAGU*
(POUCH CLASP), THE PLATE OF THE *KAGAMI* NETSUKE,
AND THE *OJIME* ALL OF GOLD AND SILVER GILT
WITH DECORATION IN *SHAKUDŌ, SHIBUICHI,* AND
COPPER; THE BOWL OF THE *KAGAMI* NETSUKE OF
STIPPLED SILVER
DŌRAN: W. 6 IN. (15.2 CM); NETSUKE: D. 2⅝ IN. (6.6 CM)
THE *KAGAMI* NETSUKE SIGNED WITH CHISELED
HIRAGANA SYLLABLES: *MITSUYOSHI;* THE OTHER PARTS
UNSIGNED; MUSEUM OF FINE ARTS, BOSTON 11.24762

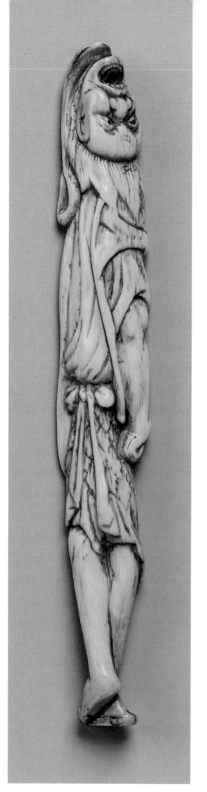

5 | TRANSFORMING SENNIN

A very tall figure of a sennin *wearing a cloak with a girdle of mugwort, his head turned upward so that one side resembles an amaryō (rain dragon, see cat. 61) and another side resembles a fish, the sennin's crossed legs forming its tail, the eyes inlaid in dark horn, the* himotōshi *formed by two holes very close to one another in the middle of the back, the larger hole below the smaller.*

Chinese printed books about *sennin*, as well as their Japanese translations and adaptations, often mention the ability of *sennin* to transform themselves into other creatures; it is only rarely, however, that these metamorphoses are actually depicted in the illustrations to the books. The absence of a pictorial model gave the carver of this early netsuke an opportunity to exercise his imagination and ingenuity by making economical use of a sector of tusk to present three manifestations of the same being.

LATE 17TH–MID-18TH CENTURY
STAINED IVORY AND HORN; H. 6⁵⁄₁₆ IN. (16 CM)
UNSIGNED
PRIVATE COLLECTION

6 | FISHERMAN *SENNIN*

A figure with a bald pate and curly hair, wearing a wide-sleeved, Chinese-style garment, carrying a basket and fishing rod with the line wound around it, his left hand at his shoulder holding a rope from which three fish hang behind his back, each of the fish with an eye of inlaid horn, the himotōshi *formed by two holes on the back arranged on either side of the girdle, the larger hole below the smaller.*

This figure cannot be identified precisely, but the facial features, hairstyle, and dress are clearly designed to define him as a foreign or otherworldly being. Although *sennin* are often depicted wearing girdles or skirts of mugwort, Chinese illustrated books of the sixteenth and seventeenth centuries also show them with other types of outlandish dress, making it reasonable to assign this fisherman to their ranks.

LATE 17TH–MID-18TH CENTURY
STAINED IVORY AND HORN; H. 4⅜ IN. (11.1 CM)
UNSIGNED
PRIVATE COLLECTION

7 | CHŌKARŌ SENNIN

A figure wearing a wide-sleeved, Chinese-style garment, with mugwort around his neck and waist, a gourd tied behind his head, the ribs visible on his ema-ciated chest, the himotōshi *formed by two holes in the center of the back, the larger hole below the smaller.*

Chōkarō is one of the Hassen (Eight Immortals), a group which originated in China during the fourteenth century but did not achieve a settled membership until the sixteenth century. He was believed to have lived during the eighth century, when he achieved fame by refusing to join the corrupt administration of the Emperor Xuan-zong. Chōkarō is depicted carrying a gourd from which he produced a magic colt or mule that could, when required, carry him thousands of miles in a single day. Early netsuke of Chōkarō tend not to show the colt, but in later pieces he is often seen releasing it from his gourd – a sculptural realization of the proverb *hyōtan kara koma*, "a colt from a gourd," used to describe any unexpected event.

MID-18TH CENTURY
STAINED IVORY; H. 3¹¹⁄₁₆ IN. (9.4 CM)
UNSIGNED
PRIVATE COLLECTION

An emaciated standing figure with curly hair and a long beard, dressed in rags and a cloak of mugwort, looking upward and grasping a crutch with both hands, his lips pursed as he prepares to exhale his spirit, the himotōshi *formed by two large holes in the back partially covered by the cloak.*

Like Chōkarō, Tekkai Sensei, or Ri Tekkai (in Chinese, Li Tieguai), is another of the select group of Hassen (Eight Immortals). The upward-looking stance, a feature already seen in Chinese carvings of Li Tieguai made a century and a half before this piece, is explained by the fact that in many graphic depictions of this immortal, he is shown blowing his soul up into the sky, an attribute not easily depicted in a compact sculpture such as this. Volume 1 of *Yūshō ressen zenden,* published in 1650, relates that Tekkai was a well-built man who "attained the Way" (achieved enlightenment) at an early age. One day, deciding that his spirit should go to meet his master at Mount Huashan, Tekkai instructed a disciple that if the spirit did not return within seven days, he should destroy Tekkai's sentient physical body. During the absence of his master's spirit, the disciple was called away to look after his sick mother and lost track of time, hurrying back on the sixth day and mistakenly destroying the body. On his return from Mount Huashan, Tekkai was forced to take up residence in the body of an emaciated beggar, losing all of his former strength.

MID-18TH CENTURY
STAINED BOXWOOD; H. 4⁵⁄₁₆ IN. (10.9 CM)
UNSIGNED
PRIVATE COLLECTION

NETSUKE OF TEKKAI SENSEI
BY YOSHIMURA SHŪZAN, FROM INABA
TSŪRYŪ, *SŌKEN KISHŌ* [1781],
VOLUME 7, PP. 3–4.
MUSEUM OF FINE ARTS, BOSTON

11 | KINKŌ SENNIN

A figure in Chinese dress riding on the back of an enormous carp, holding an open scroll which rests on the fish's head, the base in the form of waves pierced with large and small holes forming the himotōshi.

Sometimes included among the Hassen (Eight Immortals), Kinkō (in Chinese, Qin Gao) is often encountered in illustrated books, including both specialist texts such as *Yūshō ressen zenden* (1650) as well as collections of painting reproductions such as *Ehon nezashi takara*, illustrated by Tachibana Morikuni and published in Osaka in 1744. These sources give slightly different versions of his legend, but most accounts agree that Kinkō was a

retainer of the king of the early Chinese state of Song, and an accomplished performer on the drums and *kin* (in Chinese *qin*, a plucked musical instrument; the word also forms the first part of Kinkō's name). One day Kinkō went away on his travels accompanied by a group of disciples. Telling them that he planned to seize the child of a dragon, he plunged into a nearby river, emerging later on the back of a gigantic carp. After exchanging a few words with his disciples, he plunged back in again, returning later to eat and drink with them; in some versions this second reappearance is awaited by a crowd of ten thousand onlookers.

EARLY–MID-18TH CENTURY
STAINED IVORY; L. 2½ IN. (6.3 CM)
UNSIGNED
PRIVATE COLLECTION

A figure in Chinese dress riding on the back of an enormous carp, holding an open scroll, the base in the form of waves pierced with two holes forming the himotōshi.

Although the most widely available texts do not mention the scroll carried by Kinkō, it appears in virtually all netsuke of the subject. The general appearance of the required iconographic elements for netsuke depicting this famous *sennin* – waves, carp, scroll, and Kinkō himself – seems to have been established by the early eighteenth century, as in the preceding example. Subsequent carvers exercised their ingenuity by varying features such as the relative size of *sennin*, fish, and waves, and the relationship between Kinkō's head and the fish's tail.

LATE 18TH CENTURY

STAINED BOXWOOD; H. 2⅛ IN. (5.4 CM)

UNSIGNED

PRIVATE COLLECTION

An elderly Chinese figure in an embroidered robe, seated on the back of a recumbent elephant, holding a scroll in both hands, the himotōshi *formed by the legs.*

Although well known in Japan as the founder of the philosophical and religious system known in the West as Daoism, and often depicted in a grouping with Confucius and Buddha, Rōshi (in Chinese, Lao Zi or perhaps more familiarly, Lao Tzu) is also listed occasionally as a *sennin*. He appears as such on the first illustrated page of *Yūshō ressen zenden* (1650), seated on his more usual mount of a water buffalo. An elephant-seal netsuke is illustrated in *Sōken kishō* (see also number 222) and this may be an early example of a netsuke made up from several different visual sources, the elephant-seal type being combined with a figure from a book illustration.

EARLY–MID-18TH CENTURY

STAINED IVORY; H. 2¼ IN. (5.7 CM)

UNSIGNED

PRIVATE COLLECTION

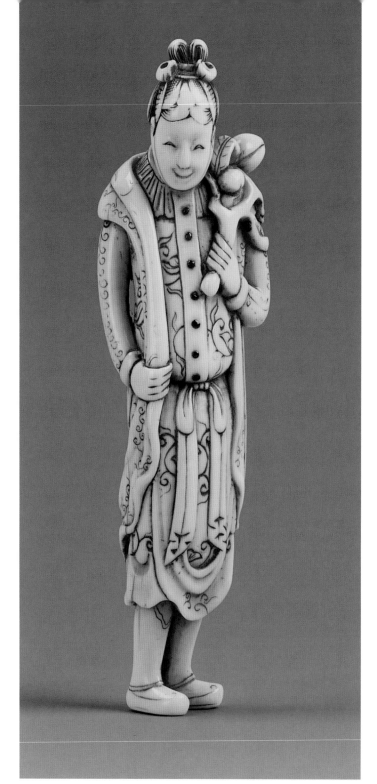

14 | SEIŌBO SENNIN

A tall standing female figure dressed in elaborate Chinese-style robes, her hair arranged in a topknot, holding a branch from a peach tree to her left shoulder, her seven buttons inlaid in dark buffalo horn, the himotōshi *formed by two holes of almost equal size in the middle of the back.*

One of the highest-ranking of all *sennin* and a member of the select group of female immortals, Seiōbo (in Chinese, Xi Wang Mu, "The Royal Mother of the West") is shown on the opening pages of *Yūshō ressen zenden* (1650). The text includes the well-known story of Seiōbo's gift of seven magic peaches to the Chinese Emperor Butei (in Chinese, Wudi). The emperor ate two of the peaches and wanted to keep the pits, but was prevented from doing so by Seiōbo, who explained that they came from a tree that bore fruit only once in three thousand years. This exchange was witnessed through a window by an enigmatic retainer named Tōbōsaku (in Chinese, Dongfangshuo), but Seiōbo spotted him and told the emperor that he already had stolen three peaches in the past. This remarkable netsuke seems to owe very little to seventeenth-century illustrated versions of the tale, whether Chinese or Japanese, and may have been influenced by larger Chinese ivory figures of Seiōbo, who enjoyed enormous popularity in China during the sixteenth and seventeenth centuries.

EARLY—MID-18TH CENTURY

STAINED IVORY AND HORN; H. 5⅝ IN. (14.2 CM)

UNSIGNED

PRIVATE COLLECTION

15 | *SENNIN* WITH SWORD ON HIS BACK

A standing figure dressed in a sleeveless tunic, his mouth wide open, with curly locks and a bald pate, pointing with his right hand to an object held in his left, a large sword and scabbard slung behind his back.

It is not certain who, if anyone, this extraordinary figure is intended to represent. The frontal pose is rather similar to that of a netsuke of Ryūjin by Shūzan illustrated in *Sōken kishō* (see page 71), and the object held in the left hand is presumably a jewel or talisman of some kind; the large sword and scabbard may derive from the same source as that worn by the later *ijin* netsuke, cat. 50. There appears to be no *himotōshi*, and since the figure would hang upside down if a cord was threaded through the small gap between the legs, it is probable that it was not intended for wear. For Yoshimura Shūzan, see page 21 and cat. 36.

ATTRIBUTED TO YOSHIMURA SHŪZAN (DIED 1773)
PAINTED CYPRESS WOOD; H. 4³⁄₁₆ IN. (10.7 CM)
UNSIGNED
PRIVATE COLLECTION

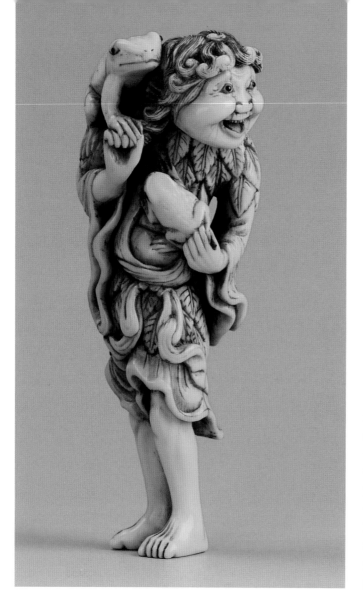

16 | KŌ SENSEI

A standing figure with curly hair and Caucasian features, wearing a Chinese-style garment with wide sleeves and a ruff and girdle of mugwort, a large toad on his right shoulder and a smaller one in his left hand, the pupils of the figure and of the larger toad inlaid in horn, the himotōshi *formed by two unequal holes in the back, signed with incised and stained characters next to the larger hole.*

Better known in the West as Gama Sennin ("Toad Immortal"), Kō Sensei was one of the most popular of the many Chinese immortals imported to Japan during the seventeenth century. The toad's origins can be traced back as far as the Western Han Dynasty (2nd–1st century BC), when it was associated particularly with the moon, even losing one of its legs so as to match a three-legged crow that was said to inhabit the sun. "White Jade Toad," or Liu Hai, to give him his most usual Chinese name, features in Ming Dynasty drama and ivory carving, where his toad invariably has three limbs, a tradition that seems to be ignored in the majority of netsuke representing Kō Sensei. This netsuke bears the signature of Yoshinaga, an important Kyoto carver mentioned in *Sōken kishō*, but it may be a later addition.

POSSIBLY BY KŌYŌKEN YOSHINAGA OF KYOTO
(ACTIVE AROUND 1781)
STAINED IVORY AND HORN; H. 4⁵/₁₆ IN. (11 CM)
SIGNED: *YOSHINAGA*
PRIVATE COLLECTION

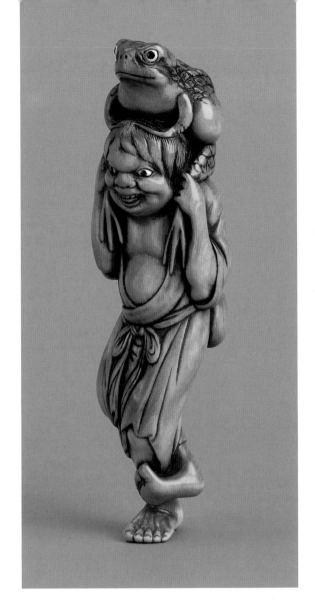

17 | KŌ SENSEI

A tall standing figure with Caucasian features, wearing a Chinese-style garment with wide sleeves, standing on one foot and carrying a large toad on his shoulders, gripping its rear flippers in his hands, the eyes of both man and toad inlaid in ivory and horn, the himotōshi formed by large and small holes on either side of a gourd slung on his back, signed with incised and stained characters next to the larger hole.

The first artist (there were possibly three successors) using the name Minkoku started working in Edo toward the end of the eighteenth century. Here he retains some of the iconography for Kō Sensei established by earlier Kyoto and Osaka artists, including the non-Japanese facial features that likely are derived from the putti seen on imported Dutch leather, as reproduced in volume 6 of *Sōken kishō*. In contrast to the netsuke signed *Yoshinaga* (cat. 16), this carving respects a written tradition, reported in *Ehon tsūhōshi* (published in Osaka in 1730), that Kō Sensei has no eyebrows.

MINKOKU (LATE 18TH–EARLY 19TH CENTURY)
STAINED BOXWOOD, IVORY AND HORN; H. 5½ IN. (14 CM)
SIGNED: *MINKOKU*
PRIVATE COLLECTION

18 | KŌ SENSEI

*A squatting, muscular figure dressed in a cloak
with a mugwort shawl and girdle, looking up
in surprise at an enormous toad that leaps up his
back and onto his head, the toad's long left hind
leg resting on his left thigh, the eyes inlaid in
horn, the* himotōshi *formed by holes in his back
and side, signed with incised and stained
characters on a raised oval reserve near the base.*

This is thought to be Toyomasa's only
depiction in ivory of Kō Sensei, one of his
favorite subjects. In nearly all of Toyomasa's
depictions of this *sennin*, the toad is no
longer a mere attribute but has become the
dominant partner.

NAITŌ TOYOMASA OF TANBA PROVINCE
(1773–1856)
STAINED IVORY AND HORN
H. 2¹⁄₁₆ IN. (5.3 CM)
SIGNED: *TOYOMASA*
PRIVATE COLLECTION

19 | KŌ SENSEI

*A similar figure to the preceding netsuke,
in stained boxwood rather than ivory.*

NAITŌ TOYOMASA OF TANBA PROVINCE
(1773–1856)
STAINED BOXWOOD AND HORN
H. 2 IN. (5.1 CM)
SIGNED: *TOYOMASA*
PRIVATE COLLECTION

SIGNATURES FOR PLATES 18 AND
19 RESPECTIVELY;
OPPOSITE PAGE SHOWS DETAIL OF
BACK SIDE OF 19

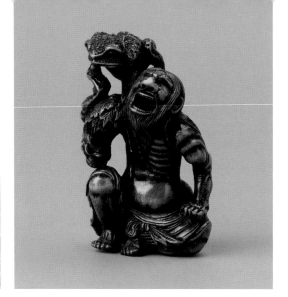

20 | KŌ SENSEI

A squatting, muscular figure dressed in a skirt and a mugwort shawl, looking up in surprise at a toad that leaps up his back and onto his head, the toad's long left hind leg resting on his left thigh, his eyes inlaid in pale horn with ebony pupils, the toad's eyes inlaid in dark horn, the himotōshi *formed by deep holes in the skirt, signed with incised and stained characters on an oval plaque near the base.*

Naitō Toyomasa is one of that rare group of netsuke carvers whose lives are documented in a fair amount of detail. A resident of the town of Sasayama in Tanba Province, he started a workshop at the beginning of the Bunka era (1804–1818), receiving his studio name of Toyomasa in 1809, and in 1835 was appointed official carver to the Aoyama family of daimyō (local lords). Surviving documents record a large number of orders placed with Toyomasa by the Aoyama family, as well as other commissions from further afield.

NAITŌ TOYOMASA OF TANBA PROVINCE (1773–1856)
STAINED BOXWOOD, HORN, AND EBONY; H. 2¹⁄₁₆ IN.
(5.3 CM)
SIGNED: *TOYOMASA*
PRIVATE COLLECTION

21 | CHINNAN SENNIN

A diminutive figure holding a bowl in his right hand and a jewel in his left, overwhelmed by an enormous dragon that has emerged from the bowl, the remainder of the netsuke made up of clouds and waves, the dragon's eyes inlaid in horn with stained pupils, the himotōshi *formed by a hole in the base, signed with stained and incised characters on a plaque next to the hole.*

Although Chinnan Sennin, as befits a Chinese immortal, should be in control of the creature that he has summoned into being, here he is overwhelmed by his own creation. The same approach is seen in Toyomasa's netsuke of Kō Sensei (cats. 18–20), and evidence of his independent approach to his work also is provided by a letter he sent to the daimyō of Mino, Aoyama Yukishige. In the letter, Toyomasa gave detailed reasons as to why he did not produce an exact copy of a design sketch that he had been shown.

NAITŌ TOYOMASA OF TANBA PROVINCE (1773–1856);
PROBABLY ABOUT 1834; STAINED BOXWOOD AND HORN;
H. 2¹⁄₁₆ IN. (5.2 CM) SIGNED: *ROKUJŪNISAI TOYOMASA*
(TOYOMASA, AGED SIXTY-TWO), WITH A *KAŌ*
MUSEUM OF FINE ARTS, BOSTON 11.23557

22 | CHINNAN SENNIN

A sturdy figure dressed in an embroidered skirt and a mugwort cloak, a dragon twined around his back and over his left shoulder, one of its claws in his mouth, a sacred jewel in his right hand and a large gourd hanging at his right side, the eyes inlaid in dark horn, no himotōshi, *signed with incised and stained characters on a raised oval reserve underneath the right foot.*

Sawaki Masaka was born in Nagoya in 1868, and moved in 1883 to Osaka. There he carved both netsuke and the larger ornamental carvings known as *okimono*, submitting one for exhibition at the Columbian World's Fair held in Chicago in 1893. Like many other ivory carvers of the period, Masaka combines the exaggerated musculature characteristic of Buddhist sculpture of the twelfth and thirteenth centuries with a Western style of naturalism first introduced by the Italian sculptor Vincenzo Ragusa (1841–1927), who taught in Japan from 1875 to 1882. In the interests of producing a carving that is very much a miniature sculpture rather than a functional netsuke, Masaka has altered radically the traditional relationship between *sennin* and dragon and dispensed with the *himotōshi*, although a cord could be threaded between the dragon and Chinnan's body.

SAWAKI MASAKA OF NAGOYA (BORN 1868); ABOUT 1900
STAINED IVORY AND HORN; H. 4$\frac{5}{16}$ IN. (11 CM)
SIGNED: *MASAKA*
PRIVATE COLLECTION

A long-haired Madonna seated on a carved wooden stool, the Christ child seated on her lap and supported by her right hand, the himotōshi *formed by the gap between her hair and the stool, signed with incised* gyōsho *(semicursive) characters on the base, the box signed in ink.*

Although nothing is known of Mr. Asai, it is quite possible that this netsuke is intended as a devotional piece, in the same tradition as the small Buddhist figures in miniature shrines that stand in many Japanese homes. The signature indicates that Sōsui wanted to recreate the appearance of a secret Christian figure as it might have appeared during the prohibition of the foreign religion between the mid-seventeenth and the mid-nineteenth century, an approach that accounts for the ambiguously part-Japanese and part-Western features. Sōsui was the son of Morita Sōko (1879–1943), a leading netsuke carver of the 1920s and 1930s.

ŌUCHI SŌSUI OF TOYKO (1911–1972)
BOXWOOD; H. 1⅝ IN. (4.1 CM)
SIGNED: *ASAI-Ō NO KONOMI NI YOTTE SŌSUI SAKU*
(MADE BY SŌSUI TO THE ORDER OF MR. ASAI)
THE BOX SIGNED: *SEIBOSHI KIBORI NETSUKE ASAI-Ō NO KONOMI NI YOTTE SŌKI KINSEI JIDAI WAYŌSHIKI SŌSUI KIZAMU* (A WOOD NETSUKE OF THE MADONNA AND CHILD, CARVED BY SŌSUI TO THE ORDER OF MR. ASAI IN AN IMAGINARY JAPANESE STYLE FROM THE PERIOD WHEN CHRISTIANITY WAS BANNED), AND SEALED: *SŌSUI*
PRIVATE COLLECTION

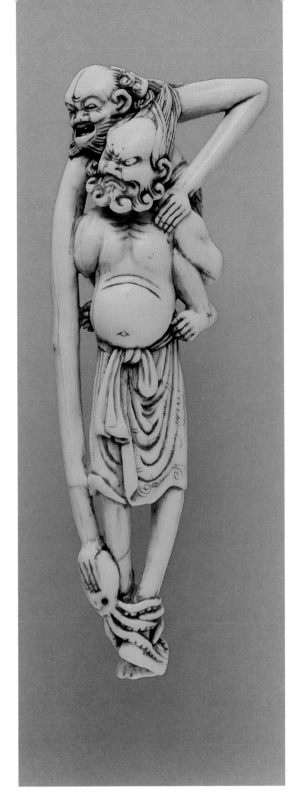

A tall netsuke of a pot-bellied ashinaga *with a curly beard, dressed in a skirt, carrying on his shoulders a* tenaga *of similar appearance who reaches down with an enormously long right arm to pull away an octopus that has entwined itself around the* ashinaga's *feet, the octopus's eyes inlaid in horn, the* himotōshi *formed by two holes very close to one another in the middle of the back, the larger hole below the smaller.*

Japanese awareness of "terrifying beings" with oversize limbs living in the stormy sea can be traced as far back as the tenth-century court lady and diarist Sei Shōnagon, who describes a screen painted with them, but depictions of *tenaga* ("long arms") and *ashinaga* ("long legs") from the Edo period are based on Chinese illustrated books and encyclopedias of the sixteenth century, and on Japanese works derived from them. Terashima Ryōan, an Osaka doctor who published his great encyclopedia *Wakan sansai zue* in 1713, includes them in a section devoted to increasingly weird and wonderful humans and humanoids from foreign lands, describing not only a "Long-Legs" and a "Long-Arms" country but also countries populated by "No-Legs" and "One-Legs." Despite the intricacies involved in representing these two outlandish creatures, the carver of this piece achieved a remarkably compact shape, enhanced by the almost flat, slightly concave back typical of many early figure netsuke.

EARLY–MID-18TH CENTURY
STAINED IVORY AND HORN; H. 5³⁄₁₆ IN. (13.2 CM)
UNSIGNED
PRIVATE COLLECTION

An almost bald ashinaga *dressed in an embroidered skirt, a drum at his side, carrying on his back a* tenaga *of similar appearance who reaches down with an enormously long left arm to pull away an octopus that has entwined itself around the* ashinaga*'s feet, the eyes of the two humanoids inlaid in horn, those of the octopus in silver and* shakudō, *the hem of the* tenaga*'s skirt decorated with gilding, coral, silver, and* shakudō, *no* himotōshi, *signed with incised and stained characters on an irregular reserve on the* ashinaga*'s skirt.*

Terashima Ryōan (see the preceding entry) relates that the inhabitants of Long-Legs Land carry the inhabitants of Long-Arms Land on their backs to help them catch fish, and *ashinaga* and *tenaga* such as this also are seen in later eighteenth-century books. The signature is probably that of Kikugawa Masamitsu, who made both netsuke and the ornamental carvings known as *okimono*, and who was the teacher of Ishikawa Kōmei, the celebrated ivory sculptor of the Meiji period. Given the carving's late date and lack of a *himotōshi*, it should be regarded perhaps as an *okimono*, even though a cord could have been threaded through one of the *tenaga*'s armpits.

KIKUGAWA MASAMITSU OF TOKYO
(MID-LATE 19TH CENTURY)
STAINED IVORY, GILDING, CORAL, SILVER, AND
SHAKUDŌ; H. 4½ IN. (11.5 CM)
SIGNED: *KIKUGAWA*
MUSEUM OF FINE ARTS, BOSTON 11.23342

A very tall standing figure with a pot belly, dressed in a loin-cloth and a cloak fastened by a coral button, holding a small drum in his left hand and a drumstick in his right, the himotōshi formed by two large holes separated by the girdle, signed in worn incised and stained characters to the right of the lower hole.

Although this celebrated figure has been identified simply as a "foreigner" since it was published in the London Red Cross Exhibition catalogue in 1916, a comparison with the two preceding *tenaga* and *ashinaga* groups suggests that while impossibly long arms are an essential attribute of *tenaga* ("long arms"), his *ashinaga* ("long legs") companion can be identified by limbs that are only slightly elongated, as here. Like the *ashinaga* in the group by Kikugawa Masamitsu, this figure holds a drum, an iconographic marker that seems to have been added at an early stage in the development of *ashinaga* netsuke. Despite the difference between their signatures, both this and the following figure are likely to be the work of the first Shūgetsu, who is listed in *Sōken kishō* with typically minimal information: "A resident of Shimanouchi in Osaka but now lives in Edo. Also a painter, in which capacity he was awarded the honorary title *hōgen*. He carves netsuke with extremely fine detail. It goes without saying that his workmanship is excellent." He is one of the few netsuke carvers mentioned in the list of the lost collection of Matsura Seizan (1760–1841), Lord of Hirado (see page 20).

HŌGEN HIGUCHI SHŪGETSU OF OSAKA AND EDO
(ACTIVE AROUND 1781)
STAINED IVORY AND CORAL; H. 5¹³⁄₁₆ IN. (14.8 CM)
SIGNED: *SHŪGETSU*
PRIVATE COLLECTION

A very worn, curly-haired shouting figure wearing a long skirt high up on his torso, holding a small drum in his right hand and a drumstick in his left, the himotōshi *formed by one extremely large and one smaller hole in the back, signed on the back to the right of the holes with two crudely formed, incised characters.*

Although not an *ashinaga*, this figure of an *ijin* or foreigner is included here for comparison with the preceding netsuke of similar design, also by Shūgetsu.

HŌGEN HIGUCHI SHŪGETSU OF OSAKA
AND EDO (ACTIVE AROUND 1781)
STAINED BOXWOOD; H. 4³⁄₁₆ IN. (10.6 CM)
SIGNED: *SHŪGETSU*
MUSEUM OF FINE ARTS, BOSTON 47.594

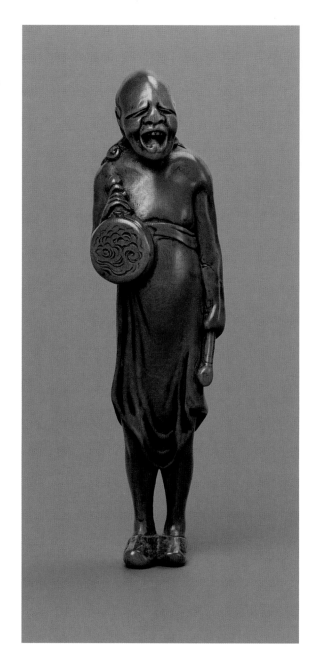

An ashinaga *standing on a rock, clinging to a tree trunk with a branch of coral at the base, wearing a huge tobacco pouch with a button netsuke, the* himotōshi *formed by the arms.*

Eighteenth-century reference works often depict *tenaga* and *ashinaga* living on small islands, and this figure stands on a tiny outcrop in the middle of the ocean, clinging to a dead tree to save himself from drowning. The artist has adopted the hairstyle and other features associated with earlier carvings of non-Japanese beings, but replaced their caricatured expressions with a look of real terror. This may be a *sashi* netsuke, intended to hang behind the wearer's *obi* leaving only the head and arms exposed, but an alternative *himotōshi* is provided by the thread supporting the *ashinaga*'s tobacco pouch, so it also could have been worn as a conventional netsuke. The use of *umimatsu* (literally, "sea-pine"), a type of marine fossilized wood, underlines the exotic, remote nature of the subject matter.

MID-19TH CENTURY

SASHI NETSUKE

UMIMATSU, STAINED STAG ANTLER, AND

MARINE FOSSILIZED WOOD;

L. 7⁹⁄₁₆ IN. (19.2 CM)

UNSIGNED

MUSEUM OF FINE ARTS, BOSTON 47.705

A tall standing figure with an oversize head, the eyes inlaid in stag antler and horn, wearing a pair of drawers with a bulging codpiece, a knife hanging at the waist, his body heavily stained and lacquered, his long legs joined at the knees and feet, his hands behind his back holding a branch of coral that forms the himotōshi.

The Japanese of the Edo period had limited knowledge of dark-skinned people, but among the sporadic encounters recorded is one in 1680 with a ship containing eighteen black crew members. Most of them died, and the rest were sent away on the next available ship in accordance with the official policy of national exclusion, leaving most Japanese free to indulge their fantasies about *Konron*, *Korondo*, or *Koronbō* – words probably derived from the name of the modern Sri Lankan capital, Colombo, but using Chinese characters from the name of another distant place, the Kunlun mountains of Central Asia, which were famous as the abode of Seiōbo (see cat. 14). *Konron* is said to be in the southwest ocean, and to be inhabited partly by people with skin like black lacquer who are enslaved by their compatriots. Terashima Ryōan, in *Wakan sansai zue* (1713), notes that these may be the same as the black people sometimes seen on Dutch ships. A later encyclopedia, *Zōho tōsho zui taisei* (1789), adds that they can swim with ease to the bottom of the sea and also are good at climbing to great heights.

18TH CENTURY

STAINED AND LACQUERED WOOD, STAG ANTLER, AND HORN; H. 5¹¹⁄₁₆ IN. (14.4 CM)

UNSIGNED

PRIVATE COLLECTION

A figure carved from ebony, with eyes inlaid in ivory, clasping a huge lump of coral, surrounded by intricately carved ivory waves, the himotōshi *formed by a metal ring, signed underneath with incised and stained characters on a rectangular reserve.*

As with the figure of *tenaga* and *ashinaga* (cat. 25), the exotic nature of the subject matter is underlined by a combination of rare and unusual imported materials. The first Genryōsai Minkoku is believed to have worked in Edo at the end of the eighteenth century, but he probably had at least one successor who used the same name.

GENRYŌSAI (MID–LATE 19TH CENTURY)
EBONY, CORAL, AND IVORY; L. 2⅜ IN. (6 CM)
SIGNED: *GENRYŌSAI*
MUSEUM OF FINE ARTS, BOSTON 47.973

31 | MERMAID

A compact carving of a long-haired mermaid, her arms folded at her sides, holding a large jewel under her chin, the head and upper torso of human form, the rest in the shape of a fish's tail with intricately carved and stained scales, the himotōshi *formed by two holes underneath, the larger hole near the tail.*

Mermaids and mermen appear frequently in illustrated versions of the early Chinese text *Shan hai jing*, where they are included among the inhabitants of "Strange Lands," described as Teijin (in Chinese, Diren), and said to have human faces, fish bodies, and no feet. The Japanese encyclopedia *Wakan sansai zue* (1713), quoting the earlier Chinese work *Sancai tuhui* (1600), adds the information that the Teijin are a tribe living in the far southwest of China. The coloration of both the mermaid and the merman (cat. 32) is typical of early ivory netsuke: the rich yellow of the outside of the tusk, protected from light during long years worn against its owner's *obi*, contrasting with the bleached white of the inner, exposed side. The positioning of the larger hole near the tail suggests that the netsuke was worn with the mermaid's face looking upward toward her owner.

LATE 17TH–EARLY 18TH CENTURY
STAINED IVORY; L. 3¹⁄₁₆ IN. (7.8 CM)
UNSIGNED
PRIVATE COLLECTION

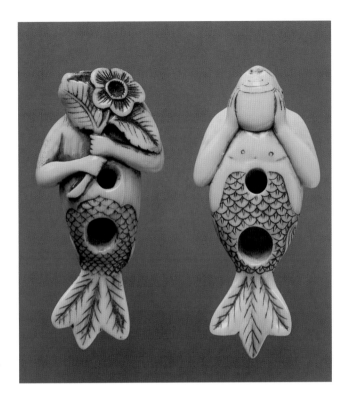

32 | MERMAN

A compact carving of a bearded merman, his arms folded underneath his body, holding a stem with a five-petaled flower and two leaves, the head and upper torso of human form, the rest in the shape of a fish's tail with intricately carved and stained scales, the himotōshi *formed by two holes underneath, the larger hole near the tail.*

LATE 17TH–EARLY 18TH CENTURY
STAINED IVORY; L. 2¹⁵⁄₁₆ IN. (7.5 CM)
UNSIGNED
PRIVATE COLLECTION

A long-haired mermaid in the embrace of an octopus, her left hand cradling its head, wearing a contented expression, her body curling with pleasure, a strand of seaweed around her tail, the eyes of the octopus inlaid in translucent horn and ebony, the himotōshi *formed by a larger hole underneath the octopus and a smaller one under the mermaid, signed with incised characters on a rounded rectangular reserve underneath the mermaid's tail.*

Sōken kishō illustrates a mermaid netsuke by Unjutō Shumemaru, a Shinto priest living in Kanijima, Osaka. The Shumemaru netsuke holds a pearl, but making allowances for the sketchy nature of the *Sōken kishō* pictures, in all other respects it is very similar to this carving, confirming Hidemasa's reputation as a copier and adapter of earlier Kyoto-style pieces. By substituting an octopus for the original jewel, Hidemasa successfully appropriated a sexually charged theme that was already popular in woodblock print form (see also cat. 196).

CHINGENDŌ HIDEMASA (LATE 18TH–EARLY 19TH CENTURY)
LIGHTLY STAINED IVORY, EBONY, AND HORN;
L. 2 IN. (5.1 CM)
SIGNED: *HIDEMASA*
PRIVATE COLLECTION

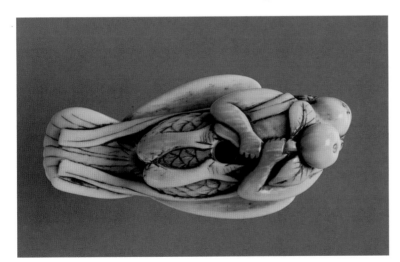

A compact carving of a bird-woman, her face with Chinese features, her hair partially tied in a topknot, her arms folded underneath her body, holding a stem with a peach and two leaves, the head and upper torso of human form, the rest in the shape of a bird, the himotōshi *formed by a smaller hole in front of the bird's feet and a larger one underneath its tail.*

The double-page spreads of illustrations to a sixteenth-century Chinese edition of *Shan hai jing* very often include a bird-monster, usually placed in the far top left of the design. Although quite clearly derived from the classical European harpy, these creatures are adapted to the requirements of the much earlier text: one has three legs and the body of a heron, while another apparently is intended to represent Seiei (in Chinese, Jingwei), a metamorphosis of Nüwa, daughter of the Emperor Yan. While playing in the East Sea she had drowned and turned into a bird, which would carry twigs and stones all the way from the West Mountains to the East Sea in an effort to fill it up. The peach branch may have been inspired by a representation of Jingwei, but this netsuke also could be interpreted as an example of the carver drawing together a selection of disparate elements with an eye to richly allusive design, rather than to strictly accurate storytelling. If so, the branch might have been borrowed from the standard iconography for Seiōbo (cat. 14).

LATE 17TH–EARLY 18TH CENTURY
STAINED IVORY; L. 2¹⁵⁄₁₆ IN. (7.5 CM)
UNSIGNED
PRIVATE COLLECTION

35 | SUIKO

A human-headed dragon with childish features and long hair, its scaly back terminating in a short tail that rests on the ground, its right hand held underneath its chin, its left hand reaching down to touch its left foot, the simple himotōshi *formed by a vertical hole passing straight through the body.*

A crude illustration of a *suiko* (literally, "water-tiger") appears in the 1713 encyclopedia *Wakan sansai zue* alongside a text, drawn from an earlier Chinese work, which explains that it resembles "a three- or four-year-old child with an impenetrable shell like a scaly anteater or pangolin." Despite this information, the encyclopedia's illustrator gave the *suiko* more or less adult features, in contrast to the netsuke carver who faithfully followed the verbal formula.

LATE 17TH–EARLY 18TH CENTURY
STAINED IVORY; H. 2½ IN. (6.4 CM)
UNSIGNED
PRIVATE COLLECTION

A standing figure of a bald, bearded deity with a fearsome expression, holding a jewel in front of his body with both hands while a dragon clings to his back and peers over the top of his head, with details painted in red, blue, and other pigments, several possible himotōshi formed by the spaces between the dragon and the figure.

This exceptionally powerful netsuke of the Dragon King of the Sea is an example of a model illustrated from three different angles in *Sōken kishō*, where it is the only carving to be shown in such detail. It is attributed there to the important early carver Yoshimura Shūzan (see page 21), who always made his netsuke from painted cypress wood, and who is said never to have signed his work. The object held by Ryūjin is the jewel that he uses to control the tides.

ATTRIBUTED TO YOSHIMURA SHŪZAN (DIED 1773)
PAINTED CYPRESS WOOD; H. 3⅞ IN. (9.9 CM)
UNSIGNED
PRIVATE COLLECTION

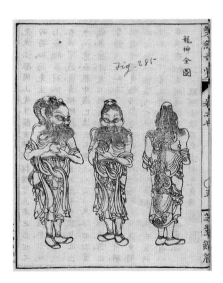

THREE VIEWS OF A NETSUKE OF RYŪJIN BY YOSHIMURA SHŪZAN, FROM INABA TSŪRYŪ, *SŌKEN KISHŌ* [1781], VOLUME 7, PP. 5–6. MUSEUM OF FINE ARTS, BOSTON

37 | KAKU SANNAN SUCKLING HER GREAT-GRANDMOTHER

A figural group of a young Chinese woman with her hair in a topknot, offering her breast to an elderly woman while her own child sits at her feet playing with a giant peach, the himotōshi *formed by holes in the younger woman's back and side, signed with incised and stained characters on the younger woman's back.*

Kaku Sannan, also called Tō Fujin (in Chinese, Hu Shannan or Tang Furen), suckled her aged great-grandmother who had lost all of her teeth and was no longer able to eat rice. She is one of the Nijūshikō (Filial Twenty-Four), a grouping of children and young people who were depicted widely in art of the Ming Dynasty. This carving is of particular interest in that, although it is undoubtedly Japanese, it appears to have been copied directly from a Ming ivory of a type represented by an example in the British Museum. The British Museum ivory, at 2⁷/₈ in., is only slightly taller than this netsuke, and has been in the museum's collection since the eighteenth century. It is drilled with two holes to form the equivalent of a *himotōshi*, so this may be one of the few cases known of a netsuke directly copied from a Chinese toggle. The signature appears to be much later and was perhaps added to enhance the purely Japanese credentials of the carving.

LATE 17TH–EARLY 18TH CENTURY
STAINED IVORY; H. 2¹¹/₁₆ IN. (6.8 CM)
WITH A LATER SIGNATURE: *MASAHIRO*
PRIVATE COLLECTION

38 | CHINESE DIGNITARY, perhaps SHO KATSURYŌ or GOMŌ

A compact standing figure with a beard, in a long gown and lobed cap, holding a scroll in his left hand and a fan made from feathers in his right, the himotōshi *formed by large and small holes in the back.*

This is another example of a netsuke that is derived more likely from a Chinese carving than from any printed source. Figures with this type of hat and fan are seen in eighteenth-century Japanese books illustrating earlier Chinese and Japanese paintings, and are often identified in the text as either the general and statesman Sho Katsuryō (181–234), or the filial exemplar and magician Gomō (in Chinese, Zhu Geliang or Wu Meng). This netsuke, however, bears a much closer resemblance to a late Ming (about 1580–1644) ivory figure of a deity or dignitary, exhibited at the British Museum in 1984; the catalogue entry suggests that the hat has mystical overtones, much like the mugwort skirts and shawls worn by *sennin*. Despite the probable origin of the design, the compact shape and concentrated facial expression exemplify the Japanese carver's success in assimilating and transforming the imported sculptural style.

EARLY–MID-18TH CENTURY

STAINED BOXWOOD; H. 4 ¹¹/₁₆ IN. (11.9 CM)

UNSIGNED

PRIVATE COLLECTION

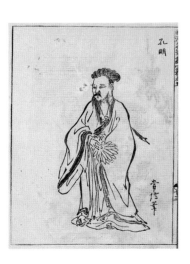

KŌMEI (SHO KATSURYŌ), AFTER KANŌ TSUNENOBU [1636–1713], FROM YOSHIMURA SHŪZAN (ILLUSTRATOR), *WAKAN MEIHITSU ZUHŌ* [1767], VOLUME 5, PP. 13–14. MUSEUM OF FINE ARTS, BOSTON

A tall figure of a Chinese general in an elaborately embroi-
dered long robe, tied at the front in a large bow, his left hand
stroking his beard and his right hand holding a halberd, the
blade curving upward over his head, the eyes inlaid in horn, the
himotōshi *formed by large and small holes in the back,*
partially concealed by the girdle.

Kan'u (in Chinese, Guanyu), originally a hero of China's
Three Kingdoms period (2nd–3rd centuries AD), is
depicted frequently in painting manuals of the eighteenth
century, usually shown in this approximate pose with
the left and right hands holding, respectively, his beard and
his halberd. He is one of the favorite subjects for figure
carving in the late Ming Dynasty, particularly after his
official deification in 1594 as Guandi, protector of the
Empire and talisman of China's armies. A seventeenth- or
early-eighteenth-century soapstone example in the
British Museum also has the left hand stroking the beard,
as in this figure.

EARLY–MID-18TH CENTURY
STAINED IVORY AND HORN; H. 5¾ IN. (14.6 CM)
UNSIGNED
PRIVATE COLLECTION

40 | KAN'U

A tall figure of a Chinese general in an elaborately embroidered long robe, tied at the front in a large bow, his left hand stroking his beard and his right hand holding a halberd with its blade pointing downward, his hand-protectors inlaid with horn studs, his shoes with green-stained ivory studs, the himotōshi *formed by one very large and one small hole in his back.*

EARLY–MID-18TH CENTURY

STAINED IVORY; H. 4⅝ IN. (11.8 CM)

UNSIGNED

PRIVATE COLLECTION

A figure of a Chinese general leaning slightly to his left in a dynamic pose, wearing an embroidered robe tied at the front in a large bow, his left hand stroking his beard and his right hand holding his halberd behind his back with its blade pointing downward, the himotōshi *formed by a small hole drilled at the back in a fold in one of the sleeves, signed with minute incised and stained characters inside the hem of the robe.*

In contrast to the two preceding netsuke, this figure almost certainly was based on a strikingly similar image of Kan'u found in volume 7 of *Ehon shahō bukuro*, illustrated by Tachibana Morikuni, originally published in 1720 and reissued in 1770. It is subtly different from the netsuke of Kan'u depicted in *Sōken kishō*, but closely follows the detail of Morikuni's design, with the sole important difference that, in Morikuni's depiction, the halberd is held away from Kan'u's body and is grasped by a demon attendant. Since this would have been impractical in a netsuke, the carver tucked the halberd away behind Kan'u's back. The change in the source of the design may account for the greater sculptural dynamism of this piece, which contrasts with the static feeling of the earlier, Chinese-derived models (cats. 39–40). A similar carving of Kan'u, with the same signature, is in the British Museum.

ATOKAMA (LATE 18TH CENTURY)
STAINED IVORY; H. 3⅛ IN. (7.9 CM)
SIGNED: *ATOKAMA*
PRIVATE COLLECTION

KAN'U AND ATTENDANT, FROM TACHIBANA MORIKUNI (ILLUSTRATOR), *EHON SHAHŌ BUKURO* [1720; THIS EDITION 1770], VOLUME 7, PP. 16–17. MUSEUM OF FINE ARTS, BOSTON

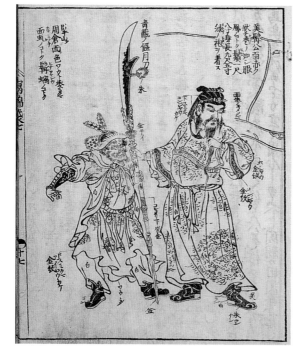

42 | KAN'U

An imposing, somewhat squat figure of a Chinese general, his left hand stroking his beard and his right hand holding a halberd with its blade pointing downward, the embroidered dragon and cloud designs on his robe represented by thick inlays of shell, the himotōshi *formed by a vertical opening in the back of the girdle.*

The shell inlaid in ebony, approximating the appearance of the Chinese technique of inlaying shell in black lacquer, emphasizes the subject's continental origins.

19TH CENTURY
EBONY AND SHELL; H. 3¾ IN. (9.5 CM)
UNSIGNED
PRIVATE COLLECTION

A massive group depicting a Chinese general, holding his beard in his left hand and his halberd in his right, riding on a horse with gigantic hooves that turns its head to the left and starts to graze, while a groom standing on the left struggles to pull the horse's head up, the himotōshi *formed by a single hole in the base, signed with incised characters on the base.*

In keeping with Hidemasa's reputation as an imitator and developer of earlier Kyoto styles (see cat. 33), Kan'u retains the basic elements of his time-honored pose but is turned into a comic figure accompanied by an undersized, incompetent groom. The dress and general appearance of this secondary figure are similar to those of the many stock Chinese figures who crowd the pages of eighteenth-century illustrated books.

CHINGENDŌ HIDEMASA
(LATE 18TH–EARLY 19TH CENTURY)
HEAVILY STAINED MARINE IVORY; H. 3⅛ IN. (7.9 CM)
SIGNED: *CHINGENDŌ HIDEMASA*
PRIVATE COLLECTION

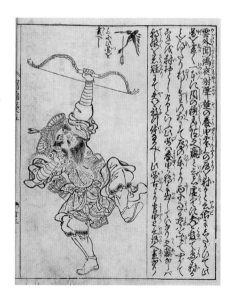

THE CHINESE ARCHER YŌ YŪKI [IN CHINESE, YANG YOUJI], FROM TACHIBANA MORIKUNI (ILLUSTRATOR), *EHON SHAHŌ BUKURO* [1720; THIS EDITION 1770], VOLUME 5, PP. 12–13. MUSEUM OF FINE ARTS, BOSTON

44 | *IJIN* AND CHILD

A tall figure with a curly beard and hair combed back, dressed in a long-sleeved coat tied at the front in a large bow, with a collar decorated with stylized cloud designs, his leggings decorated with large polka dots, his left hand held toward his face, his eyes inlaid with minute horn pupils, his right hand cradling a Chinese child with two topknots on either side of its head, the himotōshi *formed by large and small holes in the back of the carving below the sash.*

EARLY–MID-18TH CENTURY
STAINED IVORY AND HORN; H. 5⅞ IN.
(14.9 CM)
UNSIGNED
PRIVATE COLLECTION

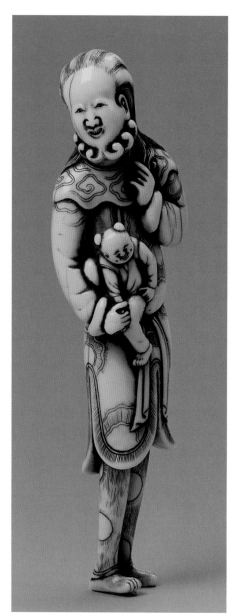

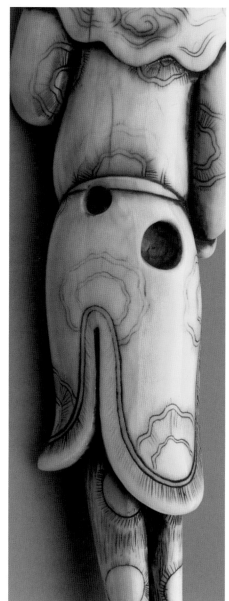

45 | *IJIN* AND MONKEY

A tall figure with a curly beard and hair, dressed in a richly embroidered long-sleeved coat with a scalloped collar, tied at the front in a large bow, his left hand holding a halberd with its blade downward, his right hand raised to his right shoulder where a monkey sits, its left paw on the top of his head and its right paw reaching down to steal something from one of the two baskets on the figure's belt, his eyes inlaid in horn, the himo-tōshi *formed by two unequal holes above and below the belt.*

In this variation on the "man and child" or "man and animal" theme, the free hand holds Kan'u's halberd (see cats. 39–41).

EARLY–MID-18TH CENTURY

STAINED IVORY AND HORN; H. 5⁷⁄₁₆ IN. (13.8 CM)

UNSIGNED

PRIVATE COLLECTION

46 | *IJIN* AND TIGER

A tall figure with a curly beard, his long hair tied in a band, dressed in a richly embroidered long-sleeved coat, tied at the front in a large bow, his right hand holding a hossu *(Buddhist priest's ritual whisk), his left hand raised to his left shoulder, the palm held outward and supporting a small tiger seated with its left front paw raised, the* himotōshi *formed by a small hole above and a large hole below the belt.*

The intricate hairwork on the small carving of a tiger, which creates such an effective contrast with the embroidered coat worn by the main figure, is reminiscent of early Osaka animals (see cat. 247). The smooth, gently curving back, as well as the arbitrary combination of basically Chinese dress with Western features, and of an exotic animal with a ritual implement, make this a classic example of an early *ijin* netsuke.

MID-18TH CENTURY

STAINED IVORY; H. 5⅝ IN. (14.3 CM)

UNSIGNED

PRIVATE COLLECTION

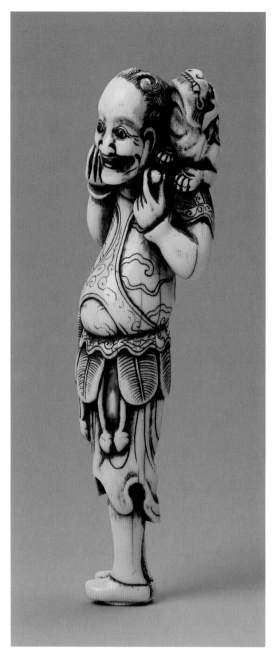

A tall standing figure of a curly-haired ijin *or* sennin, *wearing a patterned tunic and a girdle of leaves, carrying a* shishi *on his shoulders, the prominent eyes inlaid in horn, the* himotōshi *formed by two holes in the back above and below the girdle, the larger hole below the smaller.*

It probably mattered little to the carver of this netsuke whether it depicted a foreigner or a *sennin*. The *shishi* (see cat. 93), after all, is not a real creature, and the entire composition results from the creative combination of elements from a number of different pictorial sources – imaginary foreigners and beasts of the kind seen in the Japanese encyclopedia *Wakan sansai zue* (1713) perhaps jostling in the carver's imagination with the Chinese immortals depicted in earlier books about *sennin*. The bulging belly seen on this and several other early figure netsuke, not easy to depict in the simple woodblock techniques used for the illustrations to such works, is likely a feature borrowed directly from Chinese figure carvings of the late Ming Dynasty.

EARLY–MID-18TH CENTURY
STAINED IVORY AND HORN; H. 5¹⁄₁₆ IN. (12.9 CM)
UNSIGNED
PRIVATE COLLECTION

A very tall figure with a curly beard and hair, dressed in a richly embroidered long-sleeved coat tied at the front in a large bow, his left hand holding a dragon-headed halberd, his right hand raised to his right shoulder supporting the right hind leg of a shishi, *which rests its front paws on the top of his head, a basket tied at his right side, the eyes and buttons inlaid in dark horn, the* himotōshi *formed by two unequal holes on either side of the girdle.*

Like the *ijin* with a tiger (cat. 46), this unusually tall figure holds a fabulous beast that is in essence a miniature version of a netsuke, the *ijin*'s head replacing the more usual ball on which *shishi* often rest their front paws.

MID-18TH CENTURY
STAINED IVORY AND HORN; H. 6⁵⁄₁₆ IN. (16.1 CM)
UNSIGNED
PRIVATE COLLECTION

49 | *IJIN* AND CRANE

A very tall figure with a curly beard and hair, dressed in a coat decorated with stylized wave patterns and a girdle of mugwort, carved in low relief with a crane held in front of his body in both hands, the hat finished in wood, the feet forming the handle of a small knife that fits inside the body.

Several early netsuke also could be used as seals, but this is a rare example of another type of dual-purpose figurine, perhaps inspired by imitation of the samurai custom of carrying a small knife in the scabbard of the sword.

EARLY—MID-18TH CENTURY
NETSUKE INCORPORATING A HIDDEN KNIFE
STAINED IVORY, WOOD, AND STEEL; H. 6⁹⁄₁₆ IN. (16.7 CM)
UNSIGNED
PRIVATE COLLECTION

A standing figure with curly hair and a long beard, holding a cup in his left hand, his right hand gripping the hem of his garment, a sword in an enormous fish-scabbard slung over his back, the eyes inlaid (probably with horn), the himotōshi *formed by two holes in the back above and below the scabbard, inscribed with very small incised and stained characters next to the lower, larger hole.*

Clearly derived, at least in part, from the figure of Ryūjin reproduced in such detail in *Sōken kishō* (see cat. 36), with the fish-scabbard substituted for the dragon on Ryūjin's back, this is one of several netsuke of the same subject with the rare signature *Rokkon.* The deep staining of the wood and the combination of elaborate carving with a satisfyingly compact overall shape suggest the possible influence of Toyomasa of Tanba Province (see cat. 20).

EARLY–MID-19TH CENTURY

STAINED BOXWOOD AND HORN; H. 3¹¹⁄₁₆ IN. (9.4 CM)

SIGNED: *ROKKON*

PRIVATE COLLECTION

51 | CONTINENTAL MERCHANT

A simply carved, standing bearded figure, dressed in a long-sleeved coat and narrow-brimmed hat, holding a string of money against his body, the himotōshi *formed by two unequal holes in the back.*

Although it is impossible to be quite certain whether this piece represents a Chinese or Korean merchant, both the dress and the facial expression suggest that this netsuke is closer to observed reality than to the fantasy world of other works depicting wild-eyed, curly-haired foreigners carrying tigers and *shishi* on their shoulders.

EARLY–MID-18TH CENTURY

STAINED IVORY; H. 4⅜ IN. (11.1 CM)

UNSIGNED

PRIVATE COLLECTION

A figure with a long pigtail behind his back, dressed in contemporary Chinese style in a tunic with sleeves and buttons, cradling a covered jar in his right hand, his left wrist and fingertips placed against his side, the eyes and buttons inlaid in horn, the himotōshi *formed by two holes placed very close to one another on the back, signed with crudely scratched and stained characters below the higher of the two holes.*

This is a rare instance of an eighteenth-century netsuke depicting a Chinese person in recognizably contemporary dress. An early artist not listed in *Sōken kishō*, Jobun specialized in carving wood figures.

JOBUN (MID–LATE 18TH CENTURY)
STAINED BOXWOOD AND HORN; H. 4¼ IN. (10.8 CM)
SIGNED: *JOBUN*
PRIVATE COLLECTION

A very tall figure of a bearded archer in a tall brimmed hat, dressed in a long-sleeved coat edged with fur, tied at the front in a large bow, with a separate skirt edged with metal studs represented by dark horn inlay, his left hand holding his bow against his body and his right hand setting an arrow to the bowstring, an empty quiver on his back, the himotōshi *formed by a large hole in the skirt connecting with a much smaller hole above.*

This well-established type is seen in many eighteenth-century netsuke, but this is probably the largest recorded example. With an iconography standard both in netsuke and in contemporary encyclopedias, it is usually identified as a Dattanjin or Tartar. Equally, it could represent one of the male inhabitants of Orankai, a dependency of Dattan to the northeast of Korea, also depicted wearing tall brimmed hats and fur-trimmed robes.

MID-18TH CENTURY

STAINED IVORY AND HORN; H. 6⅛ IN. (15.5 CM)

UNSIGNED

PRIVATE COLLECTION

A very tall, mustached figure dressed in a long-sleeved Chinese robe, embroidered with dragons, waves, a mask, and other motifs, tied at the front in a large bow, wearing a brimmed hat and standing on one foot, playing a wide-mouthed wind instrument that he holds in both hands, the himotōshi *formed by two rather small holes in the back.*

This powerful fantasy owes its very dynamic shape to the piece of antler from which it was carved, another instance of the skill of the netsuke artist in making economical and effective use of materials.

EARLY—MID-18TH CENTURY
STAINED STAG ANTLER; H. 6 1/16 IN. (15.4 CM)
UNSIGNED
PRIVATE COLLECTION

55 | STANDING DUTCHMAN WITH BOY AND PUPPY

*A standing figure with a curly beard and wig, wearing a
brimmed hat decorated with a feather, a ruff, breeches, leather
shoes, and a long-sleeved knee-length coat, its hem embroidered with Chinese-style standing wave designs, his right arm
cradling a Chinese child, the child's right hand and his left
hand holding a leash tied around the neck of a dog that sits
at his feet, the* himotōshi *formed by a hole in the back
connecting with a larger hole drilled upward between the
figure's legs.*

Here a Chinese child, as seen in cat. 44, is combined
with an unmistakably Dutch adult, although his garment,
despite its basically Western cut, is decorated with
Chinese textile designs.

MID–LATE 18TH CENTURY

STAINED IVORY; H. 3¹³⁄₁₆ IN. (9.7 CM)

UNSIGNED

PRIVATE COLLECTION

56 | DUTCHMAN WITH A COCKEREL

*A standing, bewigged figure wearing a brimmed hat decorated
with a feather, breeches, leggings, leather shoes or clogs, and
a long-sleeved knee-length coat, its hem embroidered with floral
designs, both arms holding a large cockerel, the* himotōshi
*formed by a hole in the back connecting with a larger hole
drilled upward between the figure's legs.*

MID–LATE 18TH CENTURY

STAINED IVORY; H. 4⅝ IN. (11.7 CM)

UNSIGNED

PRIVATE COLLECTION

57 | DUTCHMAN HOLDING A WIND INSTRUMENT

A standing, bewigged figure wearing a Chinese or Tartar hat and a richly embroidered, long-sleeved Chinese robe, a ruff, breeches, leggings, and Chinese shoes, holding a large silver wind instrument to his body with both hands, the buttons and hat decorations of horn, the ruff of glass beads, the himotōshi *formed by a hole in the back connecting with a larger hole drilled upward between the figure's legs.*

The silver instrument and glass ruff, both probably later replacements, are an indication of the care that was taken to preserve early netsuke of good quality. Although it is conceivable that images of Dutchmen dressing up in Chinese clothes might have been accessible to the Kyoto or Osaka carvers, it seems much more likely that the combination of motifs seen here resulted from the workshop practice of using different facial types, garments, and attributes to produce an endlessly varied gallery of foreign beings.

MID–LATE 18TH CENTURY

IVORY, SILVER, JADE, AND HORN; H. 3⅞ IN. (9.9 CM)

UNSIGNED

PRIVATE COLLECTION

58 | DUTCHMAN WITH HARE

A standing figure wearing a long-sleeved, buttoned knee-length coat, wooden clogs, and a brimmed hat that covers most of his curly wig, carrying a dead hare tied by its hind legs to a stick held over his left shoulder, his eyes and buttons inlaid in horn, the himotōshi *formed by two unequal holes in the Dutchman's back on either side of the hare's right front paw, signed with incised and stained characters on an oval reserve underneath the right foot.*

In contrast to most netsuke of Dutchmen, which like other figures of *ijin* (see cats. 44–49) often are composed from arbitrary combinations of motifs, these two figures by Masanao (cats. 58–59) have a lifelike quality that suggests that they may have been inspired by Dutch prints, which were widely available in later eighteenth-century Japan. Even so, the rather Chinese-looking standing wave designs around the hem of the coat show that the artist was not immune to prevailing workshop practices. Masanao is praised highly in *Sōken kishō*, but nothing is known about his life and career beyond the fact that he was a resident of Kyoto. His careful visualization and delicate execution, which never sacrifices sculptural form to excessive detail, have made him one of the most highly prized of all netsuke artists.

MASANAO OF KYOTO (ACTIVE AROUND 1781)
STAINED IVORY AND HORN; H. 3¹¹⁄₁₆ IN. (9.3 CM)
SIGNED: *MASANAO*
PRIVATE COLLECTION

59 | DUTCH BOY WITH DEER

A standing figure wearing a long-sleeved, buttoned knee-length coat (unbuttoned up to the waist), buckled shoes, and a brimmed and tasseled hat (possibly intended to be Chinese), carrying a dead deer tied by its hind legs to a stick held over his right shoulder, his eyes and buttons inlaid in horn, the himotōshi *formed by the gap between his body and the deer's legs or neck, signed with incised and stained characters on an oval reserve on the right foot.*

MASANAO OF KYOTO (ACTIVE AROUND 1781)
STAINED IVORY AND HORN; H. 3 $^{15}/_{16}$ IN. (10.1 CM)
SIGNED: *MASANAO*
PRIVATE COLLECTION

Fabulous Beasts and Demons

THE IMAGINARY CREATURES GROUPED IN THIS SECTION FALL INTO TWO distinct categories. A few (cats. 102–118) have a very long history within the native Japanese tradition, but most (60–101) belong to the same China-oriented mental world as the *ijin* in the previous section, and like them are often based on models seen in illustrated books. These included not only Chinese encyclopedias and gazetteers (and their Japanese derivatives), but also painting manuals that reproduced the work of famous Chinese and Japanese artists. Several such manuals were illustrated by Yoshimura Shūzan, who was also famous as a netsuke carver.

A few of the Chinese beings depicted in early netsuke, such as the dragonlike God of Mount Shitsugozan (cats. 71 and 72), are highly unusual and have yet to be positively identified. Netsuke of this and other subjects, including the God of Mount Tenguzan (cat. 60), the *amaryō* or rain dragon, and the *hiryū* or flying dragon (cats. 65–68), are among the small number selected for reproduction in volume seven of *Sōken kishō*, published in 1781, which includes a short guide to netsuke and netsuke carvers. This suggests that they were very popular subjects, even if relatively few have survived to the present day. The exotic *amaryō* or *hiryū*, hardly seen in Japanese art before the seventeenth century, are very different from the more everyday dragons, *ryū* or *tatsu*. The latter are illustrated in their proper position between hares and snakes in the sequence of zodiac animals in the last section of this catalogue (cats. 266–269).

Several of the Chinese creatures favored by eighteenth-century netsuke buyers were prized for their auspicious significance. According to Confucian doctrine, the *hakutaku* (cats. 69–70) and the *kirin* (cats. 73–80) appear on earth only during the reign of a virtuous ruler, the *baku* (cats. 83–90) devours bad dreams, and the *shishi* (cats. 92–101) is the king of the beasts, representing elemental energy and vitality. Although the original models for most of these animals can be traced to pictures either by Chinese artists or by members of the Kanō school of Japanese academic painters, the medium that served as the immediate source of the designs – monochrome woodblock-printed books – had a profound influence on the appearance of early netsuke. The strong black lines on white paper translated naturally to ivory carving with heavy staining, and the need to turn these images into practical netsuke inspired ingenious efforts to simplify their overall forms (cat. 69). In the case of the *kirin*, this process culminated in the development of a model (cats. 75–80) that has no precedent in printed illustrations, and that has proved to be one of the most popular of all netsuke types in the West.

These Chinese subjects all originated in the Kamigata cities (Osaka and Kyoto), but later were made in provincial centers (cats. 81 and 82) as well as in the shogun's capital, Edo, where the fashion for netsuke spread toward the end of the eighteenth century. Purely Japanese imaginary creatures, such as the fishy-smelling *kappa* (cats. 102–104), the mountain-dwelling *tengu* (cats. 109 and 110), or the ubiquitous *oni* or demon (cats. 111–117), were seldom carved in the Kamigata but were extremely popular in nineteenth-century Edo. They are often featured in pattern books intended for use by netsuke carvers.

A monstrous figure wearing a demonic grin, with scaly skin and a long tail curled upward between its legs, its left hand resting on the end of its tail, its right hand pulling on a scarf that passes around its neck, standing on two balls, the eyes inlaid in pale and dark horn, the himotōshi *formed by the curl of the tail.*

The exact identity of this monster is uncertain. A very similar netsuke is illustrated in *Sōken kishō*, where it is captioned *Tenguzan no kami* (in Chinese, Tenyushanshen, The God of Mount Tenguzan; there is no connection with the better-known and purely Japanese monster called *tengu*, see cats. 109–110). The God of Mount Tenguzan is described in the text of volume 1 of the Chinese classic *Shan hai jing*, and a related creature, called simply a *Tengu* but written with the same characters, is discussed in volume 16. *Sōken kishō* claims that illustrated versions of *Shan hai jing* were much used by Yoshimura Shūzan (see page 21) as a source of subject matter, yet no illustrated edition of *Shan hai jing*, either Chinese or Japanese, has yet come to light that includes an image resembling either this netsuke or the *Sōken kishō* rendering. The assumption, therefore, must be that Shūzan or his contemporaries were inspired by one of the many popular, ephemeral editions of the work published in China during the seventeenth and eighteenth centuries. Volume 1 describes the God of Mount Tenguzan as having a dragon's body and a man's face (exactly the same words used to describe several other monsters in the text), while volume 18 states that the Tengu lives in the great western desert and is "a man with bent arms." Inaba's example is attributed to Unjutō Shumemaru, described in *Sōken kishō* as a Shinto priest who carved exclusively for special commissions and whose work is little known, but the only signed examples recorded bear the name of another artist, Kawai Yoritake (see cat. 109).

ATTRIBUTED TO KAWAI YORITAKE
OF KYOTO (ACTIVE AROUND 1781)
STAINED BOXWOOD AND HORN; H. 3⁵⁄₁₆ IN. (8.4 CM)
UNSIGNED
PRIVATE COLLECTION

NETSUKE OF THE GOD
OF MOUNT TENGUZAN BY
UNJUTŌ SHUMEMARU,
FROM INABA TSŪRYŪ,
SŌKEN KISHŌ [1781],
VOLUME 7, PP. 6–7.
MUSEUM OF FINE ARTS,
BOSTON

A tall and slender monstrous standing figure, with a dragon's head and a smooth body, its upper chest with simple spiral decorations, its right forearm stretched back to touch the top of its tail, its left hand touching its left thigh, the eyes inlaid in dark horn, the himotōshi *formed by the junction of the mane and the upper back.*

Although of ancient origin, *amaryō* or *chi* (in Chinese, *yulong* or *chi*), the smooth or rain dragon, is not much seen in Japanese art before the seventeenth century. The *amaryō* is featured frequently in written inventories of the shoguns' collections of Chinese lacquer in the fifteenth and sixteenth centuries, and its exotic, non-Japanese character is confirmed by the fact that it was used as a motif in high-quality lacquers intended for Europeans, such as the celebrated "Beckford" casket (about 1634–1640) at Chiddingstone Castle in Kent, England. *Kinmō zui*, an encyclopedia of all things continental published in 1666, lists four main types of dragon – the hornless *mizuchi*, the standard *tatsu*, the smooth *amaryō*, and the scaly *ryō* (akin to the *suiko*, see cat. 35) – while traditional Chinese references characterize the *amaryō* as being yellow, without horns, and similar to a sea horse.

18TH CENTURY

STAINED BOXWOOD AND HORN; H. 5 ¼ IN. (13.4 CM)

UNSIGNED

PRIVATE COLLECTION

*A tall monstrous standing figure with a dragon's head and a
smooth body, its long arms hanging down and touching its
thighs, its knees slightly bent, its long tail ending in a small curl,
the* himotōshi *formed by large and small holes next to the base
of the tail.*

This particular version of the *amaryō*, or rain dragon,
is illustrated in the section of *Sōken kishō* devoted to
Chinese carvings, indicating that the 1781 work continued
to influence netsuke design right up until the end of
the nineteenth century. A more conventional *amaryō* of
the type seen in Chinese art since early times is illustrated
on one of the pages of *Sōken kishō* showing netsuke by
Yoshimura Shūzan.

POSSIBLY BY OZAKI OR TAKEDA KOKUSAI (DIED 1894)

STAG ANTLER; H. 5 IN. (12.8 CM)

UNSIGNED

MUSEUM OF FINE ARTS, BOSTON 47.715

NETSUKE OF A RAIN
DRAGON, FROM INABA
TSŪRYŪ, *SŌKEN KISHŌ*
[1781], VOLUME 7, PP.
16–17. MUSEUM OF FINE
ARTS, BOSTON

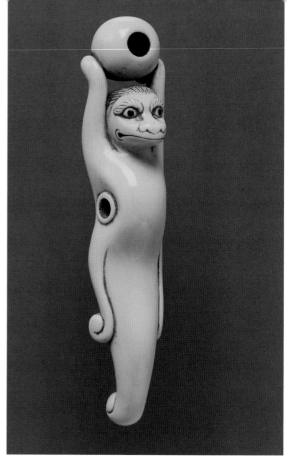

63 | DRAGON OR BIRD-MONSTER

A monstrous winged figure with a dragon's head and bird's wings, its legs folded upward against its chest and its tail looping back over the side of its body, the himotōshi formed by the junctions of the beard and breast or the legs and chest.

This creature does not conform to any of the monstrous beings illustrated in late Ming or early Edo reference works and imaginary gazetteers.

MID-LATE 18TH CENTURY

STAINED IVORY; H. 4⁹⁄₁₆ IN. (11.6 CM)

UNSIGNED

PRIVATE COLLECTION

64 | RAIN DRAGON HOLDING A BOWL ABOVE ITS HEAD

A tall monstrous creature, probably an amaryō or rain dragon, with a humanoid face, its body ending in a curled tail, its short arms holding a bowl above its head, the eyes inlaid in horn, the himotōshi formed by a hole passing transversely through the chest.

Like the preceding carving, this is a rare example of an early netsuke designed in such a way that it cannot be placed upright on a flat surface.

EARLY–MID-18TH CENTURY

STAINED IVORY AND HORN; H. 4³⁄₁₆ IN. (10.6 CM)

UNSIGNED

PRIVATE COLLECTION

A very light carving of a horned dragon's head, with a short tail ending in a curl, the surface lacquered first black and then red and polished so that the black nodules on the dragon's body show through the red layer, the design heightened with touches of gold lacquer, the himotōshi *formed by a rather narrow hole drilled transversely through the tail.*

The lacquering on this carving emulates the style traditionally associated with the temple Negoroji, founded in the twelfth century, in which a layer of black lacquer is covered with a layer of red lacquer and then rubbed, either deliberately or through prolonged use, until the black lacquer is visible again. In the case of this piece, the rubbing was probably deliberate and was intended to impart a look of greater antiquity. *Sōken kishō* mentions a certain Hata Tomofusa as a specialist in lacquered netsuke, indicating that such pieces certainly existed before 1781.

18TH CENTURY
CYPRESS WOOD WITH RED, BLACK, AND GOLD LACQUERING
L. 6⅛ IN. (15.5 CM)
UNSIGNED
PRIVATE COLLECTION

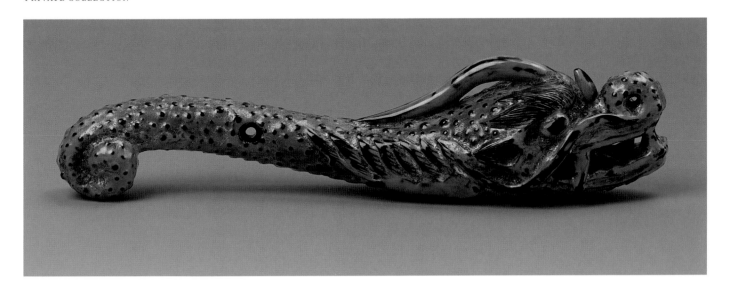

A horned dragon's head and torso terminating in a fishlike tail, which turns underneath the body, forming a loop, the wings held tightly against the sides, the mouth wide open, the underside of the body finished with a flat polished surface, drilled with a hole that connects with another very large, deep hole by the end of the tail, forming the himotōshi.

This carving is slightly different from the drawing of a *hiryū* ("flying dragon") netsuke that appears on one of the pages of *Sōken kishō* showing pieces by Unjutō Shumemaru. The tail curls downward instead of upward, the wings are smaller, and the eyes are set deeply instead of bulging prominently as in the illustrated example.

MID–LATE 18TH CENTURY

STAINED BOXWOOD; L. 3$^{7}/_{16}$ IN. (8.7 CM)

UNSIGNED

PRIVATE COLLECTION

NETSUKE OF A FLYING
DRAGON, FROM INABA
TSŪRYŪ, *SŌKEN KISHŌ*
[1781], VOLUME 7,
PP. 6–7. MUSEUM OF
FINE ARTS, BOSTON

A horned dragon's head and torso terminating in a fishlike tail, which turns to the right of the body, forming a loop, the small, finlike wings held tightly against the sides, the snout turned back, the jaws clenched around a tai *or sea-bream, the eyes of the dragon inlaid in ivory and horn and those of the* tai *in horn only, the* himotōshi *formed by one very large and one small hole carved in the underside of the dragon's lower jaw.*

This netsuke is an elaboration of the prototype illustrated in *Sōken kishō*, with bolder, deeper carving, a more dynamic shape, prominent inlay, and the addition of a fish between the dragon's jaws. If the dragon was worn with the head facing upward, as must have been intended, the larger hole of the *himotōshi* would have been uppermost, in contrast to most early figure netsuke where the smaller hole is uppermost.

LATE 18TH CENTURY

STAINED BOXWOOD, IVORY, AND HORN; L. 4⅜ IN.

(11.2 CM)

UNSIGNED

PRIVATE COLLECTION

68 | FLYING DRAGON

A horned dragon's head with a very short, fishlike body, terminating in a tail that turns to the left of the body, the small, finlike wings held tightly against the sides, the eyes set deeply behind a prominent snout and inlaid with horn, the himotōshi *formed by a hole in the base connecting with the mouth cavity.*

LATE 18TH CENTURY
STAINED IVORY AND HORN; L. 3⁵⁄₁₆ IN. (8.4 CM)
UNSIGNED
PRIVATE COLLECTION

A seated man-beast, its head with a human face, curly hair, and two horns, its body in the shape of an ox sitting with its legs folded under its body, a third eye in the center of the forehead and three more eyes and a pair of horns on either side of the body, the himotōshi *formed by large and small holes in the base, the larger hole in the fold of the left hind leg, the smaller hole behind the front legs.*

An ink painting of a standing version of this creature was reproduced in 1750 by the netsuke artist and book illustrator Yoshimura Shūzan in his *Wakan meihitsu gaei* (Glories of Japanese and Chinese Painting). The picture is captioned *Hakutaku higai no zu* (Disaster-Averting Picture of a *Hakutaku*), a reference to an early Chinese account which relates that the legendary Yellow Emperor found a magical beast at Hakutaku (in Chinese, Baize, or the "White Marsh") near Mount Kōzan (in Chinese, Hengshan). Discovering that the creature understood human speech, the emperor questioned it about the gods and spirits of heaven and earth, and ordered that its portrait be painted and made an object of worship; during the Tang Dynasty, the *hakutaku* was depicted on banners. Like the *kirin* and *hō-ō* (see cats. 73 and 215), it is believed to appear on earth only during the reign of a virtuous monarch. As both a protective talisman and a symbol of virtuous government, this *hakutaku* perfectly encapsulates the spirit of popular Confucianism that inspired so many of the earlier netsuke. It is also an outstanding example of the ability of the netsuke carver to transform a complex, spiky image with six horns and four long legs into a compact and practical toggle.

LATE 17TH–EARLY 18TH CENTURY
STAINED IVORY; L. 1¹⁵⁄₁₆ IN. (5 CM)
UNSIGNED
PRIVATE COLLECTION

STANDING HAKUTAKU, FROM YOSHIMURA SHŪZAN (ILLUSTRATOR), *WAKAN MEIHITSU GAEI* [1750; THIS EDITION 1807], VOLUME 6, PP. 3–4. MUSEUM OF FINE ARTS, BOSTON

A standing man-beast, its head with a human face, curly hair, and two horns, its body in the shape of an ox, a third eye in the center of the forehead and three more eyes and thirteen horns on either side of the body, the nine eyes all inlaid in horn, the himotōshi *formed by a large hole under the body connecting with a small hole in the side.*

Some printed illustrations of *hakutaku*, such as that in *Morokoshi kinmō zui*, an encyclopedia of all things continental published in 1719, give it a single horn and no extra eyes, but these distinctive and exotic markers were clearly irresistible to early netsuke carvers. This example owes its unusual pose to an attempt to create a compact carving without completely losing the spirit of the standard pictorial depiction of *hakutaku*, which generally are shown standing.

EARLY–MID-18TH CENTURY
STAINED BOXWOOD AND HORN; H. 1⅝ IN. (4.2 CM)
UNSIGNED
PRIVATE COLLECTION

A standing figure of a fearsome imaginary beast with a dragon-like head and forelegs, the face contorted in an angry roar, a long mane, a snake's or dragon's body, scaly haunches, and a horse's hooves and tail, supported on its tail and hooves with its body arched in an S-shape, its right foreleg grasping its right haunch, its left foreleg raised upward in a threatening gesture, flames licking around its body, painted in red, blue, and other pigments, no himotōshi.

This creature resembles one of a group of pieces illustrated in *Sōken kishō* that are said to be the work of the netsuke carver and book illustrator Yoshimura Shūzan. The *Sōken kishō* illustration is not captioned, unlike that of the God of Mount Tenguzan (see cat. 60), but has long been assumed to represent a *shokuin* (in Chinese, *zhuyin*, literally "light and shade"). The *shokuin* is a fabulous being first mentioned in the Chinese text *Shan hai jing*, which offers little information about the creature's appearance beyond telling us that it is red, has a snake's body and a human face, and is one thousand leagues long. All Chinese and Japanese captioned illustrations of *shokuin*, including that in a 1902 Japanese reprint of the sixteenth-century Chinese illustrated edition of *Shan hai jing*, show a rather harmless-looking snakelike creature in quite a different pose, with one or more heads and a forked tongue, but no hooves or haunches. This would suggest that the accepted identification is incorrect, and in fact, the 1902 work includes several standing, four-legged monsters that bear a much closer resemblance to this piece, making due allowance for the crude and formulaic nature of the book's illustrations. Of these, the most likely candidate is the God of Mount Shitsugozan (in Chinese, Qiwu-shan, volume 1, figure 5), with a dragon's torso, scaly humanoid arms, chicken claws, and flames licking around its body. Until we can identify a Chinese illustrated text

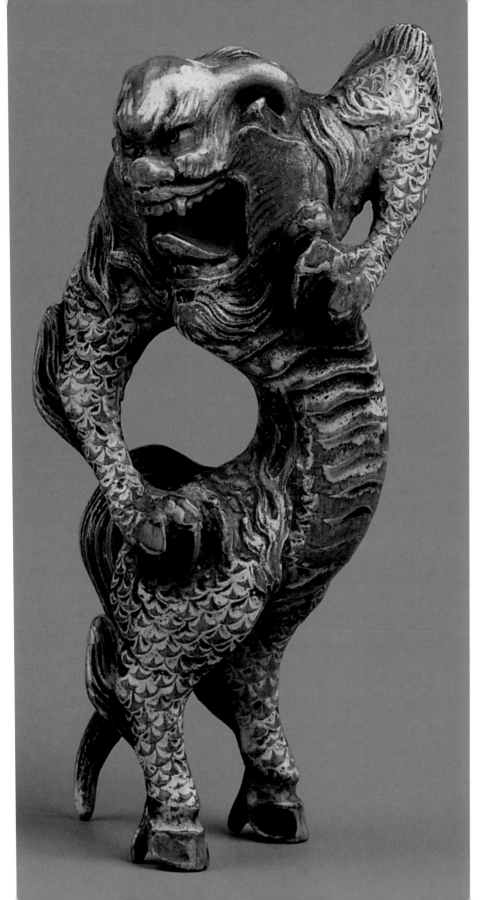

that corresponds more exactly to this type (of which about a dozen early examples are known), it will be impossible to be sure of its intended identity, but it is certainly not the same as the limbless *shokuin.*

ATTRIBUTED TO YOSHIMURA SHŪZAN
(DIED 1773)
PAINTED CYPRESS WOOD; H. 3¼ IN. (8.3 CM)
UNSIGNED
PRIVATE COLLECTION

NETSUKE OF THE GOD OF
MOUNT SHITSUGOZAN BY
YOSHIMURA SHŪZAN,
FROM INABA TSŪRYŪ,
SŌKEN KISHŌ [1781],
VOLUME 7, PP. 2–3.
MUSEUM OF FINE ARTS,
BOSTON

A creature with a dragon's head, a single horn on its forehead,
a scaly body, and a long tail arranged upward along its back,
crouching on its haunches, its forelegs supporting its long neck
as it looks directly upward with its mouth slightly open,
flames licking around its body, the tiny pupils inlaid in horn,
the himotōshi *formed by two holes of almost equal size in*
its right side, signed with incised and stained characters on a
rectangular reserve underneath the right hind leg.

Despite the highly sculptural quality of this piece, the
unusual material, the slightly different modeling of
the neck, and the very crisp and easily breakable under-
cutting in some areas suggest that it may be a somewhat
later workshop production.

IZUMIYA TOMOTADA OF KYOTO (ACTIVE AROUND 1781);
POSSIBLY EARLY 19TH CENTURY
STAINED BOXWOOD AND HORN; H. 4⁷⁄₁₆ IN. (11.3 CM)
SIGNED: *TOMOTADA*
MUSEUM OF FINE ARTS, BOSTON 47.796

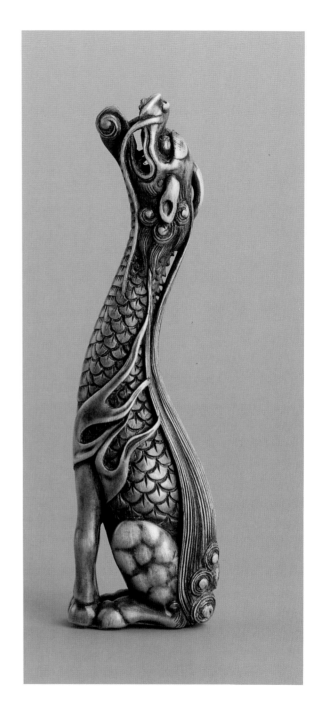

A creature with a dragon's head, a single horn on its forehead, a scaly body, and a long tail arranged upward along its back, crouching on its haunches, its forelegs supporting its long neck as it looks directly upward with its mouth slightly open, flames licking around its body, the tiny pupils inlaid in dark horn, the himotōshi *formed by two holes of almost equal size in its left side, signed with incised and stained characters on a rectangular reserve underneath the left hind leg.*

This is a rare example of a howling *kirin* facing to the right, with the *himotōshi* holes and signature on the left. Virtually nothing is known of Yoshimasa, who is not listed in *Sōken kishō* and is assumed to be a slightly later follower of Yoshinaga.

YOSHIMASA (LATE 18TH–EARLY 19TH CENTURY)
STAINED IVORY AND DARK HORN; H. 4½ IN. (11.4 CM)
SIGNED: *YOSHIMASA*
PRIVATE COLLECTION

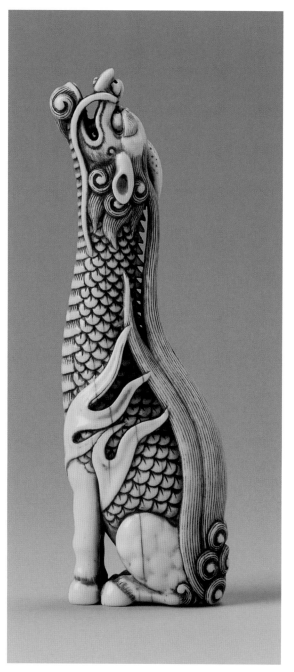

80 | HOWLING *KIRIN*

A creature with a dragon's head, a single horn on its forehead, a scaly body, and a long tail arranged upward along its back, crouching on its haunches, its forelegs supporting its long neck as it looks directly upward with its mouth slightly open, flames licking around its body, the tiny pupils inlaid in ebony, the himotōshi *formed by two holes of almost equal size in its right side, signed with incised and stained characters on a rectangular reserve underneath the right hind leg.*

YOSHIMASA (LATE 18TH–EARLY 19TH CENTURY)
STAINED IVORY AND EBONY; H. 4⅛ IN. (10.5 CM)
SIGNED: *YOSHIMASA*
PRIVATE COLLECTION

A creature with an ox's body, a dragonlike face, a single horn, and a shaggy tail, squatting on its haunches with its body twisted to the left, the eyes inlaid in pale and dark horn, the himotōshi *formed by the junction of the left legs, signed with incised and stained characters on a rounded rectangular reserve underneath the right haunch.*

Ikkan of Nagoya is one of those rare netsuke artists whose precise life dates have been established, thanks to local research by Japanese amateur historians. The younger brother of the head priest of a minor temple in Nagoya with a meager congregation, he was forced to seek a living as a netsuke artist, but also carved religious images including a small Amida Buddha that he completed at the age of seventy-two. His netsuke are prized for their depiction of animals, and this netsuke, although of an imaginary beast, is a good example of the work of the generation of regional carvers who inherited and adapted the Kyoto style, moving in the direction of a studied naturalism inspired by painters of the Shijō school. The animal's *kirin*-like attributes are minimized, making it look more like an ox or buffalo with an outlandish head and tail.

TAKAOKA IKKAN OF NAGOYA (1817–1893)
STAINED CHERRY WOOD AND HORN; H. 1⁵⁄₁₆ IN. (3.3 CM)
SIGNED: *IKKAN*
MUSEUM OF FINE ARTS, BOSTON 11.23252

A very small carving of a creature with a dragon's head, a single horn on its forehead, a scaly body, and a luxuriant long tail arranged in a mass of curls, crouching on its haunches with its head turned sharply to the left, the eyes inlaid in pale horn, the himotōshi *formed by the right hind leg, signed underneath with very small incised and stained characters on a polished oval reserve.*

Toyomasa shows his usual skill in integrating intricate, almost baroque carving into a compact shape.

NAITŌ TOYOMASA OF TANBA PROVINCE (1773–1856)
STAINED BOXWOOD AND HORN; H. 1⁷⁄₁₆ IN. (3.7 CM)
SIGNED: *TOYOMASA*
PRIVATE COLLECTION

83 | *BAKU*

*A creature with a long trunk, two tusks, a luxuriant, curly mane and tail,
and a spotted coat, squatting with its head raised in the air, the pupils drilled
and stained black, the* himotōshi *formed by the junction of the end of the
tail and the animal's back, signed with incised and stained characters on a
rectangular reserve between the hind legs.*

Like many of the other fantastic Chinese beasts favored by early
netsuke carvers, the *baku* is an amalgam of features drawn from real
animals. In *Wakan sansai zue* (1713), it is said to have an elephant's
trunk, the eyes of a *sai* (another mythical beast akin to the rhinoceros), an ox's tail, and tiger's feet. Early-eighteenth-century painting
manuals, such as *Ehon shahō bukuro* (1720), show the *baku* with a
spotted coat and a luxuriant mane and tail. These features are
included in this and the following piece (although the spots are

much worn on this example), but were often ignored by later carvers.
In contrast to the rather abstract political virtues associated with the
hakutaku and *kirin*, *baku* served the eminently practical function of
devouring bad dreams, and were therefore often depicted on the sides
of lacquered pillows made as part of formal wedding gift sets. Gechū,
an artist listed in *Sōken kishō* but with no information beyond the fact
that "netsuke with this signature exist," is best known for his *baku*,
shishi, and tigers.

GECHŪ (EARLY–MID-18TH CENTURY)
STAINED IVORY; H. 3⅛ IN. (7.9 CM)
SIGNED: *GECHŪ*
PRIVATE COLLECTION

84 | *BAKU*

85 | *BAKU*

A creature with a short trunk, two tusks, a luxuriant, curly mane and tail, and a spotted coat, squatting with its head turned sharply to the left, the pupils inlaid in dark horn, two himotōshi *formed by the junction of the left and right legs.*

A creature with a long trunk, two small tusks, and a luxuriant, curly mane and tail, sitting up on its haunches and looking downward, its trunk extended, the elaborate carving creating numerous himotōshi.

This tiny netsuke was probably carved from the tip of an elephant tusk. Its compact shape and neat arrangement of the oversized hooves underneath the body prefigure the mature Kyoto animal style seen in the work of artists such as Tomotada and Masanao.

LATE 18TH CENTURY

STAINED BOXWOOD; H. 2¹⁄₁₆ IN. (5.3 CM)

UNSIGNED

PRIVATE COLLECTION

MID-18TH CENTURY

STAINED IVORY AND HORN; H. 1¹⁄₄ IN. (3.2 CM)

UNSIGNED

PRIVATE COLLECTION

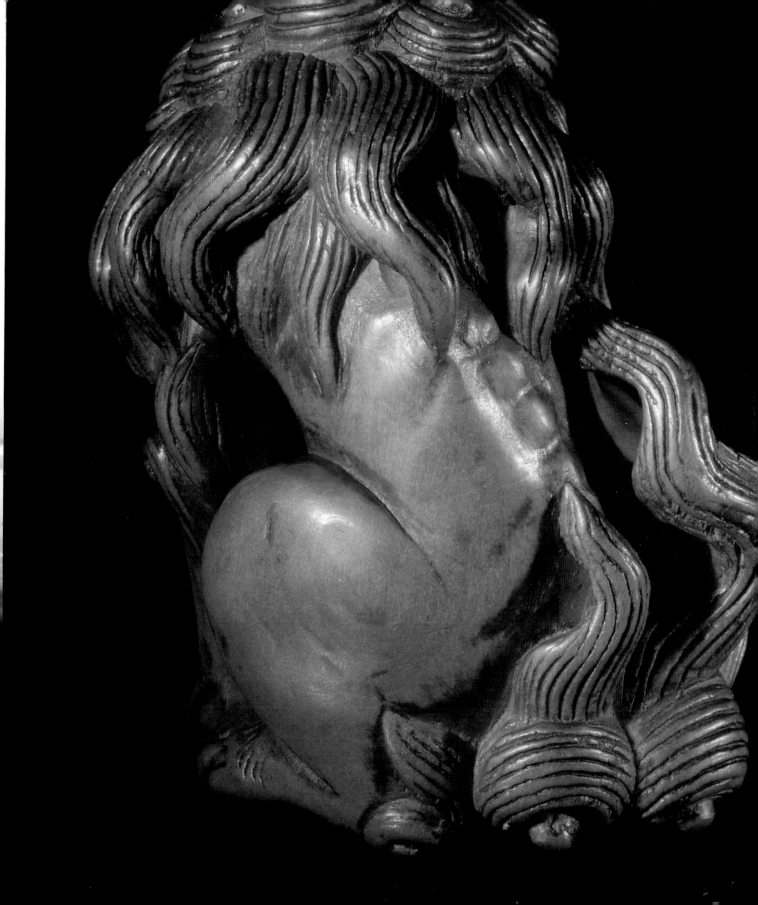

A human-headed beast standing on a rounded rectangular base, wearing a cap, its head turned to the right, its mane and tail meeting on its back, the pupils inlaid in horn, the himotōshi formed by a single hole in the base, signed underneath with incised and stained characters.

This figure appears to be copied from an almost identical type illustrated (but not captioned) in *Sōken kishō*, in a section devoted to carvings of continental origin. Some of these also serve as seals, which can be adapted to function as netsuke by drilling holes through them or winding threads around them. The origin of the design is perhaps a large, late-seventeenth-century image in the temple Gohyakurakanji in Edo, known as the *baku* king and representing a different iconographic tradition from the *baku* netsuke shown on the preceding pages (cats. 83–88).

GYOKUMIN (MID–LATE 19TH CENTURY)
STAINED BOXWOOD AND HORN; H. 1 $\frac{7}{16}$ IN. (3.6 CM)
SIGNED: *GYOKUMIN*, WITH A *KAŌ*
MUSEUM OF FINE ARTS, BOSTON 17.25

NETSUKE OF A HUMAN-HEADED CREATURE, FROM INABA TSŪRYŪ, *SŌKEN KISHŌ* [1781], VOLUME 7, PP. 16–17. MUSEUM OF FINE ARTS, BOSTON

91 | MYTHICAL BEAST

A beast with a demonic two-horned head, a curly mane, a feathered back, mammalian forelegs and scaly hind legs, sitting over a ball perched on top of a stand carved with openwork demon designs, its forelegs resting on the stand and holding the ball, its hind legs on either side of the stand, its tail curled in a loop, the himotōshi *formed by a hole drilled under the right foreleg connecting to the inside of the stand.*

The *himotōshi* appears to have been added later, suggesting that this powerful miniature may well have started life as a seal. The unusual style of carving would also support the hypothesis that this was perhaps originally a Chinese artifact imported to Japan and later remodeled to form a netsuke.

LATE 17TH–EARLY 18TH CENTURY

STAINED IVORY; H. 2^{11}/$_{16}$ IN. (6.8 CM)

UNSIGNED

PRIVATE COLLECTION

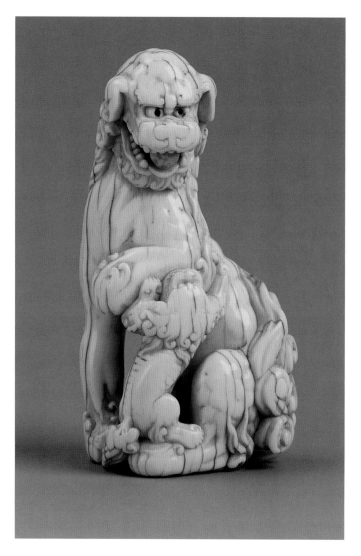

A parent shishi *seated on its haunches and raised up on its right foreleg, its head, with a curly beard and mane, turned to the left with its mouth slightly open, the cub standing up on the parent's left foot and reaching up to bite playfully on the parent's left foreleg, the* himotōshi *formed by a hole in the base connecting with another in the parent's right side, signed with incised characters on a rectangular panel under the left hind leg.*

This powerful netsuke is a magnificent example of a style of *shishi* carving that is very distinct from the more familiar type seen on the following pages (cats. 93–98). Although all of the surfaces are well worn and there are extensive cracks from age, it is not necessarily much older than some in the other group. Garaku is listed in *Sōken kishō*, which also (and uncharacteristically) gives the name of his teacher, Tawaraya Denbei, suggesting perhaps that he was of the second generation of professional carvers, and thus was unlikely to have been active much before the early eighteenth century. Unfortunately, *Sōken kishō* tends not to make it clear whether the artists listed are alive or dead, or whether more than one artist used the same name, but in this particular case it does seem reasonable to speculate that there was more than one artist or generation of artists using the name Garaku.

GARAKU RISUKE OF OSAKA (EARLY–MID-18TH CENTURY)
STAINED IVORY; H. 3⅝ IN. (9.2 CM)
SIGNED: *GARAKU*
PRIVATE COLLECTION

A shishi or sangei *with its hind legs on a ball and its forelegs on the ground, looking upward towards its tail of five curls, which folds down over its body to reach its face, the eyes inlaid in dark horn, the ball polished so as to bring out the criss-cross texture of the ivory, the* himotōshi *formed by the junction of the tail and head.*

Famed for its ability to run five hundred leagues in a single day, often called the "king of beasts" as in the West, and known as the mount of Monjū, a Buddhist goddess of wisdom, the *shishi* has been a favorite subject in East Asian art since early times. Of all the fabulous beasts seen in both eighteenth-century painting manuals and netsuke, the prancing, gamboling *shishi* (often under the alternative names *sangei* or *gei*) offers the clearest visual evidence of the debt owed by the early carvers to printed images. The need to convey the animals' luxuriant manes, vividly patterned coats, and lively behavior in the woodblock medium encouraged the development of a highly mannered graphic style that translated perfectly from carved block to carved ivory, another basically monochromatic medium, although the radiating marks around each of the *shishi*'s spots usually are omitted, as in this example. It was this two-dimensional source material that enabled the Kyoto and Osaka carvers to break away from earlier varieties of miniature *shishi*, probably based on actual Chinese seals and other carvings, and to develop a highly distinctive type that is particular to the netsuke medium. The cord for this netsuke probably was threaded through the gap between head and tail, so that when worn it would have appeared to be leaping down the wearer's *obi*, just as printed versions are often shown leaping down the page.

MID-18TH CENTURY

STAINED IVORY AND HORN; H. 2⁷⁄₁₆ IN. (6.2 CM)

UNSIGNED

PRIVATE COLLECTION

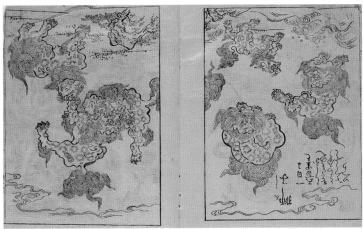

SHISHI, FROM ANON.,
EHON SHOSHIN HASHIRADATE
[1715; THIS EDITION 1761],
VOLUME 1, PP. 1–2.
VICTORIA AND ALBERT
MUSEUM

94 | *SHISHI*

A recumbent shishi *with its head turned to the left, licking its outstretched left front paw, the curls of its mane and tail boldly modeled, the eyes inlaid in horn, the* himotōshi *formed from two rather small holes underneath the body, the* kaō *incised and stained next to the smaller hole.*

This is a rare case of a netsuke signed only with a *kaō*, a kind of cursive monogram. The use of the *kaō* originally was restricted to members of the aristocratic, priestly, and artistic elite, but later was extended to other social classes.

MID-18TH CENTURY

STAINED IVORY AND HORN; L. 2⅞ IN. (7.3 CM)

SIGNED WITH A *KAŌ*

PRIVATE COLLECTION

95 | *SHISHI*

A shishi in a contorted pose, with its chin touching the ground and its left hind leg scratching the top of its head, its tail with the standard five curls laid flat along its back, one curl on each of the legs and three on the mane, a loose ball in its mouth, the eyes inlaid in dark horn, the* himotōshi *formed by a larger hole in the right haunch connecting with a smaller hole in the body.*

Both sides of this classic *shishi* netsuke bear all of the marks of long and careful use.

MID-18TH CENTURY

STAINED IVORY AND HORN; H. 2 IN. (5.1 CM)

UNSIGNED

PRIVATE COLLECTION

96 | SHISHI

A very vigorous carving of a shishi *with a luxuriant tail and mane, squatting down on its front paws, its tail curled over its body, its head turned to the left, wearing a characteristically ferocious expression, a loose ball in its mouth, the eyes inlaid in horn, alternative* himotōshi *formed by the tail and feet, signed underneath with small incised and stained characters on a rectangular reserve.*

This very compact carving, only slightly more refined than the unsigned examples shown on the preceding pages (cats. 93–95), achieves a perfect balance between the contrasting qualities of raw natural energy and grotesque caricature seen in eighteenth-century *shishi* netsuke. Matsura Seizan (1760–1841), Lord of Hirado, owned a netsuke of two "crazy" *shishi* that must have looked something like this.

IZUMIYA TOMOTADA OF KYOTO (ACTIVE AROUND 1781)
STAINED IVORY AND HORN; H. 2 $\frac{1}{16}$ IN. (5.3 CM)
SIGNED: *TOMOTADA*
PRIVATE COLLECTION

97 | SEATED *SHISHI*

A seated shishi *about to scratch its chin with its left hind leg, its head turned to the left, a loose ball in its mouth, its weight supported on its forelegs, the five wavelike endings of its tail stretching up its back, the eyes inlaid in dark horn, the* himotōshi *formed by a very large and a small hole in its right side, signed underneath with incised and stained characters on a rectangular reserve next to the larger hole.*

IZUMIYA TOMOTADA OF KYOTO (ACTIVE AROUND 1781)
STAINED IVORY AND HORN; H. 2 IN. (5.1 CM)
SIGNED: *TOMOTADA*
PRIVATE COLLECTION

98 | STANDING *SHISHI*

A powerfully carved figure of a shishi standing with its left foreleg and hind leg touching, a loose ball in its mouth, its tail curling upward over its back, its head turned sharply upward to the left, the curls and patterns on the coat emphasized by heavy staining, the himotōshi formed by a large hole underneath the body connecting with a smaller hole in the side.

Although carved from wood instead of the more usual ivory, this standing *shishi* is probably based on a book illustration, just like the gamboling and prancing creatures seen in the preceding examples.

MID–LATE 18TH CENTURY

STAINED BOXWOOD; H. 3 IN. (7.7 CM)

UNSIGNED

PRIVATE COLLECTION

99 | *SHISHI*

A shishi crouching down on all fours, most of its body covered by the curls of its mane and tail, its head turned sharply back to the left, a loose ball in its mouth, the eyes inlaid in pale horn with dark horn pupils, several himotōshi formed by the tail and feet, signed with incised characters on a rounded rectangular reserve underneath the right hind leg.

As usual, Toyomasa develops the earlier prototype, in this case exaggerating the animal's curls and contrasting their traditional whirling lines with more up-to-date, naturalistic fur markings incised on the body in place of the standard spots.

NAITŌ TOYOMASA OF TANBA PROVINCE (1773–1856)

STAINED BOXWOOD AND HORN; H. 1⁵⁄₁₆ IN. (3.4 CM)

SIGNED: *TOYOMASA*

PRIVATE COLLECTION

A button netsuke intricately carved in openwork, with two gamboling shishi *on one side and peony blossoms on the other, the eyes of both animals inlaid in dark horn, the* himotōshi *formed by a hole through the central peony blossom on the reverse and a larger hole to its side, signed with a single incised and stained character on a square plaque.*

The association of the *shishi*, the king of beasts, with the *botan* or tree peony, traditionally the king (or queen) of flowers, is emblematic of royal power. The phrase *botan ni karashishi* ("a Chinese lion on a peony") also stands proverbially for a good fit or happy coincidence. This is an example of a *Ryūsa manjū* netsuke, a buttonlike openwork carving associated with Ryūsa, an eighteenth-century specialist in wood-turning. Most *Ryūsa manjū* date, however, from the middle or late nineteenth century. An artist usually linked with Ozaki Kokusai (see the following entry), Rensai often carved in a more conventional manner than his celebrated contemporary, but with no less skill. Two artists are said to have used the name, the first of them retiring in 1876.

ISHIKAWA RENSAI OF TOKYO (MID–LATE 19TH CENTURY)
RYŪSA MANJŪ NETSUKE
STAINED IVORY AND HORN; D. 1¹⁵⁄₁₆ IN. (4.9 CM)
SEALED: *REN*
PRIVATE COLLECTION

103 | *KAPPA* ON A TURTLE

A long-haired kappa *crouching on the back of a turtle, its large webbed front feet spread out in front of it, its head turned to the left, its mouth closed and showing two small fangs, the deep-set eyes inlaid in pale horn with black stained pupils, its body with toadlike skin, the turtle's limbs, head, and tail retracted, the* himotōshi *formed by a very large hole next to the turtle's tail connecting with a smaller hole in the center of the base, signed with incised and stained characters within an oval reserve.*

Ueda Reikichi claims that Chūichi was active in the early twentieth century, but a piece with this signature in the Trumpf Collection of the Linden Museum in Stuttgart can be dated firmly to the year 1893, and the present netsuke also appears to be of nineteenth-century date. Chūichi is presumed to be a pupil of Masakazu (see preceding entry), and the pairing of these two works allows a comparison between the work of master and pupil, showing a range of subtle differences in approach to the overall form, the positioning of the different elements, and the treatment of surface textures.

KAWAMI CHŪICHI OF OSAKA (LATE 19TH CENTURY)
STAINED BOXWOOD AND HORN; H. 1½ IN. (3.8 CM)
SIGNED: *CHŪICHI*
PRIVATE COLLECTION

104 | *KAPPA* LICKING CLAM JUICE FROM ITS FINGERS

A kappa in a leaf skirt, sitting next to a slightly opened clam, gripping the shell with its hind flippers and its left fore-flipper, and licking the fingers of its right flipper, the contrasting textures of the kappa's body, the skirt, and the shell carefully rendered, the eyes inlaid in dark horn, the himotōshi formed by a hole next to the kappa's right thigh lined in green-stained ivory, signed underneath with incised and stained characters on a rounded rectangular reserve.

Kappa often are shown with one foot trapped by a clam shell, making a vain attempt to escape, but in this later variation, the *kappa* has triumphed and is shown devouring its would-be captor. Suketada is thought to have been a pupil of Matsuda Sukenaga (see cat. 183).

EGURO SUKETADA OF TAKAYAMA,

HIDA PROVINCE (1852–1915)

STAINED BOXWOOD, HORN, AND STAINED IVORY;

H. 1½ IN. (3.9 CM)

SIGNED: *SUKETADA*

PRIVATE COLLECTION

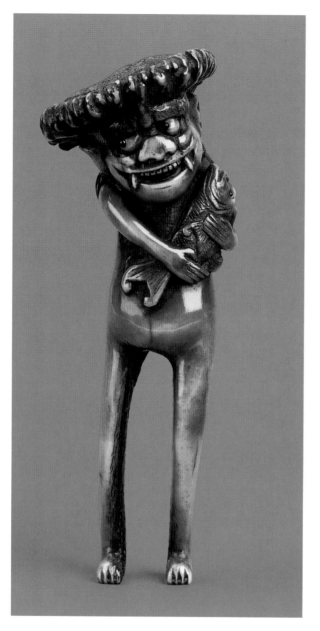

105 | *KAPPA* HOLDING A FISH

A very tall figure of a grinning kappa, *clasping a fish to its body, the back of its torso covered in scales, the top of its head formed from the root of the antler, the eyes of both* kappa *and fish inlaid in black horn, the* himotōshi *formed by a small hole in the back connecting to a central cavity.*

This very unusual netsuke exploits the ambiguity inherent in the *kappa*'s nature: as with carvings of *shishi*, the expression may be interpreted as either a grotesque caricature or a genuinely fearsome expression of monstrous rage.

19TH CENTURY

STAINED STAG ANTLER; H. 5$\frac{7}{16}$ IN. (13.8 CM)

UNSIGNED

PRIVATE COLLECTION

The stylized head of a kappa with a frightened, quizzical expression, its hair represented by the deer's natural fur, its long movable tongue carved from a separate piece of antler, terminating in a hook, the himotōshi *possibly formed by a hole through the nose, signed on the back with a single character in relief within a sunken square reserve.*

Ozaki Kokusai specialized in exploiting the root and hair of stag antler, often using it as an integral part of his carvings.

OZAKI OR TAKEDA KOKUSAI (DIED 1894)

SASHI NETSUKE

STAINED STAG ANTLER AND FUR; H. 4¹⁵⁄₁₆ IN. (12.5 CM)

SEALED: *KOKUSAI*

MUSEUM OF FINE ARTS, BOSTON 11.23722 A . B

A very light standing figure of a horned and bearded demon, supporting a lantern on its head, its arms folded together in front of its chest, its legs slightly apart, the wood partly painted with bluish pigments, now much worn, the himotōshi *formed by large and small holes on the back on either side of the girdle, the larger hole below the smaller.*

This carving is very similar to an illustration in *Sōken kishō* in the section devoted to work by Yoshimura Shūzan, but it is impossible to be certain whether the netsuke is copied from the printed version or antedates it. The classical model for the figure is a famous painted wood figure dating from 1215 in the temple Kōfukuji in Nara, attributed to the sculptor Kōben. The figure might have come to Shūzan's attention in 1717, when it was rescued from a fire that engulfed the building in which it was housed. Following this incident, inscriptions were discovered inside the image that gave details both of its authorship and of the exact date of its completion or dedication. The thirteenth-century model, one of a pair with another demon carrying a lantern on its left shoulder, differs from the netsuke version in several respects. In Kōben's work, the lantern has six sides and an elaborate cover, while the demon wears a scarf from which the head of a small dragon peeps out; the demon is dressed in a simple loincloth rather than the elaborate skirt seen here, and looks upward at the load on its head rather than straight out at the viewer.

ATTRIBUTED TO YOSHIMURA SHŪZAN (DIED 1773)
PAINTED CYPRESS WOOD; H. 5¾ IN. (14.6 CM)
UNSIGNED
PRIVATE COLLECTION

NETSUKE OF RYŪTŌKI BY YOSHIMURA SHŪZAN, FROM INABA TSŪRYŪ, *SŌKEN KISHŌ* [1781], VOLUME 7, PP. 2–3. MUSEUM OF FINE ARTS, BOSTON

A tall bearded figure with a huge sword slung on his back, dressed in a cloth cap and a gown embroidered with a dragon, tied with a long tasseled girdle from which hangs a double gourd, towering over a demonic figure who looks up at him with a mixture of fear and defiance, the himotōshi *formed by large and small holes in the back, the larger hole below the smaller.*

This early unsigned image of Shōki the Demon Queller and an *oni* or demon exemplifies the characteristics of Shōki that had become established in Japan as early as the thirteenth century: awesome power and the ruthless imposition of the Buddhist law. Shōki (in Chinese, Zhong Kui) first made his appearance in eighth-century China, when the Tang Emperor Ming Huang had a dream in which he saw a large demon capturing and eating a smaller demon. The larger demon explained that in a former life he had been granted the funeral rites appropriate to a minister of state, despite failing the Imperial examinations. In gratitude for this special treatment, he resolved to devote his existence in the after-life to the pursuit and destruction of demons and other evil spirits. Upon waking, Ming Huang ordered the court painter Go Dōshi (in Chinese, Wu Daozi) to paint a likeness of Shōki. This became the standard image of the great Demon Queller, dressed in court robes, wearing a long beard, and wielding or carrying a huge sword. In Japan, Shōki was assimilated rapidly into popular folklore and eventually became associated with the Boys' Festival, held on the fifth day of the fifth lunar month.

EARLY—MID-18TH CENTURY

STAINED IVORY; H. 4 IN. (10.2 CM)

UNSIGNED

PRIVATE COLLECTION

113 | *ONI* HOLDING A ROPE

A crouching figure of a demon wearing a distressed expression, its right arm across its breast, its left hand behind its back holding a rope carved from ivory, the eyes inlaid in dark horn, the himotōshi *probably formed by the crook of the left arm.*

Even in these earlier depictions of *oni*, there is often some deliberate ambiguity about the artist's narrative intention. Along with his mighty sword, Shōki the Demon Queller often wields a rope with which to bind any miscreant *oni* that cross his path. The demon's dejected look might be intended to suggest that he is about to be tied up. An alternative interpretation, in keeping with popular belief in the *oni*'s mischievous cunning, might be that he has stolen the rope and plans to use it on Shōki.

MID–LATE 18TH CENTURY
STAINED BOXWOOD, IVORY, AND HORN; H. 2¹⁄₁₆ IN.
(5.2 CM)
UNSIGNED
PRIVATE COLLECTION

114 | *ONI* WEARING A SHŌKI MASK

A sturdy figure of a pot-bellied oni, *mimicking the pose normally adopted by Shōki the Demon Queller, a long sword in his right hand, his left hand holding a Shōki mask with a long beard and a Chinese court cap, wearing a loincloth tied in a knot at the back, the* oni's *grinning face partly visible behind the mask, the* himotōshi *probably formed by the junction of the right arm and right thigh, signed with crudely incised characters on the left buttock.*

Little is known about Gesshō beyond the facts that he appears to have specialized in humorous wood figures, and that he probably was active toward the end of the eighteenth century. Both the shared character *Getsu* and the style of signature suggest a connection with the *Sōken kishō* artist Shūgetsu (see cat. 26).

GESSHŌ (LATE 18TH CENTURY)
STAINED BOXWOOD; H. 4¼ IN. (10.8 CM)
SIGNED: *GESSHŌ*
PRIVATE COLLECTION

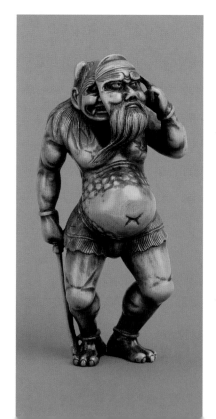

115 | *ONI* RECITING A PRAYER

A standing oni *in the guise of a wandering Buddhist monk or priest, its ample cloak failing to hide its horned feet and hands, bony ribcage, and skeletal chest, in the act of using a mallet in its right hand to strike a wooden drum held in its left hand and suspended from a rope around its neck, the* himotōshi *formed by a small hole in the center of the back connecting with a larger angled hole to the left of the skirt, signed with small incised and stained characters on the hem of the robe.*

The dynamic carving and dramatic staining are typical of Sanko, an artist praised in *Sōken kishō*, which notes with regret that his netsuke were much copied.

SANKO SHŌBEI OF OSAKA (ACTIVE AROUND 1781)
STAINED BOXWOOD; H. 3⁵⁄₁₆ IN. (8.4 CM)
SIGNED: *SANKO*
PRIVATE COLLECTION

(cat. 144), are often based closely on earlier animal carvings with the simple addition of a human figure, but later examples can be carved very intricately with complicated narrative scenes (cat. 145). Other netsuke of myths and legends focus on a single element in the story: for example, a tea kettle turning into a badger (cat. 148), a basket releasing a crowd of monsters (cat. 149), or a famous hero's severed head (cat. 150). In contrast to the two previous sections featuring carvings of imaginary people and animals, about half of the pieces in this section were made outside the Kamigata area; most come from Edo, where popular Japanese (as opposed to Chinese) narrative and belief were very important sources of netsuke subject matter.

A tall figure of Raijin, God of Thunder, carrying a smaller Fūjin, God of Wind, on his back, the larger god with a pouch in his right hand decorated with lightning and cloud designs, a smaller pouch carried on his left side decorated with a mitsudomoe (three-comma) design, the smaller god with a large sack of wind on his back, both gods with human characteristics except for their heads, hands, and feet, each dressed in a loincloth tied in a knot at the back, the eyes inlaid in horn, no himotōshi, signed on Raijin's loincloth with incised and stained characters on an oval reserve.

Masaka (see cat. 22) here applies some of the conventions of Western classical art to a pairing of deities that had inspired some of Japan's most celebrated sculptors and painters – in particular the great Tankei, whose near life-size figures of the two gods were already regarded during the Meiji period as among the greatest masterpieces of Japanese sculpture. Strictly speaking, this figure probably should not be regarded as a netsuke, although in theory a *himotōshi* could be formed by the junction of Fūjin's right arm and Raijin's right shoulder. On earlier netsuke, the three-comma motif on the smaller pouch is also seen on Raijin's thunder-creating drum.

SAWAKI MASAKA OF NAGOYA (BORN 1868); ABOUT 1900
STAINED IVORY AND HORN; H. 4⅝ IN. (11.8 CM)
SIGNED: *MASAKA*
PRIVATE COLLECTION

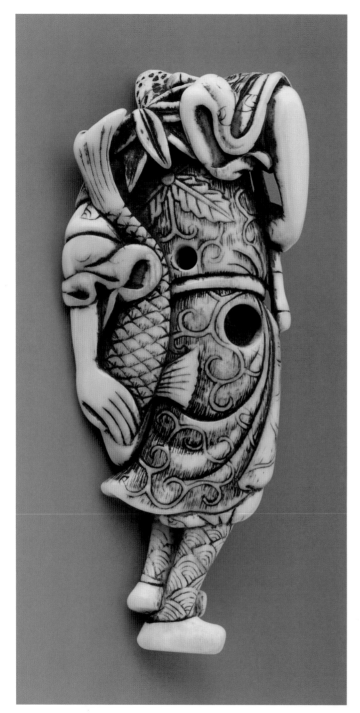

119 | EBISU HOLDING A CARP

A tall figure of Ebisu wearing a patterned coat tied at the waist, an undergarment covering his chest decorated with a leaf design, a small cap on his head, a bamboo fishing rod held over his right shoulder, his leggings decorated with stylized wave patterns, holding a large carp under his left arm, the carp with an eye inlaid in ebony, the himotōshi *formed by large and small holes in the back arranged on either side of the girdle.*

The only one of the Shichifukujin (Seven Gods of Good Fortune) with a purely Japanese origin, Ebisu is a patron saint of seafaring, fishing, and trade. According to a long-established tradition, his legs did not develop until he was three years old, with the result that he is often depicted, as here, in a slightly awkward, twisted pose. This netsuke possesses many of the attributes that have come to be associated with the finest early figure carvings. The details on the reverse are simplified ingeniously so as to present a flat, gently curving surface, and the whole shape is designed to make the best possible use of a piece of ivory from the tip of the tusk. In addition, the netsuke is pleasingly worn and patinated, and there is a marked difference in color between the two sides.

EARLY—MID-18TH CENTURY
STAINED IVORY AND EBONY; H. 4½ IN. (11.5 CM)
UNSIGNED
PRIVATE COLLECTION

120 | HOTEI RIDING A MULE

A figure of Hotei riding on a mule, dressed in a robe that leaves his fat belly exposed, wearing a Chinese hat, his sack held on a stick over his left shoulder, the himotōshi *formed by a large hole underneath the mule connecting with a smaller hole in its side.*

By origin both a Chinese recluse and a manifestation of Miroku, the Buddha of the future who is destined to be reborn 5,670,000,000 years after the death of the historical Buddha, Hotei became associated in popular belief during the Edo period with wealth and good fortune. He is always shown carrying a sack of treasure, hence his name, which literally means "cloth sack." The carver of this unusual netsuke has combined a Kyoto-style animal study with a pictorial prototype that can be traced to Chinese paintings imported during the medieval period, but this prototype is transformed here by the addition of an incongruous Chinese hat.

MID—LATE 18TH CENTURY
STAINED IVORY; H. 2¹³⁄₁₆ IN. (7.2 CM)
UNSIGNED
PRIVATE COLLECTION

121 | HOTEI ON A WATER BUFFALO

A well-worn, compact figure of Hotei mounted on a grazing water buffalo, its four hooves placed close together, its halter held in Hotei's left hand, the very deep himotōshi *starting under the animal and emerging through the top of its left flank behind Hotei.*

EARLY–MID-18TH CENTURY
STAINED BOXWOOD; H. 2¹⁵⁄₁₆ IN. (7.5 CM)
UNSIGNED
MUSEUM OF FINE ARTS, BOSTON 47.540

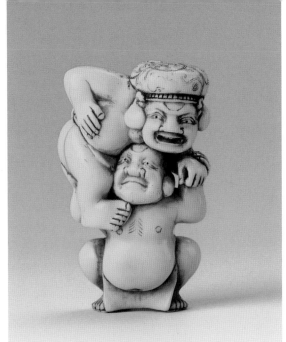

122 | HOTEI AND DAIKOKU SUMO WRESTLING

A figural group depicting a squatting Hotei lifting Daikoku above his head, both figures dressed in sumo wrestlers' keshōmawashi (formal aprons), Daikoku wearing his usual distinctive headgear, both gods with pendulous earlobes, the himotōshi formed by an opening between Daikoku's left leg and Hotei's right arm.

As the Shichifukujin were assimilated into the iconography of popular urban culture during the Edo period, they increasingly were depicted engaged in everyday human activities. Because they are associated very closely and often shown together, this model, of which many examples are extant, has sometimes been described as a depiction of Daikoku and Ebisu (see cat. 119), but while the hat clearly identifies the upper figure as Daikoku, the lack of any special attributes other than the bulging belly and pendulous earlobes makes it more likely that the lower figure is intended to be Hotei (see cat. 120).

EARLY–MID-18TH CENTURY
STAINED STAG ANTLER; H. 2¹⁵/₁₆ IN. (7.4 CM)
UNSIGNED
PRIVATE COLLECTION

123 | HOTEI AND DAIKOKU SUMO WRESTLING

A figural group very similar to the preceding example, but slightly smaller and carved from ivory rather than stag antler.

MID–LATE 18TH CENTURY
STAINED IVORY; H. 2³/₈ IN. (6.1 CM)
UNSIGNED
PRIVATE COLLECTION

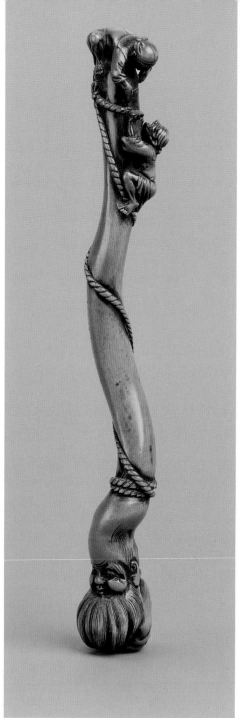

124 | TWO BARBERS CLIMBING ON FUKUROKUJU'S HEAD

An extremely tall figure of Fukurokuju, his long beard completely covering the front of his body, two laughing figures having just succeeded in using a rope to climb to the top of his enormously exaggerated cranium, which they are shaving with razors, a tiny himotōshi *formed by one of their arms, signed with incised and stained* sōsho *characters on Fukurokuju's cranium.*

Fukurokuju (literally, "good luck, high rank, and long life") is associated closely with Jurōjin, another of the Shichi-fukujin, but is distinguished by his tall cranium. Sessai is known to have worked for the *daimyō* (local lord) of Echizen Province, who awarded the honorary Buddhist title of *hokkyō* to the artist, probably for his work on Buddhist sculpture rather than on netsuke.

HOKKYŌ SHIMA SESSAI OF MIKUNI, ECHIZEN
PROVINCE (1822–1880)
STAINED BOXWOOD; H. 6⁵⁄₁₆ IN. (16 CM)
SIGNED: *SESSAI TŌ* (CARVED BY SESSAI)

125 | FUKUROKUJU DISGUISED AS A TURTLE

An ingeniously carved netsuke which looks like a turtle with its head, tail, and feet exposed when viewed from above, but turns over to reveal Fukurokuju holding the sleeves of his cloak wide apart, the himotōshi *formed by two small holes just above his girdle, signed with incised characters between his feet.*

An example of the transformational powers possessed by many Chinese and Japanese deities (see also cat. 1), this netsuke combines one emblem of longevity, Fukurokuju, with another, the turtle.

KIGYOKU (PROBABLY EDO, EARLY 19TH CENTURY)
STAINED BOXWOOD; L. 2⅛ IN. (5.4 CM)
SIGNED: *KIGYOKU*
MUSEUM OF FINE ARTS, BOSTON 11.23286

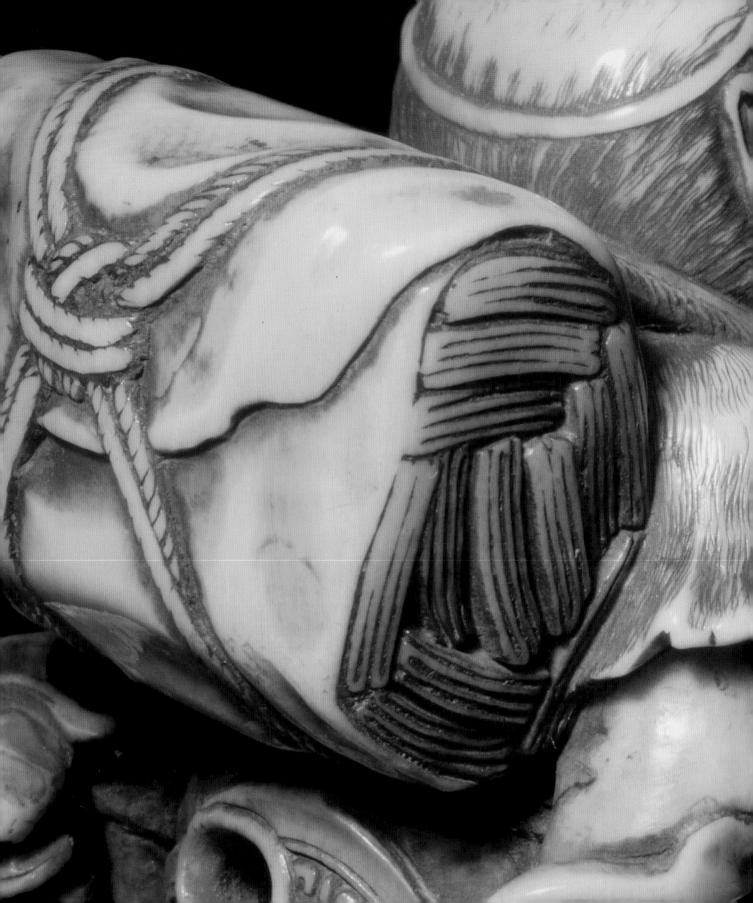

A standing figure of a monkey, dressed in Chinese armor of the Tang Dynasty, his left hand holding a kongō, *a Buddhist ritual implement symbolizing a thunderbolt, carrying a satchel of books on his back, the* himotōshi *formed by large and small holes drilled in the back on either side of the girdle, signed with incised and stained characters on the back near the hem.*

The monkey Songokū (in Chinese, Sun Wukong, translated by the British sinologue Arthur Waley as "aware of vacuity"), is one of the heroes of the novel *Saiyūki* (in Chinese, *Xiyouji*, "The Journey to the West"). Starting out as a troublesome magician with the power to transform himself into seventy-two different shapes, he quickly submits to the will of the Buddha and becomes the faithful companion of the Chinese pilgrim Gensō Sanzō (in Chinese, Xuanzang Sanzang). Songokū accompanies the pilgrim on an epic journey to India, during which they endure eighty-one adventures and eventually succeed in bringing back the 5,048 volumes of the Buddhist scriptural canon, some of which can be seen here on the monkey's back. Little is known about Yūsō, but his signature is recorded on a *sashi* netsuke in the style of Kokusai (see cat. 101), suggesting that he probably worked in Tokyo toward the end of the nineteenth century.

YŪSŌ (LATE 19TH CENTURY)

HEAVILY STAINED IVORY; H. 3¹³⁄₁₆ IN. (9.7 CM)

SIGNED: *YŪSŌ TŌ* (CARVED BY YŪSŌ)

MUSEUM OF FINE ARTS, BOSTON 47.510

A tall figure of a bald rakan *dressed in a* kesa *(priest's robe), which leaves his right shoulder uncovered, holding a frightened* shishi *upside down, the pupils of both* rakan *and* shishi *inlaid in horn, the* himotōshi *formed by a central hole in the back connecting with another underneath.*

Rakan (in Sanskrit, *arhat,* "one worthy of respect") are direct disciples of the historical Buddha, said to be sixteen or five hundred in number. Although their true nature was much debated during the early history of Buddhism, they are regarded generally as beings who have reached a point of spiritual development just below that of a true Buddha or Enlightened One. Their distinctive appearance, with noble, craggy features, bald heads, beardless faces, and large ears, was established firmly in medieval Japan through imported Chinese paintings. They often are depicted in their role as staunch protectors of the Buddhist law, in this case perhaps chastising a wayward *shishi* that has failed to perform its duty as a guardian.

MID–LATE 18TH CENTURY
STAINED BOXWOOD AND HORN; H. 5³⁄₁₆ IN. (13.1 CM)
UNSIGNED
PRIVATE COLLECTION

A ghostly figure with a shaved head and pendulous earlobes, his body wrapped in a cloak that twists around to end in a narrow curl, the surface very carefully polished to bring out the grain of the wood, the eyes inlaid in horn, the himotōshi *formed by two unequal holes, the larger hole partially concealed by the cloak, signed with incised and stained characters on an oval reserve on the reverse of the torso below the smaller hole.*

This elegant, haunting figure has been identified in the past as a *rakan* (see cat. 127), but the lack of legs may be a reference to a story about Daruma (in Sanskrit, Bodhidharma), the founder of Zen Buddhism. Daruma spent so long seated in meditation that his legs atrophied, a tradition also represented by the legless, roly-poly Daruma doll (see next entry). This netsuke bears the signature of Hōshin, an artist described by *Sōken kishō* as carving ivory clams with miniature palaces inside them (see cat. 146), while in *Netsuke no kenkyū* (*A Study of Netsuke*, 1942), Ueda Reikichi adds the information that he also carved in wood. As usual with Ueda, it is impossible to know whether this information was derived from an independent source or if it simply reflects the fact that he had seen wood netsuke with Hōshin's signature.

HŌSHIN OF KYOTO (ACTIVE AROUND 1781)
STAINED BOXWOOD AND HORN; H. 3¹⁵⁄₁₆ IN. (10.1 CM)
SIGNED: *HŌSHIN*
PRIVATE COLLECTION

129 | DARUMA DOLL HOLDING A *HOSSU*

A legless Daruma doll, the cloak raised leaving only the eyes and nose visible, holding a hossu *(ritual whisk) in its hidden left hand, the brush falling down behind the doll in a scythelike shape, the two enormous eyes inlaid with horn pupils, the* himotōshi *formed by two almost equal holes in the back, signed and dated on the back with incised and heavily stained characters.*

Daruma's iconography in Japan can be traced back to Chinese paintings imported in the medieval period, but in the Edo period the Indian sage was transformed into the legless doll seen here, often carrying a ritual *hossu* that he uses to brush away the petty distractions and attachments of worldly life. This compact, humorous figure is free of the fussy detail seen all too often in ivory netsuke carved in Edo during the middle years of the nineteenth century.

ANRAKU; DATED 1850
STAINED IVORY AND HORN; H. 1⁵⁄₁₆ IN. (3.3 CM)
SIGNED: *KAEI SANNEN KICHIJITSU ANRAKU KORE O TSUKURU* (ANRAKU MADE THIS ON AN AUSPICIOUS DAY IN THE THIRD YEAR OF THE KAEI ERA [1850])
PRIVATE COLLECTION

Two muscular figures wearing caps and loose robes, one bracing himself with his left hand on his left knee, the other using both arms to grasp the other's right arm, the himotōshi *formed by a very large hole in his buttocks and emerging through his neck, signed with incised and stained characters above the hole.*

Niō ("Virtuous Kings") often stand guard outside Buddhist temples, their muscular bodies making them ideal material for caricature in miniature – emphasized in this case by the irreverent positioning of the *himotōshi*. The signature on this striking carving, one of the most remarkable netsuke in the Museum of Fine Arts, refers to an official position rather than a personal name, as *Higo no daijō* literally means "steward of Higo (Province)." This ancient honorary title is seen on a number of similar pieces in other collections, but the name also might be connected with Kameya Higo, a carver mentioned in *Sōken kishō* who also made *karakuri* (automata) and false teeth.

HIGO NO DAIJŌ (MID–18TH CENTURY)

STAINED BOXWOOD; L. 3 IN. (7.7 CM)

SIGNED: *HIGO NO DAIJŌ SAKU* (MADE BY HIGO NO DAIJŌ)

MUSEUM OF FINE ARTS, BOSTON 47.716

131 | KIYOHIME AND THE BELL OF DŌJŌJI

A demonic female figure with a snake's tail wrapped around a Buddhist temple bell, peering through an opening in the side at a revolving fitting, turned by twisting the handle of the bell and showing a series of four faces, the himotōshi *formed by a hole in the base emerging by the demon's right side, sealed with incised and stained characters on a square reserve underneath the bell.*

This netsuke depicts the key episode in the story of the temple Dōjōji, originally the subject of a Nō play incorporating a transformational dance sequence that later became extremely popular on the kabuki stage. The witch Kiyohime is shown turning into a monstrous serpent, about to burn to death the unfortunate priest Anchin, who had resisted her amorous advances and sought refuge under a huge temple bell. In an ingenious twist, the interior of the bell contains a revolving fitting depicting Anchin's changing face as he endures his death agonies, based on the *mawari karakuri* and other mechanical-optical entertainments that were devised during the eighteenth century. This model was conceived originally by Tanaka Minkō (see cat. 155).

SESSEN (EARLY 19TH CENTURY)

STAINED BOXWOOD; H. 1¾ IN. (4.5 CM)

SEALED: *SESSEN*

MUSEUM OF FINE ARTS, BOSTON 47.432

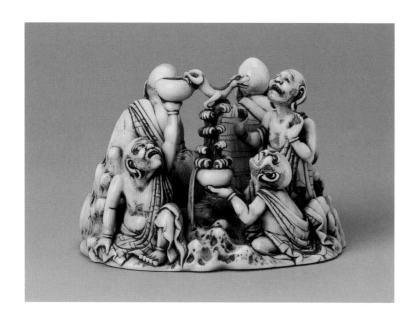

A group of five rakan *with their attributes arranged on an irregularly shaped base, no* himotōshi, *signed on the base with incised and stained characters, and sealed with a single carved and red-stained character within a square reserve.*

This virtuoso little carving, made from the tip of an elephant tusk, is a miniature version of a larger type of figure group that was made for the export market during the early Meiji period; several examples of such groups are preserved in older museum collections. The remarkable detail makes it possible to identify some of the *rakan* (see cat. 127) by their attributes. The figure with an alms bowl containing a fountain, for example, is Nakasaina, the dragon in a bowl is held by Handaka, while the tiger is the companion of Hattara.

GYOKUSHINSAI (ABOUT 1880–1890)
OKIMONO
STAINED IVORY; H. 1¹¹⁄₁₆ IN. (4.3 CM)
SIGNED: *GYOKUSHINSAI*
SEALED: *SADA*
MUSEUM OF FINE ARTS, BOSTON 11.23669

133 | UMBRELLA *BAKEMONO*

A one-legged figure with its head and body in the shape of a folded umbrella of bamboo and paper, decorated with cloud designs, sticking out its tongue, its ghoulish eyes inlaid in ivory and dark horn, one hand held to its chest and another to the top of its head, the himotōshi *formed by one very large and one smaller hole in the back.*

Bakemono ("transmogrified beings") abound in the popular literature and theater of the Edo period. The origins of this peculiar figure can be traced to a kabuki dance including seven costume changes that was illustrated by the print designer Utagawa Toyokuni (1769–1825) around 1810.

EARLY 19TH CENTURY

STAINED BOXWOOD, IVORY, AND HORN; H. 3⅝ IN.

(9.2 CM)

UNSIGNED

PRIVATE COLLECTION

134 | MITSUME-KOZŌ

A dancing figure dressed in a kimono, standing on one leg, sticking out its tongue, a third eye in its forehead, wearing a court cap, around which hangs the cord of a straw hat worn on the back of its head, the three eyes inlaid in ivory and horn, the himotōshi *formed by large and small holes on either side of the* obi.

Probably a transformation of the Buddhist deity Aizen, whose third eye is placed vertically on the forehead, Mitsume-Kozō ("Little Three-Eyes") seems to have entered the popular imagination, along with Hitotsume-Nyūdō ("Saint One-Eye") and similar monstrosities, during the late Muromachi period. Such beings are depicted frequently in seventeenth-century paintings, including a scroll by Hishikawa Moronobu in the Museum of Fine Arts, Boston.

MID–LATE 18TH CENTURY

STAINED BOXWOOD, IVORY, AND HORN; H. 3⅝ IN.

(9.2 CM)

UNSIGNED

PRIVATE COLLECTION

135 | MIKOSHI NYŪDŌ LOOMING OVER A MAN

A monstrous figure with an extendable neck, looming over a tiny, terrified human being, its eyes inlaid in shell and its teeth in ivory, its back with a simple zigzag pattern representing lightning, the himotōshi *formed by two unequal holes above and below the* obi, *signed with incised and stained characters below the holes.*

A very similar Mikoshi Nyūdō ("Saint Overlooking," also known as Santo) is reproduced in the encyclopedia *Wakan sansai zue* (1713), but with the freak terrorizing a samurai rather than a commoner, as seen here. The encyclopedia tells us that the creature is more than twenty feet tall, has black skin, red eyes, and yellow hair, and lives deep in the mountains in a nest like a bird's, where it lays eggs more than three feet long. The use of the suffix Nyūdō (literally, "one who has entered the way") in the names of these monsters not only refers to their shaven heads, which resemble those of Buddhist monks, but also has a pacificatory function, in much the same way that the ancient Greeks referred to the Furies as Eumenides ("Kindly Ones"). The carving of the victim's face is a miracle of miniaturized expressionism.

HASEGAWA IKKO OF EDO (EARLY–MID-19TH CENTURY)
STAINED BOXWOOD, SHELL, AND IVORY
H. 2⅜ IN. (6 CM), RETRACTED; SIGNED: *IKKO*
PRIVATE COLLECTION

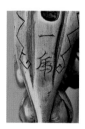

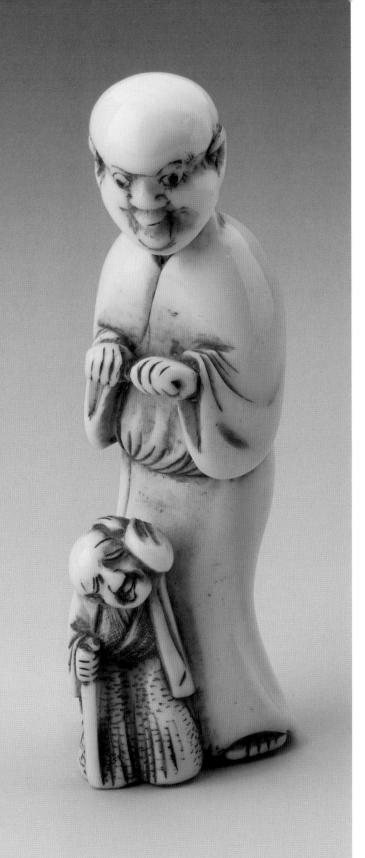

A monstrous figure with an extendable neck, towering over a tiny, terrified human being, its hands in a threatening gesture, the little figure protecting his head with his left hand and arm, the monster's eyes inlaid in black horn, the himotōshi *formed by holes near the bottom of its robe.*

Like Mikoshi Nyūdō (see preceding entry), *rokurokubi* ("Lathe-Heads") are discussed in *Wakan sansai zue.* Interestingly, they appear in the section devoted to foreign races (with the alternative name *hitōban,* "Flying-Head Barbarians"), whereas Mikoshi is treated as a variety of ape. The encyclopedia relates that the eyes of *rokurokubi* have no pupils (a tradition ignored by the carver of this piece), and traces their origin back to the time of the Chinese Emperor Butei (see cat. 14).

LATE 18TH CENTURY
STAINED IVORY AND HORN; H. 2¹¹⁄₁₆ IN. (6.8 CM), RETRACTED
UNSIGNED
PRIVATE COLLECTION

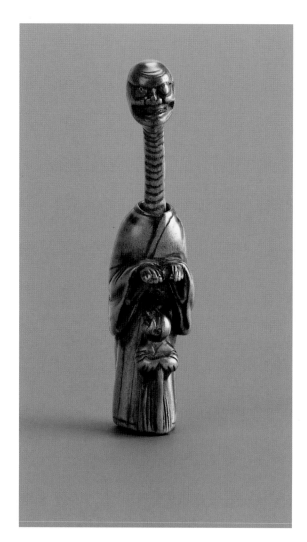

A monstrous figure with an extendable neck, towering over a tiny, terrified human being, its hands in a threatening gesture, the little figure looking up in puzzlement, the monster's eyes inlaid in black horn, the himotōshi *formed by two rather large holes in the back, signed with incised and stained characters on an oval reserve next to the holes.*

In *Netsuke no kenkyū* (1942), Ueda Reikichi gives a detailed listing of four generations of artists called Shūgetsu, and on the grounds of dating, this fine old Edo-style carving probably should be attributed to the second user of the name.

PROBABLY BY SHŪGETSU II OF EDO
(LATE 18TH–EARLY 19TH CENTURY)
STAINED BOXWOOD; H. 2⅛ IN. (5.4 CM), RETRACTED
SIGNED: *SHŪGETSU*
MUSEUM OF FINE ARTS, BOSTON 11.23535

138 | SKULL, SNAKE, FROG, AND SEVERED HEADS

A group consisting of a skull surmounted by the severed heads of a woman and a child, entwined by a snake that bites at the woman's hair, a frog to one side of the skull, the hair and other details minutely carved and stained black, other details in red pigment, the animals' eyes inlaid in horn, signed on the skull with incised and red-stained characters.

This grotesque group is an example of an *okimono*, a nonfunctional ornament of a type often carved by netsuke artists after netsuke had fallen out of use during the early Meiji period. The subject is possibly the witch of Adachigara, a sorceress who hunts down and kills young children, using their blood to cure a prince in her care before eating them. Added to this are the snake and toad, elements from the netsuke theme of the *sansukumi* (see cat. 184). The treatment shows the influence of the late nineteenth-century print designer

Tsukioka Yoshitoshi (1839–1892), whose prints often depict macabre legendary scenes. Asahi Gyokuzan, a frequent exhibitor at international and domestic expositions around 1900, was especially renowned for the anatomical accuracy of his ivory skulls and skeletons.

ASAHI GYOKUZAN OF TOKYO (1843–1923);
ABOUT 1900
OKIMONO
STAINED IVORY AND HORN, WITH PIGMENT; H. 4⅜ IN. (11.2 CM)
SIGNED: *TŌKYŌ ASAHI GYOKUZAN KORE O SAKU* (ASAHI GYOKUZAN
OF TOKYO MADE THIS)
MUSEUM OF FINE ARTS, BOSTON 11.23727

139 | FROG IN THE GUISE OF ONO NO TŌFŪ

A long-legged frog wearing a lacquered court cap, standing on a pair of high geta (clogs), resting its front legs on the top of a folded umbrella, the eyes inlaid in light and dark horn, the himotōshi *probably formed by the junction of the arms and the umbrella, signed with incised and stained characters on the frog's left thigh.*

A popular story (remarkably similar to that of the Scottish King Robert the Bruce and the spider) tells how the calligrapher and courtier Ono no Tōfū (or Michikaze, 894–966), having failed several times to win promotion, was about to renounce public office for good when he noticed a tiny frog trying to jump up from a river onto the leaf of a weeping willow. The frog finally succeeded at the eighth attempt (Bruce's spider managed to fix its web at the seventh attempt). Ono resumed his efforts, and became a minister. Here he is eliminated from the story and a huge frog leans on a furled umbrella, Ono's usual iconographic marker, in a typical netsuke metamorphosis.

GARAKU RISUKE OF OSAKA (MID–LATE
18TH CENTURY)
STAINED BOXWOOD AND HORN; H. 4⅛ IN.
(10.5 CM)
SIGNED: *GARAKU*
PRIVATE COLLECTION

140 | *NUE*

A crouching monster made up of a tiger's body, a monkey's head, and a snake's tail, scratching its chin with its right hind leg, the snake curled up on top of its back, the pupils inlaid in horn (one missing), the himotōshi *formed by a large oval in the left haunch connecting with another by the left hind paw.*

In this unique carving, a Kyoto artist, almost certainly Tomotada, has adapted the monstrous *nue* (see the following catalogue entry) to the conventions of late-eighteenth-century carving, producing what is essentially a very compact tiger netsuke with a substituted head and tail.

ATTRIBUTED TO IZUMIYA TOMOTADA OF KYOTO
(ACTIVE AROUND 1781)
STAINED IVORY AND HORN; H. 1⁵⁄₁₆ IN. (3.4 CM)
UNSIGNED
PRIVATE COLLECTION

I NO HAYATA KILLING THE *NUE*,
FROM TACHIBANA MORIKUNI
(ILLUSTRATOR), *EHON SHAHŌ
BUKURO* [1720; THIS EDITION
1770], VOLUME 3, PP. 7–8.
MUSEUM OF FINE ARTS,
BOSTON

141 | I NO HAYATA KILLING THE *NUE*

A warrior dressed in court costume and cap, using a tantō
*(short sword) to dispatch a monstrous creature with a tiger's
body, a monkey's head, and a snake for a tail, an arrow already
sticking in its side, the snake's head biting the warrior's left
shoulder, the* himotōshi *formed by two holes in the base on
either side of the monster's left hind leg, signed with incised and
stained characters on a rectangular reserve on the creature's left
haunch.*

The thirteenth-century chronicle *Heike monogatari*
relates that in 1153, the famous archer and poet
Minamoto no Yorimasa spotted an extraordinary beast
on the roof of the Imperial Palace. The creature only
appeared during the hours of darkness (the character
used for its name is made up of the elements "night" and
"bird"), and its malign influence was believed to have
brought on the fatal illness of the Emperor Konoe.
One night Yorimasa succeeded in shooting the monster
but did not kill it, and on closer inspection, it turned
out to have the head of a monkey, tiger's paws, a badger's
body, a snake for a tail, and a song like that of the
toratsugumi (golden mountain thrush). The creature
finally was put out of its misery by Yorimasa's retainer
I no Hayata. It is interesting to note that, in the interests
of preserving the conventions of Kyoto-style animal
carving, both Okakoto and Tomotada (see preceding
entry) dispensed with the textual and pictorial tradition
which holds that the creature has a badger's body, pre-
ferring to substitute the more standard and familiar tiger.

OKAKOTO OF KYOTO (LATE 18TH–EARLY 19TH CENTURY)
IVORY AND HORN; H. 1^{13}⁄₁₆ IN. (4.6 CM)
SIGNED: *OKAKOTO*
PRIVATE COLLECTION

A Japanese warrior with a quiver on his back, riding backward on a boar, holding onto its tail with his left hand while he prepares to draw his sword with his right, the boar's eyes inlaid in dark horn, the himotōshi *formed by a large hole in the underside connecting with a smaller hole in the back, signed underneath with incised and lightly stained characters on a rectangular reserve.*

The subject of this netsuke is a minor incident in the popular cycle of legends concerning the revenge of the Soga brothers. Nitta no Shirō or Tadatsune (died 1203) was a retainer of Minamoto no Yoritomo, who became the first shogun of all Japan at the end of the twelfth century, and who was also the murderer of the brothers' grandfather. During a great boar hunt held by Yoritomo in 1193, which provides the backdrop to the denouement of the Soga story, Nitta sought to demonstrate his valor by riding a boar backward and killing it in his master's presence. Unfortunately, the boar was actually a mountain *kami* (Shinto deity), and Nitta fell under a curse, with the result that Yoritomo began to suspect him of disloyalty. In keeping with Okakoto's training as a carver of animal netsuke in the Kyoto style, this is essentially a beautifully executed figure of a charging boar, with the addition of a miniaturized figural element.

OKAKOTO OF KYOTO (LATE 18TH–EARLY 19TH CENTURY)
STAINED IVORY AND HORN; H. 1¹⁵⁄₁₆ IN. (5 CM)
SIGNED: *OKAKOTO*
PRIVATE COLLECTION

NITTA NO SHIRŌ
SLAYING A BOAR, FROM
TACHIBANA MORIKUNI
(ILLUSTRATOR), *EHON
KOJIDAN* [1715],
VOLUME 5B, PP. 19–20.
MUSEUM OF FINE ARTS,
BOSTON

A warrior in Chinese dress, dispatching a giant snake with a sword held in his right hand, his pupils inlaid in black, the eyes of the snake inlaid in another unidentified material, the snake's mouth stained red, the himotōshi *formed by two small holes in the back, signed with incised and stained characters on a rounded rectangular reserve underneath the snake.*

Before ascending the Imperial throne, Kan no Kōso (in Chinese, Han Gaozu, reigned 206–194 BC) once slew a giant snake that had attacked one of the horses of the preceding emperor and had thrown a servant to the ground. This is an example of the work of the regional carver Matsushita Otoman, who worked at the port of Hakata in the southern island of Kyushu. According to a Western collecting tradition, he first signed his name with two characters Oto-man, and later, as here, with three characters O-to-man.

MATSUSHITA OTOMAN OF CHIKUZEN PROVINCE
(EARLY–MID-19TH CENTURY)
STAINED IVORY; H. 1⅜ IN. (3.5 CM)
SIGNED: *OTOMAN*
PRIVATE COLLECTION

A Kyoto-style carving of a water buffalo, with carefully textured fur and inlaid horn pupils, a halter around its muzzle and passing over its back, its hide cut open and partially concealing a figure dressed in simple clothes who seems about to flee, the himotōshi *probably formed by a hole in the hide just above the cavity in the animal's body.*

Kidōmaru ("Little Devil"), the villain in a complex cycle of medieval legends, was an associate of the monstrous brigand Shuten Dōji ("Dead-Drunk Lad"), who was slain in the year 947 by Minamoto no Yorimitsu. Stealing away from Shuten Dōji's camp, where Yorimitsu and four other warriors were feigning drunkenness in preparation for their attempt on the monster's life, Kidōmaru killed a large buffalo and hid inside its carcass. He left a small peephole through which he kept watch for the five returning heroes, who stopped nearby to rest and admire the view. One of the five, Watanabe no Tsuna, was about to fire a practice arrow at the dead buffalo when he noticed that the carcass was wriggling. Kidōmaru was discovered, and Yorimitsu struck off his head with a single blow from his sword.

LATE 18TH–EARLY 19TH CENTURY
STAINED IVORY AND HORN; L. 2¹⁵⁄₁₆ IN. (7.4 CM)
UNSIGNED
PRIVATE COLLECTION

A figure in aristocratic dress, mounted on a stocky horse that is about to climb onto a go board supported by four stout legs, the horse's pupils inlaid in horn, the himotōshi *probably formed by the horse's tail or the junction of its legs and the board, signed underneath with incised and heavily stained characters.*

The popular semihistorical personality Oguri Hangan is the hero of a complex cycle of legends that first appeared in print in the seventeenth century. Most stories about him concern his undying love for Princess Terutahime, and her efforts to save him from his enemies, who on one occasion even infected him with leprosy in an attempt to kill him. His mount Onikage is said to have been able to perch on a space as small as a board for the Japanese game of go.

KAZUSHIGE (LATE 18TH–EARLY 19TH CENTURY)
STAINED IVORY AND HORN; H. 2 IN. (5.1 CM)
SIGNED: *KAZUSHIGE*
PRIVATE COLLECTION

146 | CLAM SHELL WITH THE VINDICATION OF ONO NO KOMACHI

A carving of an open clam shell containing a tableau of one female and two male courtiers in a rustic dwelling, with a thin band of cloud above and below, the female washing a book in a basin, the himotōshi *formed by a large hole in the base near the hinge of the shell connecting with another in the center, signed underneath with incised and heavily stained characters.*

This netsuke depicts the *Sōshi arai* ("Book-Washing"), the first of seven well-established episodes in the life of the ninth-century poet Ono no Komachi. Komachi won first prize at one of the regular poetry competitions held at court, but a jealous male rival, Ōtomo no Kuronushi, accused her of having copied her poem from the great early anthology *Man'yōshū*, and produced a copy of the book as proof. Komachi washed the book in a basin and the characters of the poem disappeared, leaving only genuine *Man'yōshū* verses. The ink of the offending poem was still fresh and soluble because Kuronushi had added it hastily to the manuscript when he heard Komachi reciting it to herself the previous evening. Shūōsai Hidemasa generally is believed to have been a successor of Chingendō Hidemasa (see cat. 33).

SHŪŌSAI HIDEMASA (EARLY 19TH CENTURY)
STAINED IVORY; H. 1³⁄₁₆ IN. (3 CM)
SIGNED: *SHŪŌSAI HIDEMASA*, WITH A *KAŌ*
MUSEUM OF FINE ARTS, BOSTON 11.23212

147 | ONO NO KOMACHI IN OLD AGE

An elderly, emaciated woman dressed in a ragged garment, with a weather-beaten hat on her right arm and a basket on her left, both hands placed on the handle of her staff, her long hair tied behind her neck, the himotōshi *formed from a hole in the back connecting with a vertical hole drilled upward from the base.*

This netsuke depicts the ninth-century poet Ono no Komachi in one of the final stages of her life, wandering alone and destitute in expiation of the cruel treatment she meted out to her male admirers when she was young and beautiful. The same rather undignified *himotōshi* is seen in eighteenth-century carvings of Dutchmen (see cats. 55 and 56).

LATE 18TH–EARLY 19TH CENTURY
STAINED BOXWOOD; H. 3½ IN. (8.9 CM)
UNSIGNED
PRIVATE COLLECTION

A tea kettle with a lid, two fittings for rings, and a flange around its widest part, the rough iron surface carefully simulated, a badger's head growing out of the front of the kettle and its tail out of the back, the eyes inlaid in light and dark horn, the himotōshi formed by two almost equal holes in the base, signed underneath with deeply incised and stained characters on a polished reserve.

Like the most popular tales in any folk culture, the story of the *Bunbuku chagama* exists in several different versions. Once upon a time, a poor junk dealer (or sometimes a bamboo cutter) decided to better himself by requesting a favor of a badger (alternatively, the favor is offered by the badger in return for the junk dealer's kindness in rescuing it from some cruel boys). He asks the badger to transform itself into a tea kettle, which he sells to a local temple. When a novice monk takes the kettle to a river and scours it with sand, the tea kettle cries out, "It hurts! Scour more gently, boy!" The kettle is eventually put on to boil, whereupon it gradually turns itself back into a badger and scuttles away. According to one tradition, this story dates back to the Ōei era (1394–1428) and was associated originally with a magical kettle belonging to the temple Morinji in Kōzuke Province.

ŌHARA MITSUHIRO OF OSAKA (1810–1875)
STAINED BOXWOOD AND HORN; H. 1⅛ IN. (2.8 CM)
SIGNED: *MITSUHIRO*, WITH A *KAŌ*
MUSEUM OF FINE ARTS, BOSTON 11.23409

A miniature tsuzura *(wicker basket) from which a variety of monsters and freaks emerge, the two small* himotōshi *holes underneath lined with green ivory, signed underneath with incised characters on a rectangular red lacquer plaque.*

The origins of the tale of the *Shitakiri suzume* ("Tongue-Cut Sparrow") can be traced back to the thirteenth century. Accusing a sparrow of eating some of her rice gruel, a mean old woman cut off its tongue. Her kind husband visited the sparrow's house to seek forgiveness, and the sparrow, in return, offered him a choice of baskets containing local produce. The old man modestly took the smallest, but when he brought it home, he found it was full of treasure. The greedy old crone copied her husband's actions but chose the largest basket. When she opened it impatiently before she got home, frightful snakes, centipedes, and monsters came out and chased her away. On this netsuke, one of the creatures is a combination of a *rokurokubi* and Mitsume Kozō (see cats. 136 and 134), two monsters depicted in the *Manga*, a vast collection of sketches by Katsushika Hokusai (1760–1849) in eighteen volumes, published (some of them posthumously) between 1814 and 1878.

KŪSAI (LATE 19TH CENTURY)

HARDWOOD AND STAINED IVORY; H. 1¼ IN. (3.2 CM)

SEALED: *KŪSAI*

PRIVATE COLLECTION

A grimacing severed head, the hair arranged in a neat topknot, the cut surface revealing the vertebrae and arteries, painted with red pigment simulating blood, the himotōshi *formed by two holes in the back of the head, signed with incised characters between the holes on a smooth area of the hair.*

Nitta no Yoshisada (1301–1338) is one of a number of celebrated loyalist warriors who devoted their lives to the struggle against the Hōjō family of regents and the Ashikaga shoguns, hoping to restore real political power to the emperor. After some initial successes, Yoshisada, like so many other Japanese heroes before and since, made a hopeless last stand against overwhelmingly superior Ashikaga forces, finally striking off his own head with a single blow from his sword. The carver of this piece would have been able to study, "from the death" as it were, the severed heads that were displayed at the execution grounds in Edo, as recorded in early photographs of Japan. The signature of Ōe Shunzō is recorded on a small number of netsuke, including two more of severed heads, and another, by contrast, of a Chinese child playing with a turtle.

ŌE SHUNZŌ (LATE 19TH CENTURY)
STAINED BOXWOOD WITH RED PIGMENT
H. 1½ IN. (3.9 CM)
SIGNED: *ŌE SHUNZŌ*
MUSEUM OF FINE ARTS, BOSTON 11.23547

Daily Life

OST OF THE FIGURES IN THIS SECTION WERE CARVED FROM WOOD rather than from ivory, and many of them come from Edo, the shogun's capital, which was the largest city in the world by the end of the eighteenth century, with more than one million inhabitants. During the Edo period, a sophisticated mass urban culture developed both there and in the Kamigata cities of Osaka and Kyoto, and some of these carvings offer a glimpse of the range of popular entertainments that were to be found. These include street performances, kabuki theater, festivals, and sumo wrestling (cats. 151–159), while other netsuke depict everyday scenes from the public bathhouse (cats. 164–166), or erotica (cats. 167 and 168), both explicit and disguised. A smaller group, sometimes unfairly neglected by today's netsuke collectors, depicts everyday objects such as toys, tea bowls, or brooms (cats. 174–178).

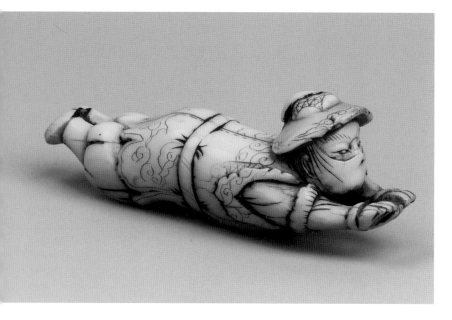

A masked figure with outstretched arms and legs, wearing a tasseled hat and embroidered tunic, the himotōshi *formed by holes underneath on either side of the girdle.*

This figure is a *kagonuke*, one of a number of specialists in *karuwaza* ("lightweight tricks"), a form of entertainment that was popular from the eighteenth century. Other forms of *karuwaza* included tightrope walking, climbing on unsupported ladders, and *kyokugei*, or contortionism (see the following entry). In the *kagonuke* performance, a cylindrical, woven bamboo tube about eight and half feet long and eighteen inches in diameter is set up on a table about six feet long. The *kagonuke* then runs up, adopts a diving posture and, if successful, springs through the basket without touching its sides. Such performers are often depicted wearing outlandish, vaguely *Kara* (continental) costume.

EARLY 18TH CENTURY
STAINED IVORY; L. 3⁵⁄₁₆ IN. (8.5 CM)
UNSIGNED
PRIVATE COLLECTION

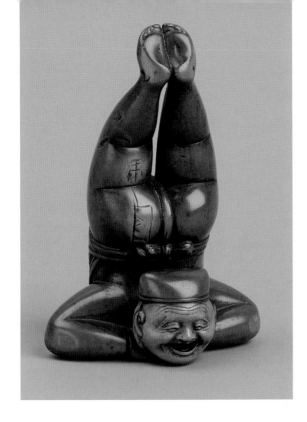

152 | CONTORTIONIST

A grinning figure wearing a loincloth and cap, his chest on the ground, his legs in the air and his hands under his chin, the himotōshi *formed by large and small holes in the chest, signed with crudely scratched characters on the right buttock and thigh.*

An illustration in *Zōho tōsho kinmō zui taisei,* an encyclopedia published in 1789, reveals that there was more to this act than simple contortionism. Volume 10 shows a very similar figure performing to the accompaniment of three musicians, while balancing on a small tray perched, in turn, on a precarious assembly of two *sanpodai* (bottle stands), some blocks of wood, a bowl, and finally, another block of wood.

GESSHŌ (LATE 18TH CENTURY)
STAINED BOXWOOD; H. 2⅝ IN. (6.6 CM)
SIGNED: *GESSHŌ*
PRIVATE COLLECTION

153 | DANCER IMITATING A CRANE

A cloaked dancer using his fan to create the silhouette of a crane with its beak on its breast, wearing a pipe case, pouch, and plain manjū *netsuke, the pouch studs inlaid in ivory, the* himotōshi *formed by a very large and a smaller hole arranged on either side of the* obi, *signed with incised characters on the back.*

This dancer's performance would have been lit from behind by lanterns, so that a crane-shaped shadow fell on a *shōji* screen stretched with translucent paper, with the audience observing from the other side of the screen. This technique, known as *utsushi-e* ("reflected picture"), was popular in the late eighteenth century. Matsura Seizan (1760–1841), Lord of Hirado, owned a wood netsuke like this that he described as follows: "Crane dance netsuke. As an entertainment, the dancer covers his head with his *haori* (jacket), and stretches out one hand holding a fan to form the crane's beak. He picks up the skirt of his kimono and sticks his legs out so that he looks like a crane walking along."

MINKOKU (LATE 18TH–EARLY 19TH CENTURY)
STAINED BOXWOOD AND IVORY;
H. 4⅛ IN. (10.5 CM)
SIGNED: *MINKOKU*
MUSEUM OF FINE ARTS, BOSTON 47.774

154 | DANCER IMITATING A CRANE

A cloaked dancer using his fan to create the silhouette of a crane with its beak on its breast, the himotōshi *formed by a very large and a smaller hole arranged on either side of the* obi, *signed on the back with simply formed, incised characters.*

This second crane dancer illustrates the variety in detail that could be achieved within a popular subject. Like many netsuke donated to the Museum of Fine Arts by William Sturgis Bigelow in 1911, it is unusually small for its type.

PROBABLY BY SHŪGETSU II OF EDO (LATE 18TH–
EARLY 19TH CENTURY)
STAINED BOXWOOD; H. 2¾ IN. (7 CM)
SIGNED: *SHŪGETSU SAKU* (MADE BY SHŪGETSU)
MUSEUM OF FINE ARTS, BOSTON 11.23534

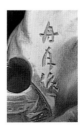

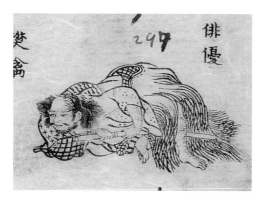

NETSUKE OF AN ACTOR
IN THE ROLE OF A
WARRIOR LYING IN
AMBUSH BY OGASAWARA
ISSAI, FROM INABA
TSŪRYŪ, *SŌKEN KISHŌ*
[1781], VOLUME 7, PP.
7–8. MUSEUM OF FINE
ARTS, BOSTON

A watchful, crouching figure wearing a large straw hat and a minutely textured straw cloak, drawing a sword with his right hand from a scabbard held in his left, the end of the scabbard just protruding from his cloak, the himotōshi *formed by the junction of the leg and crotch, signed with deeply incised characters on the left leg.*

This design, several examples of which are recorded, follows a prototype illustrated in *Sōken kishō*, where it is attributed to Ogasawara Issai. The drawing is captioned *haiyū* (actor), and it is likely that the role depicted is from the hugely popular play *Kanadehon Chūshingura*, first produced in 1748. This play tells the story of the revenge of the Forty-seven *Rōnin* (masterless samurai) on Kōno Moronao, who had engineered the suicide of their lord, En'ya Hangan. Central sections of the lengthy plot are concerned with the adventures of Hayano Kanpei, who adopts a simple rustic lifestyle, partly in order to deceive Moronao into thinking that the *rōnin* have abandoned all hope of revenge. He often wears a straw cloak, but since the action also requires that he be armed with a gun, the netsuke is intended perhaps to convey a more general impression of the *rōnin*'s patient watchfulness. The important provincial artist Tanaka (or Gose) Minkō worked mainly for the Tōdō clan.

TANAKA MINKŌ OF TSU, ISE PROVINCE (1735–1816)
STAINED BOXWOOD; L. 2³⁄₁₆ IN. (5.5 CM)
SIGNED: *GOSE MINKŌ ZU* (DRAWN BY GOSE MINKŌ),
WITH A *KAŌ*
MUSEUM OF FINE ARTS, BOSTON 47.839

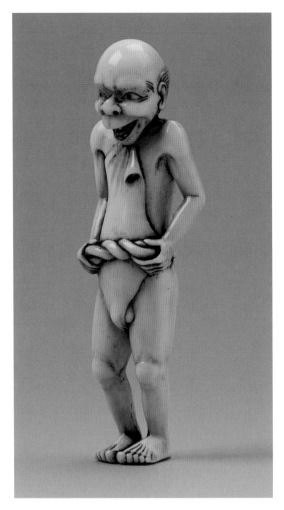

A standing bather with his towel in his left hand, looking at his reflection in a tub of water and making a face, the eyes inlaid in crystal, the himotōshi *formed by two large, crude holes on the reverse.*

Although previously described as a *bakemono* (see cat. 133), this figure is intended more likely to represent two views of the same subject: both the bather and the reflection in his water tub of the faces he is making at himself. This particular grimace is known as *hyottoko*, a term supposedly derived from *hi* (fire) and *otoko* (man), meaning a male trying to blow out a fire.

18TH CENTURY

STAINED BOXWOOD AND CRYSTAL; H. 2¹³⁄₁₆ IN. (7.1 CM)

UNSIGNED

PRIVATE COLLECTION

165 | **MAN PULLING UP HIS *FUNDOSHI***

A standing figure tying up his fundoshi *(loincloth) after taking a bath, holding a fold of cloth under his chin, wincing as he catches one of his testicles against the edge of the material, the eyes inlaid in horn, the* himotōshi *probably formed by the left arm.*

EARLY–MID-19TH CENTURY

STAINED IVORY AND HORN; H. 3⁹⁄₁₆ IN. (9 CM)

UNSIGNED

PRIVATE COLLECTION

167 | GENITALIA AND CHILD

A naturalistically rendered model of the end of an erect penis, the underside modeled as a vagina from which a child's head is about to emerge, the himotōshi *formed as a hole in the top through which a cord is passed to connect with another in the child's head.*

Feminist cultural historians have drawn attention recently to the prevalence of female self-gratification in the culture of the Edo period. This carefully modeled netsuke of the human sexual organs, and of the consequence of their interaction, may be a development of the *harigata* (dildoes) which were used more widely by Japanese women than has been acknowledged previously.

19TH CENTURY
STAINED WOOD; L. 4¹³⁄₁₆ IN. (12.2 CM)
UNSIGNED
PRIVATE COLLECTION

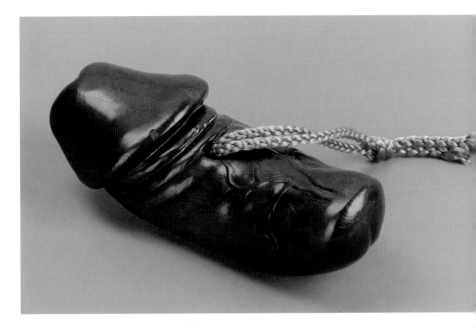

168 | OKAME IN THE GUISE OF A PROSTITUTE

Okame dressed in a kimono, with one hand to her cap, her kimono held slightly open and embroidered with silk-winder designs, the himo-tōshi *formed by two very worn holes in the back.*

Okame, the Shinto goddess of sexuality and fertility, is identifiable here by her chubby cheeks and contented expression. The silk-winder design symbolizes the Tanabata Festival, held during the seventh month to celebrate the one day of the year when the celestial Herd Boy and Weaving Girl, living on either side of the Milky Way, are allowed to meet. The imagery of happy sexual union is completed by the decidedly phallic shape of the whole carving.

MID–LATE 18TH CENTURY
STAINED BOXWOOD; H. 3¹⁵⁄₁₆ IN. (10.1 CM)
UNSIGNED
PRIVATE COLLECTION

169 | BLIND MAN WITH DOG

A carving of a figure in a striped haori *and* hakama *(jacket and trousers), standing on one leg, a staff in his right hand, his left hand held on top of his head, a small dog reaching up his back, the* himotōshi *formed by a large hole in his left thigh connecting to a smaller hole in his back.*

This very substantial carving is one of the most powerful known examples of an early wood netsuke in the style associated with Shūgetsu of Osaka and Edo.

MID–LATE 18TH CENTURY
STAINED BOXWOOD; H. 4³⁄₁₆ IN. (10.6 CM)
UNSIGNED
PRIVATE COLLECTION

A smiling figure dressed in a wide-sleeved robe and a formal lacquered hat, holding a fan in his right hand and a gohei *over his left shoulder, the* gohei *with a central flowerlike element from which the paper streamers hang, the detailed carving all in very low relief, the* himotōshi *formed by two holes on the back, signed with incised* sōsho *characters on the back in a raised area next to the lower, larger hole.*

This figure shows a *gohei-katsugi* or *engiya*, a Shinto priest carrying a *gohei*, a ritual staff terminating in strips of white paper used to summon the spirit of a particular *kami* or deity. The term *gohei-katsugi* is also used to refer to a generally superstitious person. Tametaka of Nagoya is one of the few *Sōken kishō* artists who is listed as a resident of somewhere other than Osaka, Kyoto, and Edo. He is described as having his own distinctive style, and is said to be famous for carving raised designs on the costumes of his figure netsuke. In fact, few such netsuke with his signature are known, but several of the larger carvings discovered a few years ago in the Nagoya temples Dairyūji and Enpukuji have brightly colored motifs on the clothing.

TAMETAKA KITAEMON OF NAGOYA (ACTIVE AROUND 1781)

STAINED BOXWOOD; H. 2¹¹⁄₁₆ IN. (6.8 CM)

SIGNED: *TAMETAKA*

MUSEUM OF FINE ARTS, BOSTON 47.746

171 | BOY WITH BOOK ON HIS HEAD

A boy dressed in court robes over striped hakama *(formal trousers), holding a fan and wearing a book on his head in imitation of a courtier's cap, with staining on the cords and binding of the book, the eyes, and the* mon *(crests) on the robe, the book inscribed* Monogatari *(Tales), the* himotōshi *formed by an opening underneath the* obi *at the back connecting to a fold in the skirt, signed with a single incised and stained character on the back.*

This netsuke has recently been identified as a close copy of the figure in *Fumiya no Yasuhide*, a print by Kitagawa Utamaro from a series entitled *Tōsei kodomo Rokkasen*, which depicts children as the Six Great Poets of early times. This choice of subject reflects the artist's awareness of Utamaro's immense popularity in Europe and the United States, and the netsuke was almost certainly carved with the export market in mind.

KAWAHARA RYŌ OF TOKYO (LATE 19TH–EARLY 20TH CENTURY)
IVORY WITH VERY LIGHT STAINING; H. 2⁷⁄₁₆ IN. (6.2 CM)
SIGNED: *RYŌ*
PRIVATE COLLECTION

172 | TRAVELERS IN A FERRY BOAT

A minutely detailed study of a group of traditionally dressed men, women, and a tame monkey in a ferry boat, details added in inlays of lacquer and ivory, the himotōshi *formed by two holes in the base lined with stained ivory, signed with incised characters on an inlaid, rectangular shell plaque on the base, the seal carved in relief on an inlaid, square, red lacquer plaque.*

This unashamedly nostalgic carving, probably intended for sale outside Japan and certainly of little use as a functional netsuke, is a three-dimensional realization of one of the many ferry-boat designs found on *inrō* and other items of lacquer ware from the later Edo period. Gyokusō was the father of Sōsui (see the following entry and cat. 23).

ŌUCHI GYOKUSŌ OF TOYKO (1879–1944)
BOXWOOD, LACQUER, IVORY, AND SHELL;
L. 2³⁄₁₆ IN. (5.6 CM)
SIGNED: *GYOKUSŌ*; SEALED: *JI*
PRIVATE COLLECTION

173 | GROUP SHELTERING UNDER A TREE

An extremely detailed study of a group of travelers and a horse, sheltering under a tree, including a man drying himself with a towel, a peddler with a sack, a man hiding under a leaf, another man with a fan, a lion-mask dancer, and a horse and groom, signed underneath with incised characters on a raised, rounded, rectangular reserve.

The tiny figures under the tree are essentially a miniature version of types seen in figural netsuke made in Edo from about the second quarter of the nineteenth century. Such carvings are currently at the nadir of their critical esteem (no examples are included in this catalogue), and one cannot help but admire Sōsui for his success in rejuvenating one of the more moribund strands within the netsuke tradition.

ŌUCHI SŌSUI OF TOYKO (1911–1972)
BOXWOOD; H. 1⅝ IN. (4.1 CM)
SIGNED: *SŌSUI*
PRIVATE COLLECTION

174 | TOY TIGER

A toy tiger standing on a base, carved in wood with stained stripes, fitted with a movable head and tongue made from stag antler, signed underneath with stylized relief characters imitating a seal on a sunken reserve.

The tiger with a shaking head, made from clay, wood, or papier mâché, is a popular toy all over Japan. In keeping with Kokusai's love of witty functional ambiguity, it is uncertain whether this example is simply a miniature toy, fitted with a base as many such tigers are, or actually is intended to be seen as a seal, alluding to the design of some of the very earliest netsuke.

OZAKI OR TAKEDA KOKUSAI (DIED 1894)

SEAL NETSUKE

STAINED BOXWOOD AND STAG ANTLER;

L. 1⅝ IN. (4.2 CM)

SEALED: *KOKUSAI*

PRIVATE COLLECTION

175 | TEA BOWL AND WHISK

A tea whisk lying in a square Raku-ware tea bowl with rounded corners, the bamboo whisk in stained ivory, the glazed ceramic bowl in lacquer, the underside carefully stippled to resemble unglazed pottery, the very small himotōshi *formed by two holes on either side of a simulated stamped* Raku *mark, signed with incised characters in the lacquer on the underside.*

First active in the sixteenth century, the line of potters using the name Raku produced some of the most highly regarded low-fired ceramic tea bowls throughout the Edo period, and Mitsuhiro specialized in making miniature copies such as this. The very small *himotōshi* indicates that this is not a netsuke intended for use. Like many pieces made by both Mitsuhiro and his Osaka contemporary Kaigyokusai Masatsugu (see cat. 203) in the second half of their careers, it almost certainly was intended for sale outside Japan.

ŌHARA MITSUHIRO OF OSAKA (1810–1875)

LACQUERED AND STAINED IVORY; H. 1⁵⁄₁₆ IN. (3.3 CM)

SIGNED: *MITSUHIRO*

PRIVATE COLLECTION

The head of a straw broom, the end worn down at an angle through prolonged use, the straw bound into three separate sections, the himotōshi *formed by a large hole in the polished base connecting with a smaller hole in the side.*

So that this little broom would not slip down behind the *obi* when it was in use, the carver deliberately made the base much wider than strict realism would require.

LATE 18TH–EARLY 19TH CENTURY

STAINED BOXWOOD; H. 2¹³⁄₁₆ IN. (7.1 CM)

UNSIGNED

MUSEUM OF FINE ARTS, BOSTON 47.466

A collection of local produce from Tokyo (see below), the himo-tōshi *formed by a hole in the* karashitsuke *packet, signed underneath with incised* sōsho *characters, sealed with incised characters on a square gold plaque.*

The souvenir gifts depicted on this carving (itself, ironically, a souvenir rather than a functional netsuke) include a bag of *kaminari-okoshi* sweets, named after the Kaminarimon (Thunder Gate) in eastern Tokyo, and appropriately decorated with the drums used by Raijin, God of Thunder (see cat. 118); a carved wooden bird, probably from the Kameido Tenmangū shrine, also in eastern Tokyo; some *karashitsuke* (pickles) from Ōmori in southern Tokyo; a necklace of so-called *donguri* (acorn) sweets; some *nattō* (fermented soybeans) wrapped in straw; and a *kukurizaru* (cloth doll).

SUZUKI TŌKOKU OF TOKYO (1845–AFTER 1912)
STAINED BOXWOOD, IVORY, LACQUER, AND GOLD
D. 1⅜ IN. (3.5 CM)
SIGNED: *TŌKOKU*; SEALED: *BAIRYŪ*
PRIVATE COLLECTION

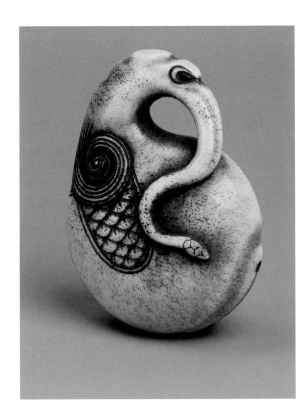

178 | *MOKUGYO* WITH MONSTROUS HEAD

A curiously shaped mokugyo, *its surface partially carved with fish scales, its handle with eyes of inlaid horn like those of a rain dragon (see cat. 61), terminating in a snake's body and head, the* himotōshi *formed by the junction of the snake's body with the side of the* mokugyo, *signed with a stylized, incised, and stained character on a square reserve on the side.*

A *mokugyo* is a type of wooden gong that is beaten as an accompaniment to the chanting of Buddhist scriptures. Kokusai creates a mysterious, ambiguous effect by combining this familiar ritual object with unexpected textures and monstrous forms derived from earlier netsuke history.

OZAKI OR TAKEDA KOKUSAI (DIED 1894)

STAINED STAG ANTLER AND HORN; L. 2$\frac{1}{16}$ IN. (5.3 CM)

SEALED: *KOKU*

PRIVATE COLLECTION

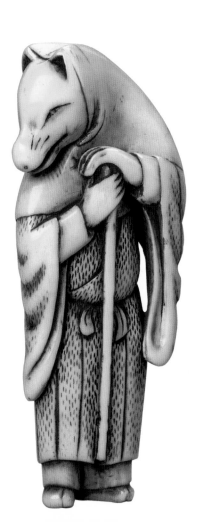

Flora and Fauna

T HIS SECTION STARTS WITH A VERY SMALL GROUP OF PLANTS, AND continues with netsuke depicting living creatures other than zodiac animals, including reptiles, amphibians, insects, fish and other marine life, birds, and mammals. Some of the humbler creatures were produced by a distinctive group of carvers who lived and worked in the remote provinces of Iwami and Aki, specializing in unusual netsuke subjects such as centipedes, lizards, frogs, snails, and crabs (cats. 182, 186, 187, 188, 194, 219). A number of these subjects were later adopted and copied by urban netsuke makers. Marine subjects were especially favored by the two Osaka carvers Mitsuhiro and Masatsugu (cats. 190, 193, 203, 208, 210, 211, 238), whose highly finished ivory carvings of sea creatures and insects were extremely popular with nineteenth-century visitors to Japan; such carvings continued to be made, chiefly for the Western market, during the twentieth century (cats. 204, 207, and 212).

The earliest piece in this group is the elephant on a base (cat. 222), a seal netsuke that was probably copied directly from a Chinese original. A few of the other nonzodiac mammals seen in netsuke, such as the *tanuki* in disguise (cat. 234) and the mischievous fox (cats. 235–237), are central characters in popular Japanese folklore. Others, such as the deer (cats. 224–226), carry rather more sophisticated cultural baggage, the cry of the deer having been an elite literary emblem of autumnal melancholy for more than a thousand years. Along with the wolf (cats. 227 and 228) and the cat (cats. 231 and 232), the deer attracted a comparable level of skill and attention to that lavished on the all-important zodiac creatures grouped in the next section (cats. 239–300). These three probably were favored because of their resemblance to three of the classic Kyoto animal types, the dog (cats. 286–294), the tiger (cats. 248–252), and the *kirin* (cats. 73–80), respectively. The best wolves, cats, and deer were carved by such well-known Osaka and Kyoto names as Garaku (cat. 224), Masanao (cats. 218 and 231), Okatomo (cats. 225 and 226), and Tomotada (cats. 227 and 232), while the wolf by Tomochika (cat. 228) shows how the Kyoto animal style was introduced to Edo from Kyoto around the beginning of the nineteenth century.

179 | MUSHROOMS

A highly polished group of nine mushrooms, the largest with a snail crawling up its side, the gills carefully rendered, the himotōshi formed by a single hole drilled through the base.

Although not regarded highly by contemporary collectors, netsuke depicting plants are often of the finest quality, and sometimes appear to be the result of direct observation rather than reproduction of established prototypes. These mushrooms are immature *Daikoku-shimeji* or *honshimeji*, valued for their delicate flavor, in contrast to the more familiar *matsutake*, which is prized for its rich aroma.

EARLY—MID-19TH CENTURY
STAINED AND POLISHED BOXWOOD
H. 1¹³⁄₁₆ IN. (4.6 CM)
UNSIGNED
MUSEUM OF FINE ARTS, BOSTON 47.474

180 | TREE FUNGUS AND SNAIL

A clump of mannentake (tree fungus) across which crawl a tiny copper spider and a large ivory snail with a shell of buffalo horn, its eyes inlaid in horn, the underside of the fungus minutely textured, the narrow himotōshi drilled through one of the stalks and lined with green-stained ivory, signed underneath with incised sōsho characters and sealed with incised characters on a square gold plaque.

SUZUKI TŌKOKU OF TOKYO (1845–AFTER 1912)
STAINED WOOD, IVORY, GOLD, HORN, AND COPPER;
L. 1⅞ IN. (4.8 CM)
SIGNED: *TŌKOKU*
SEALED: *BAIRYŪ*
PRIVATE COLLECTION

181 | MAGNOLIA AND MOON

A circular netsuke delicately carved in openwork, with a magnolia tree against a moon and stylized clouds, the moon in silver, the buds in gold and silver, the himotōshi *formed by large and small holes on the reverse, each lined with silver, sealed with incised characters on a rectangular gold plaque.*

Like several other late-nineteenth- and early-twentieth-century netsuke artists, Tōkoku often called upon the unmatched skills of the large pool of decorative metalworkers living in Tokyo, who had lost their traditional employment as makers of swordfittings when samurai privileges were abolished in 1876.

SUZUKI TŌKOKU OF TOKYO (1845–AFTER 1912)
RYŪSA MANJŪ NETSUKE
STAINED IVORY, GOLD, AND SILVER; D. 1^{11}/₁₆ IN. (4.3 CM)
SEALED: *FUZUI*
PRIVATE COLLECTION

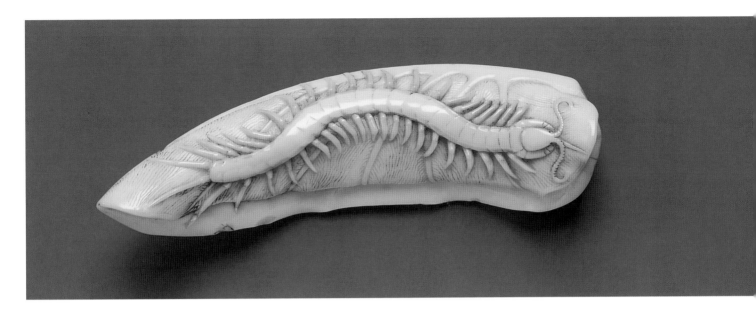

182 | CENTIPEDE ON A TARO LEAF

*A model of a centipede on a folded taro leaf, the very pale ivory
minutely incised and stained to indicate the sections of the
centipede's body and the veins of the leaf, the* himotōshi *formed
by two holes drilled in the underside, signed underneath with
minute stained and incised characters within an irregular
reserve.*

The daughter of Tomiharu (see cat. 187), founder of the
Iwami style, Bunshō is one of the few recorded female
netsuke carvers. Like her father, she specialized in
depictions of centipedes, spiders, slugs, snails, and frogs,
which she carved mainly from either boar's tusks or ivory.
She also continued her father's practice of adding long,
minutely incised signatures, but only seems to have
started including the date toward the end of her long
career.

SEIYŌDŌ BUNSHŌ OF IWAMI PROVINCE (1764–1838); DATED 1837;
STAINED IVORY; L. 3¼ IN. (8.2 CM)
SIGNED: *IWAMI NO KUNI KAAIGAWA SEIYŌDŌ BUNSHŌ-JO CHŌKOKU
TOKI NI TENPŌ HINOTO-TORI HARU NARI*
(CARVED BY MS. SEIYŌDŌ BUNSHŌ BY THE KAAIGAWA
RIVER IN IWAMI PROVINCE IN SPRING OF THE *HINOTO-
TORI* YEAR OF THE TENPŌ ERA [1837])
MUSEUM OF FINE ARTS, BOSTON 11.23662

183 | FROG CROUCHED ON A WATER LILY ROOT

A frog crouching with its back legs on the stalk and its front legs on the bulb of a water lily root, its eyes inlaid in light and dark horn, the himotōshi *formed by two unequal holes in the stalk, signed with incised and deeply stained characters on the stalk.*

At the start of his career, Sukenaga specialized in *ittōbori*, a style of carving using simple knife strokes to produce a faceted surface. Later he received instruction from an Edo carver called Suketomo, and started to produce the finely detailed, beautifully finished insect, reptile, and amphibian studies for which he is best known, although he also carved some larger figures of Shinto deities that have been preserved in local collections. Renowned as an uncompromising perfectionist, at his death Sukenaga left a mass of carvings he had rejected as failing to meet his high standards. A piece similar to this one is reproduced in Ueda Reikichi's *Netsuke no kenkyū*, where it is described as a frog on a *kabocha* (pumpkin), but it seems more likely that the frog is crouching on a water lily root. This subject is also occasionally seen in Chinese toggles.

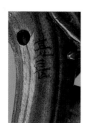

MATSUDA SUKENAGA OF TAKAYAMA,
HIDA PROVINCE (1800–1871)
STAINED BOXWOOD AND HORN; L. 2 1/16 IN. (5.3 CM)
SIGNED: *SUKENAGA*
PRIVATE COLLECTION

184 | SNAKE, SNAIL, AND FROG IN *SANSUKUMI* POSE

A snake surmounted by a frog and snail, its head on the frog's back, the minute eyes inlaid in dark horn, numerous himotōshi *formed by the snake's body, signed with incised and stained characters in a rectangular reserve on the snake's side near one of the frog's feet.*

The proverbial stalemate endured by a slug (later a snail) trying to eat a snake, which tries to eat a frog (later sometimes a toad), which tries in turn to eat the slug, dates back to *Kan'inshi* (in Chinese, *Guanyinzi*), a Tang Dynasty work; the eponymous author is supposed to have lived in the first millennium BC. In this version, Sukenaga downplays the ancient symbolism of the motif in favor of a more straightforward, detailed depiction of three of his favorite creatures.

MATSUDA SUKENAGA OF TAKAYAMA,
HIDA PROVINCE (1800–1871)
STAINED BOXWOOD AND HORN; H. 1 1/16 IN. (2.7 CM)
SIGNED: *SUKENAGA*
PRIVATE COLLECTION

186 | LIZARD ON A

A detailed and natu
mushroom, the worr
horn, the himotōshi
with ukibori *charac*

The birth and deat
Kimimichi), are ur
the years 1801–1811.
that he came from
western end of Japa
significance of the
is uncertain. In add
shellfish, Gohō is b
of frogs and lizards
mushrooms, and o

192 | CUCUMBER AND WASP

A very long netsuke in the form of a cucumber that has been colonized by a solitary wasp, the eyes inlaid in horn, the himo-tōshi formed by large and small holes on the reverse, signed with incised and stained sōsho *characters near the wider end.*

Ittokusai is thought to have been a member of the group of artists working in and around the cities of Nagoya in Owari Province and Gifu in Mino Province in the early to mid-nineteenth century. This carving is essentially a development of a model originated by an artist called Bazan, who lived at Ōgaki in Mino Province and carved netsuke of a solitary wasp in the rotted side of a pear.

ITTOKUSAI (EARLY 19TH CENTURY)
STAINED BOXWOOD AND HORN; L. 6⁵⁄₁₆ IN. (16.1 CM)
SIGNED: *ITTOKUSAI*
PRIVATE COLLECTION

193 | DRAGONFLY ON A NODE OF BAMBOO

A dragonfly resting on a node of bamboo, the wings and legs undercut, slightly stained to represent the veining on the wings and the texture of the bamboo, the himotōshi *formed by a single hole in the side connecting with the hollow of the stalk, signed with incised and stained characters just above the node.*

This is a superb example of Mitsuhiro's mature style, with every detail painstakingly rendered by minute carving and staining; the freely formed signature, which contrasts with the stiff characters seen in Mitsuhiro's early work, is another sign of a late date.

ŌHARA MITSUHIRO OF OSAKA (1810–1875)
STAINED IVORY; H. 2¼ IN. (5.8 CM)
SIGNED: *MITSUHIRO*
PRIVATE COLLECTION

194 | CRAB ON DRIFTWOOD

A crab on a piece of old driftwood, the harder year rings on the sides jutting out over the softer rotted wood, the himotōshi formed by two unequal holes in the polished base.

This is another favorite Tomiharu model (see also cat. 187), reflecting his love of both nonmammalian life and decayed materials; a very similar model in a private collection is dated to the year 1789 or 1790.

SHIMIZU TOMIHARU (1733–1810)
BLACK PERSIMMON WOOD; L. 2^{15}⁄$_{16}$ IN. (7.5 CM)
SIGNED: *SEIYŌDŌ TOMIHARU*
PRIVATE COLLECTION

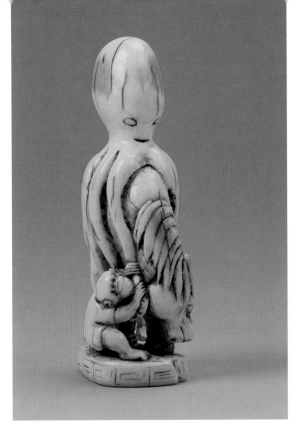

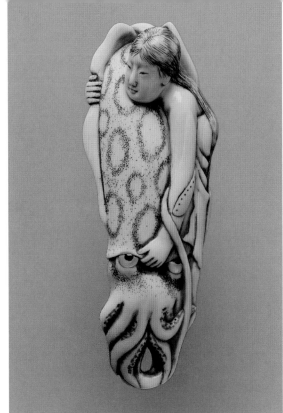

195 | OCTOPUS RIDING A HORSE

An octopus riding on a horse that stands on a rounded rectangular base, where a tiny monkey sits playing with one of the tentacles, the sides of the base incised and stained with a key-fret pattern, the himotōshi *formed by the legs.*

The shape of this carving has its origins in Chinese seals, which are often surmounted by animals that serve as handles, but this example is unusually elongated and would not hang neatly at the *obi* when worn as a netsuke. The sexual connotations of the subject (as seen in cats. 33 and 196) make it likely that this is another example of a *harigata* or dildo (see also cat. 167).

LATE 17TH–EARLY 18TH CENTURY

STAINED IVORY; H. 3⅛ IN. (8 CM)

UNSIGNED

PRIVATE COLLECTION

196 | PEARL DIVER EMBRACED BY A CUTTLEFISH

An ama *(pearl diver) embraced by a cuttlefish, its mottled body rendered in fine stippling and staining, its eyes inlaid in shell and polished horn, the* himotōshi *formed by large and small holes in back.*

The sexual union of a human female with an octopus or cuttlefish is a common theme in pornography of the later Edo period. This carving leaves a good deal to the imagination, unlike the highly graphic treatments of the subject in illustrated books and woodblock prints, such as Katsushika Hokusai's *Kinoe no komatsu,* published in 1814.

EARLY 19TH CENTURY

STAINED IVORY, SHELL, AND HORN; H. 4¹⁄₁₆ IN. (10.3 CM)

UNSIGNED

PRIVATE COLLECTION

An octopus looming over a monkey, which stands on an abalone shell and looks up in terror, the octopus's eyes inlaid in light and dark horn, the himotōshi *formed by a hole drilled upward through the octopus connecting with one in its back, signed with deeply incised and stained characters on the back of the octopus.*

This is a clear case of the adaptation of an existing type by variation of the subject matter. The composition is derived from the same type as Ikko's netsuke depicting Mikoshi Nyūdō terrorizing a man (see number 135, which is based on an encyclopedia illustration), while the combination of an octopus and monkey refers to a children's tale in which Ryūjin, the Dragon King of the Sea, falls ill and is told by his doctor, an octopus, that the only remedy for his sickness is the liver of a live monkey. In the story, a jellyfish sent to trick a monkey into following it to the bottom of the sea fails in its mission, but here the ruse has been successful and the monkey is about to meet its end.

TANAKA MINKŌ OF TSU, ISE PROVINCE (1735–1816)
STAINED BOXWOOD AND HORN; H. 1¹⁵⁄₁₆ IN. (5 CM)
SIGNED: *MINKŌ*, WITH A *KAŌ*
MUSEUM OF FINE ARTS, BOSTON 11.23397

A monkey in the grip of an octopus, its fur meticulously rendered and forming an effective contrast with the smooth surface of the octopus, the monkey's eyes inlaid in light and dark horn, the octopus's eyes inlaid in dark horn, the himo-tōshi *formed by the left leg, signed with incised and stained characters on a rectangular reserve underneath the monkey.*

In addition to the account given by Ueda Reikichi (himself a native of Gifu) in *Netsuke no kenkyū*, which reports that Tomokazu sketched animals from life, further scant details of this artist's career are provided in *Giyō gajinden* (Lives of Gifu Men of Culture, 1935). Here it is claimed that he traveled to Kyoto and became a pupil of Izumiya Tomotada, taking a character from his master's name to form his own signature. Netsuke signed *Tomokazu* have recently been the subject of intense but inconclusive debate on questions of authenticity and, as in the case of Jugyoku (see cat. 200), a series of different users of the name has been hypothesized. The most that can be said with any confidence about this example is that it exhibits all of the features associated with other Tomokazu netsuke that are widely accepted as genuine, including the compact, almost spherical form (a feature perhaps showing the influence of Masanao of Yamada), careful hairwork, and subtly contrasted textures.

KANŌ TOMOKAZU OF GIFU, MINO PROVINCE
(EARLY 19TH CENTURY)
STAINED CHERRY WOOD AND HORN; H. 1½ IN. (3.9 CM)
SIGNED: *TOMOKAZU*
MUSEUM OF FINE ARTS, BOSTON 11.23597

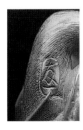

A compact model of a cuttlefish, the eyes inlaid in dark horn, the himotōshi *formed by one of the tentacles, signed underneath in deeply incised and stained characters.*

Masakatsu, son and pupil of the famous Masanao of Ise Province (who is a different artist from Masanao of Kyoto and not featured in this catalogue), here follows in the family traditions of naturalism, compactness, and high finish. This is a rare instance of a netsuke carved from wood that is left mostly unstained (apart from the signature and the stippling on the creature's head), revealing a color that explains the Chinese characters *kōyō* ("yellow willow") normally used to write the Japanese word *tsuge* (boxwood).

MASAKATSU (DIED 1899)
STAINED BOXWOOD AND HORN; L. 1¾ IN. (4.5 CM)
SIGNED: *MASAKATSU*
MUSEUM OF FINE ARTS, BOSTON 47.628

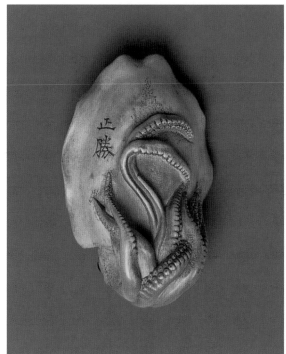

A compact carving of an octopus, the body and the outside of the tentacles virtually unstained, the inner surfaces of the tentacles carved and stained in great detail, the large eyes inlaid in black horn, several himotōshi *formed by the tentacles, signed with incised and stained characters on one of the tentacles.*

Much ingenuity has been devoted recently to analyzing different types of netsuke bearing the signature *Jugyoku*, as well as the variations in the way the characters are written, with the aim of assigning the surviving oeuvre to a number of distinct artists with the same name. As a result, it is now generally accepted in Western netsuke circles that the orthography of the signature on this piece, which preserves most of the fourteen strokes of the complex first character, should be associated with the first Jugyoku, if one excludes Chōunsai Jugyoku, another artist listed by Ueda Reikichi in *Netsuke no kenkyū*. However, in this and most other cases, the documentary evidence is so meager and unverifiable that such distinctions would be unlikely to stand up to the stricter criteria demanded by other fields of art history. The best we can do, perhaps, is to attempt a more general chronology without attempting to assign each netsuke to a particular artist.

UEDA JUGYOKU OF EDO (EARLY–MID-19TH CENTURY)
STAINED IVORY AND HORN; L. 2⅛ IN. (5.4 CM)
SIGNED: *JUGYOKU*
PRIVATE COLLECTION

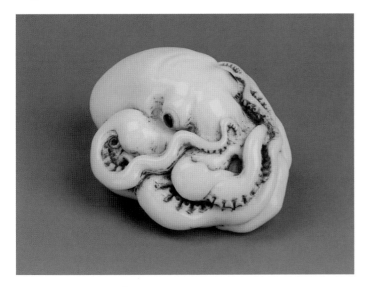

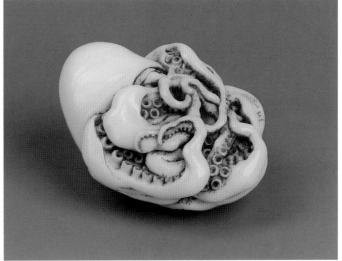

201 | OCTOPUS IN TRAP, WITH HAIKU

An octopus trap with two handles threaded with a rope, carved from wood, carefully textured to imitate the surface of the ceramic original, encrusted with barnacles in ivory and other materials, the interior with an octopus carved in great detail, the outside incised with a poem, sealed in raised characters on one end.

Several versions of this subject are known, including one that is a collaboration between the two great Osaka artists Kaigyokusai Masatsugu and Ōhara Mitsuhiro. The theme of the haiku, by Matsuo Bashō (1644–1694), is a careless octopus being deceived by a fisherman's lanterns: *An octopus trap / Dreaming empty dreams / The summer moon!*

SUZUKI TŌKOKU OF TOKYO (1845–AFTER 1912)
STAINED WOOD, IVORY, AND OTHER MATERIALS;
H. 1⁷⁄₈ IN. (4.7 CM)
SEALED: *BAIRYŪ* AND INSCRIBED WITH A HAIKU:
TAKOTSUBO YA / HAKANAKI YUME O / NATSU NO TSUKI
(SEE ABOVE FOR TRANSLATION)
PRIVATE COLLECTION

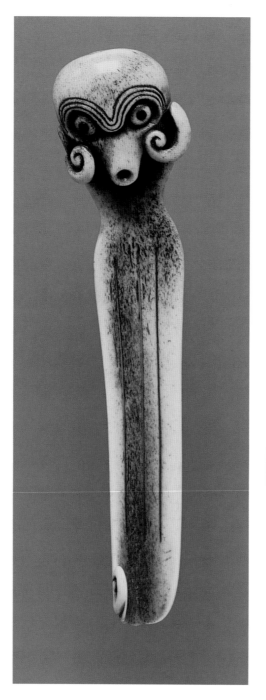

202 | OCTOPUS

An abbreviated rendering of an octopus, with a humanoid nose and eyes and two short tentacles ending in tight curls, four other tentacles, almost conjoined but with very narrow slits between them, descending to form the part of the netsuke worn behind the obi, signed with a single stylized character in sunken relief on a circular reserve on the back of the head, partially obscured by a tentacle.

This is a variation on one of Kokusai's preferred netsuke types; see also cat. 101.

OZAKI OR TAKEDA KOKUSAI (DIED 1894)
SASHI NETSUKE
STAINED STAG ANTLER; H. 4⅞ IN. (12.4 CM)
SEALED: *KOKU*
PRIVATE COLLECTION

203 | OCTOPUS

A tonkotsu (tobacco box) *formed from a polished nut, the ivory lid in the form of an octopus, its eyes inlaid in light and dark horn, signed with very lightly stained, incised characters inside the lid, the seal on a rectangular reserve with a double outline, the* ojime *in the form of an octopus and monkey, with horn and shell inlay.*

Kaigyokusai Masatsugu is perhaps the most famous of all netsuke artists, yet for much of his working life, Japan was playing an increasingly active role in the global economy; according to Ueda Reikichi, seventy to eighty percent of Masatsugu's work was exported and probably never was intended for actual use. If Ueda's information about Masatsugu's signature is believable, the use of his art name in its fullest and longest form – Kaigyokusai instead of Kaigyoku or Kaigyokudō – would indicate that this very fine piece was made after he reached the age of about fifty.

KAIGYOKUSAI MASATSUGU OF OSAKA (1813–1892);
ABOUT 1860–1892
TONKOTSU
POLISHED NUT, WITH THE LID
IN IVORY AND HORN; H. ⅝ IN. (6.6 CM)
SIGNED: *KAIGYOKUSAI*
SEALED: *MASATSUGU*
PRIVATE COLLECTION

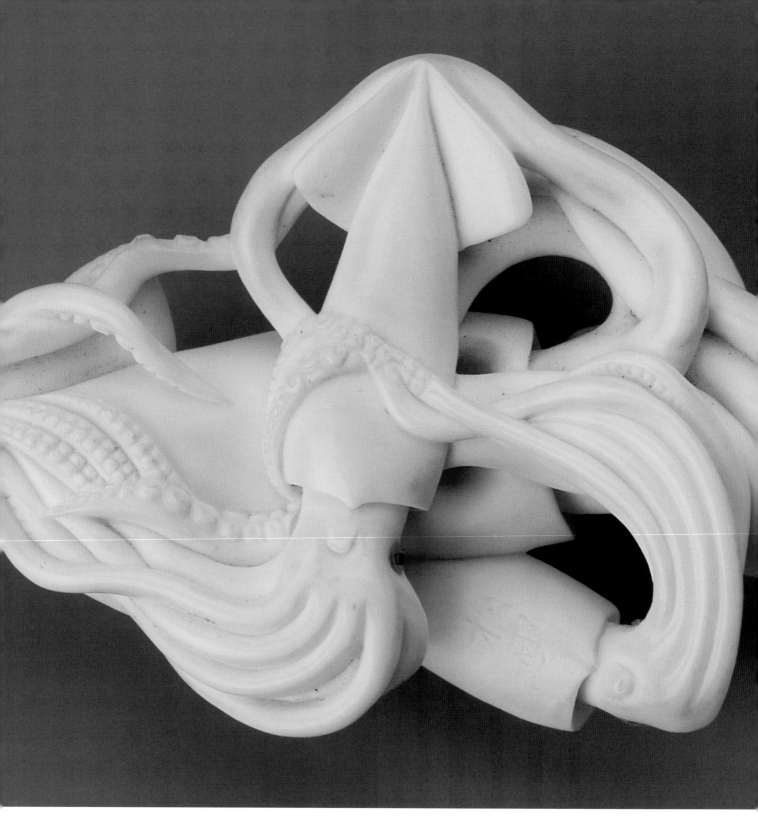

204 | SQUID AND YOUNG

A large and two small, naturalistically carved squid, each with eyes inlaid in light and dark horn, the mouths in dark horn, signed with incised characters on one of the smaller squid.

This piece is reproduced in one of the very grainy photographs included in Ueda Reikichi's *Netsuke no kenkyū*, completed at the end of 1942 and published in October of 1943. Ueda's biography states that the artist, who changed his name from Hōkunsai to Shōun in February of 1940, regarded Kaigyokusai Masatsugu (see cat. 203) as his ideal, and this is borne out by Shōun's use of milk-white, highly polished, unstained ivory, as well as his almost obsessive attention to detail.

YAMAMOTO SHŌUN OF KYOTO (BORN 1913); 1940–1943
IVORY AND HORN; L. 2⅛ IN. (5.4 CM)
SIGNED: *SHŌUN*
PRIVATE COLLECTION

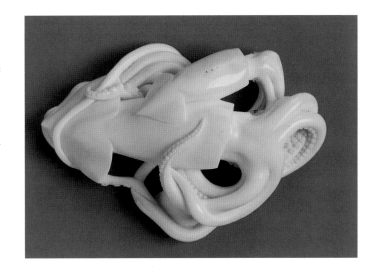

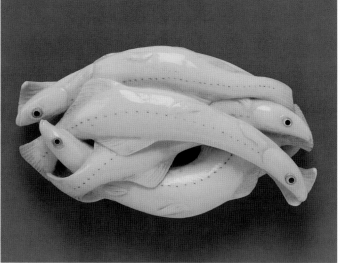

205 | THREE *NAMAZU*

A compact carving of three interlocking namazu *(catfish), the
eyes inlaid in dark horn, a natural* himotōshi *under the head of
the largest fish, signed underneath with incised and stained
characters.*

In the Edo period, it was popularly believed that
earthquakes were caused by the thrashings of a giant
namazu that lay underground, its head pinned down by a
huge rock. Recent research in local records has uncovered
life dates for a number of carvers who worked in the cities
of Nagoya and Gifu, including Masatami; the compact
shape is typical of netsuke carved in that part of Japan.

MASATAMI OF NAGOYA (1854–1928)
STAINED BOXWOOD AND HORN; D. 1⅝ IN. (4.1 CM)
SIGNED: *MASATAMI TŌ* (CARVED BY MASATAMI)
MUSEUM OF FINE ARTS, BOSTON 47.454

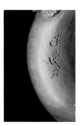

206 | *SHIRAUO*

Seven shirauo *(whitebait), the lateral markings incised and
stained, the dorsal fins shown in low relief against the bodies,
the eyes inlaid in shell and dark horn, several* himotōshi
*formed by the intersections of the fish, signed with incised and
lightly stained characters on the side of one of the fish.*

UEDA JUGYOKU OF EDO (EARLY–MID-19TH CENTURY)
STAINED IVORY, SHELL, AND HORN; L. 1¹⁵⁄₁₆ IN. (5 CM)
SIGNED: *JUGYOKU*
PRIVATE COLLECTION

207 | *SHIRAUO*

A close copy of the preceding entry.

In 1972, the netsuke dealer Bernard Hurtig encouraged Seihōsai Meikei to become a fully independent carver, and at Hurtig's suggestion Meikei carved a large number of close copies of earlier netsuke. He later abandoned ivory and started to work mostly in imported boxwood.

SEIHŌSAI MEIKEI (BORN 1932); AFTER 1972
STAINED IVORY, SHELL, AND HORN; L. 2 IN. (5.1 CM)
SIGNED: *MEIKEI*
PRIVATE COLLECTION

208 | DRIED FISH

Two dried and salted sardines, the ivory unstained, the eyes inlaid in light and dark horn within translucent amber, which allows the light to show through from both sides, the himotōshi *formed by the overlap of the tails, signed with incised characters near the tail of one of the fish.*

KAIGYOKUSAI MASATSUGU OF OSAKA (1813–1892)
IVORY, AMBER, AND HORN; L. 3½ IN. (8.9 CM)
SIGNED: *KAIGYOKUSAI*
PRIVATE COLLECTION

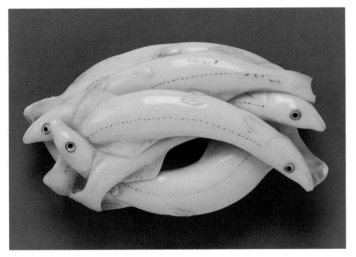

213 | CARP AT THE DRAGON GATE WATERFALL

A rather light netsuke representing a carp leaping up a waterfall, the himotōshi *formed by a single hole in the back connecting with the hollow interior.*

Despite some minor differences in detail, this is one of those rare cases in which one can be fairly confident that a certain netsuke type (another example of which is in the collection of the Museum of Fine Arts) derives either directly or indirectly from a specific printed source. In this case, that source is the influential design book *Ehon shoshin hashiradate*, originally published in 1715. There the motif is entitled *Ryūmon no taki koi* (Carp at the Dragon Gate Waterfall), referring to the traditional Chinese analogy between success in the official examinations and a carp transforming into a dragon when it ascends the Dragon Gate.

EARLY–MID-19TH CENTURY

HEAVILY STAINED FRUITWOOD; L. 2⅝ IN. (6.7 CM)

UNSIGNED

PRIVATE COLLECTION

CARP AT THE DRAGON
GATE WATERFALL, FROM
ANON., *EHON SHOSHIN
HASHIRADATE* [1715;
THIS EDITION 1761],
VOLUME 1, PP. 14–15.
VICTORIA AND ALBERT
MUSEUM

214 | PARROT

A stylized model of a parrot, with its feet drawn up under its beak, the eyes inlaid in polished horn, many other details incised and stained, the himotōshi *formed by a large hole under the legs connecting with a smaller hole in the side.*

No parallel has been discovered for this netsuke in either printed sources or in other carvings, although the basic composition is clearly related to other early creatures such as rain dragons (see cat. 61). It combines many of the features most sought after by today's collectors, including simple shape, original design, deep patination, and noticeable but not excessive wear, a pleasing reminder that the netsuke was cherished by earlier owners.

LATE 17TH–EARLY 18TH CENTURY
STAINED IVORY AND HORN; H. 4⁵⁄₁₆ IN. (11 CM)
UNSIGNED
PRIVATE COLLECTION

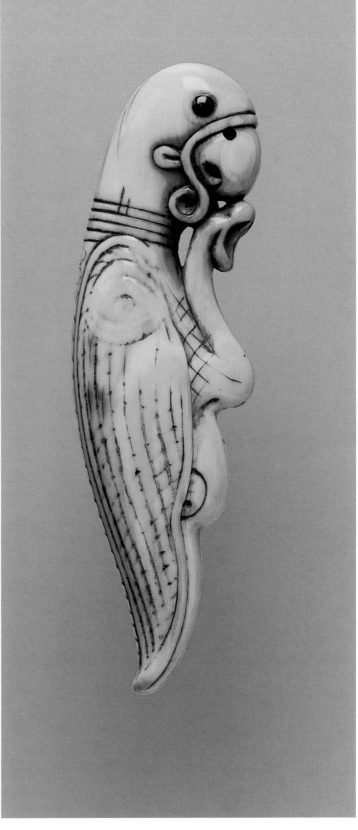

A stylized model of a hō-ō *bird preening its tail feathers, the feathers carved in openwork, the details of the bird's patterning deeply incised and heavily stained, the* himotōshi *formed by a hole underneath the bird connecting with one in the side.*

Like the *hakutaku* and the *kirin* (see cats. 69 and 73), the *hō-ō* bird, according to early Confucian teaching, only appears on earth when the empire is under the rule of a virtuous monarch. For this reason it was often depicted as a legitimizing motif by the artists who decorated the palaces and castles of the warlord Toyotomi Hideyoshi (1536–1598), and was subsequently a frequent theme of official paintings under the Tokugawa shoguns. Along with netsuke depicting Chinese *sennin* and heroes, early netsuke such as these bear witness to the spread of Confucian teaching during the first half of the Edo period. Although the design appears to create an ideal opening for the hanging cord, the artist drilled a conventional *himotōshi* so as to prevent the bird from jutting out inelegantly when worn.

EARLY–MID 18TH CENTURY
HEAVILY STAINED IVORY; D. 2¹⁵/₁₆ IN. (7.4 CM)
UNSIGNED
PRIVATE COLLECTION

216 | PARROT ON A PINE BRANCH

A parrot perched on a pine branch, the eyes and beak inlaid in ebony, the himotōshi *formed by a hole in the side connecting with the hollow of the branch, signed underneath with crudely scratched characters.*

This is another instance (see the following entry and cat. 213) of a netsuke type that appears to be based closely on a printed source, in this case *Ehon shahō bukuro,* a work that is already well known as a source of lacquer designs. The carver (about whom nothing is known) made use not only of the image, but also of the written instructions which direct that the eyes and beak should be rendered in black ink, represented here by ebony.

SŌSHIN (EARLY–MID-19TH CENTURY)
STAINED BOXWOOD AND EBONY; H. 1⅞ IN. (4.7 CM)
SIGNED: *SŌSHIN*
PRIVATE COLLECTION

PARROT ON A PINE BRANCH, FROM TACHIBANA MORIKUNI (ILLUSTRATOR), *EHON SHAHŌ BUKURO* [1720; THIS EDITION 1770], VOLUME 8, PP. 12–3. MUSEUM OF FINE ARTS, BOSTON

217 | OWL AND OWLET ON A PINE BRANCH

An owl perched on a gnarled old tree, a movable owlet hidden in a hollow branch next to the adult bird, the eyes inlaid in light and dark horn, the himotōshi *formed by a hole through the trunk.*

This popular model appears to be derived, like the previous entry, from *Ehon shahō bukuro*, where the owl is described as a "wheel-headed bird." As usual the ears have been eliminated, presumably because they would be easily breakable; a base has been added so that the netsuke can stand upright when not in use (this feature is absent in some other netsuke of the same subject); and the hole in the branch, empty in the illustration, is occupied by a movable owlet. Matsura Seizan (1760–1841), Lord of Hirado, described a similar device on one of his netsuke: "... one chestnut has the insect's head appearing from inside its cocoon, but when you push it with your finger, it goes back in."

MID-19TH CENTURY
STAINED BOXWOOD AND HORN; H. 2¹¹⁄₁₆ IN. (6.8 CM)
UNSIGNED
MUSEUM OF FINE ARTS, BOSTON 47.561

OWL ON A PINE BRANCH,
FROM TACHIBANA MORI-
KUNI (ILLUSTRATOR), *EHON
SHAHŌ BUKURO* [1720; THIS
EDITION 1770], VOLUME 8,
PP. 8–9. MUSEUM OF FINE
ARTS, BOSTON

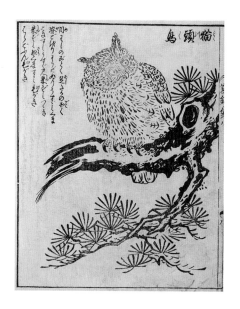

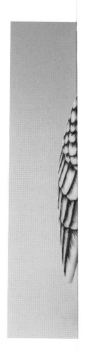

218 | MANDARIN DUCK

A compact model of a mandarin duck, the eyes inlaid in dark horn, the himotōshi *formed by a large hole under the tail connecting with a smaller hole in the center of the underside, signed under the breast with boldly incised and stained characters on an ovoid reserve, the main element of the second character narrowing toward the base in Masanao's typical manner.*

This very high-quality carving by Masanao, now one of the most highly prized of all netsuke artists, is something of an object lesson in the transformation of a motif from the printed image to a sculptural form. Thanks to their importance as symbols of marital fidelity, mandarin ducks were illustrated so widely in books and encyclopedias that it would be impossible to point to a single graphic source, but it is worth making a comparison with the example selected for reproduction here, from the influential compilation *Ehon tsūhōshi*. In the interests of compactness and durability, the head is

sunk deep into the breast and the wing feathers are low against the back, while the retracted feet, by definition not visible in illustrations, probably owe as much to the artist's imagination as they do to direct observation from nature. Other netsuke carvers might have carved more realistic birds, but few were as successful in exploiting the limitations imposed by functionality to achieve a satisfying sculptural result.

MASANAO OF KYOTO (ACTIVE AROUND 1781)
STAINED BOXWOOD AND HORN; L. 2¹⁄₁₆ IN. (5.2 CM)
SIGNED: *MASANAO*
PRIVATE COLLECTION

MANDARIN DUCK, FROM
TACHIBANA MORIKUNI
(ILLUSTRATOR), *EHON
TSŪHŌSHI*
[1729–30], VOLUME 6,
PP. 6–7. MUSEUM OF
FINE ARTS, BOSTON

220 | EAGLE CL

*An intricate car∖
the hairwork an∖
pale and dark h∖
limbs, signed wi∖
rounded rectang∖*

Despite many d∖
the prolific illus∖
apparent in this∖
collectors and c∖
were at least tw∖
signature Rante∖
appear to be the∖
in a rather mor∖
Rantei.

RANTEI II OF K∖
STAINED IVORY∖
SIGNED: *RANTE∖
MUSEUM OF FIN∖

221 | QUAIL AND MILLET

A stylized, compact carving of a quail, with a stalk of millet in its beak, a leaf trailing over its back, the stalk unstained, the seed head very finely cross-hatched and stained, contrasting with the bird's lightly incised and stained breast, which is carved so as to bring out the grain of the ivory, the himotōshi *formed by two small holes under the tail, signed underneath with minute incised and heavily stained characters on a rounded rectangular reserve in a millet leaf.*

Ueda Reikichi, in *Netsuke no kenkyū*, claims that Mitsusada had the surname Ōhara and worked after the Kansei era (1789–1801) and into the Bunsei era (1818–1830). As usual, Ueda gives no evidence to support this information, but the shared use of the character *Mitsu*, the minutely detailed carving and heavy staining, and the small *himotōshi* all suggest that this artist probably influenced the great Ōhara Mitsuhiro (see cat. 185) during his early career.

ŌHARA MITSUSADA OF OSAKA (EARLY–MID-19TH CENTURY)
STAINED IVORY; H. 1^{7}/$_{16}$ IN. (3.6 CM)
SIGNED: *MITSUSADA*
PRIVATE COLLECTION

223 | RESTING ELEPHANT

A very worn, simple carving of a recumbent elephant, with its head turned to the right, the end of its trunk touching its side, the shape of its ribs visible through its hide, very little surface texture except on the tail, the himotōshi *formed by an exceptionally large (10 mm) hole by the tail and a smaller hole behind the front legs.*

222 | ELEPHANT ON BASE

A very worn carving representing a harnessed elephant standing on a rounded rectangular base, the inner surfaces heavily stained, the himotōshi *formed by a single hole in the base.*

Sōken kishō illustrates a similar, simple carving with the caption "there is a seal underneath." These early seal-type animal figures seem to be based closely on Chinese originals, which were fashioned increasingly from ivory rather than from jade during the late Ming Dynasty, and which are among the earliest netsuke to be mentioned in Japanese literature.

This figure, attributed to Gechū, is essentially the imported Chinese elephant as seen in seal carvings, transformed through assimilation to depictions of other beasts drawn from printed sources. Gechū is credited with establishing many of the conventions of animal carving in early Kansai (Osaka and Kyoto) netsuke, and this pose, with minor variations, is seen often in mid- and late-eighteenth-century deer, dogs, tigers, water buffaloes, and other quadrupeds.

LATE 17TH OR EARLY 18TH CENTURY
SEAL NETSUKE
STAINED IVORY; H. 2½ IN. (6.3 CM)
UNSIGNED
PRIVATE COLLECTION

STYLE OF GECHŪ (EARLY–MID-18TH CENTURY)
STAINED IVORY; L. 2⅛ IN. (5.4 CM)
UNSIGNED
PRIVATE COLLECTION

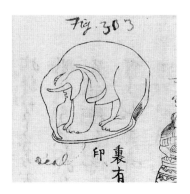

ELEPHANT ON BASE,
FROM INABA TSŪRYŪ,
SŌKEN KISHŌ [1781],
VOLUME 7, PP. 15–16.
MUSEUM OF FINE ARTS,
BOSTON

224 | RESTING DEER

A recumbent stag with its head turned to the right, licking its right haunch, the fur rendered by thick, heavily stained incisions contrasting with the plain ivory dappling, the large eyes inlaid in dark horn, the himotōshi *formed by a very large hole in the left haunch connecting with a smaller hole in the center of the underside, signed underneath with incised and stained characters on an oval reserve next to the smaller hole.*

The relatively unsophisticated treatment of the hairwork, the very flat base, and the exceptionally large *himotōshi* make it likely that this is an early work by the artist or artists using the name Garaku.

GARAKU RISUKE OF OSAKA (EARLY–MID-18TH CENTURY)
STAINED IVORY AND HORN; L. 1^{15}⁄$_{16}$ IN. (5 CM)
SIGNED: *GARAKU*
PRIVATE COLLECTION

225 | RECUMBENT DEER

A recumbent stag with its head raised and turned to the left, its mouth slightly open, the fur rendered by fine, lightly stained striations, the outline of the ribs visible beneath the coat, the himotōshi *formed by a large and a slightly smaller hole in the center of the underside, signed underneath with incised and stained characters on a rectangular reserve on the right haunch.*

Okatomo receives only the briefest of mentions in *Sōken kishō*, described merely as "like the previous." The previous artist listed is the great Masanao, whose work is said to be deserving of the highest praise, but contemporary connoisseurship has tended to rank Okatomo slightly below Masanao, not only because his work is more common, but also because some figures bearing his signature are somewhat formulaic in character despite their satisfying sculptural qualities and high finish. This is a particularly striking example of his work, with especially skillful use of the ivory grain on the right side of the neck and on the left haunch.

OKATOMO OF KYOTO (LATE 18TH–EARLY 19TH CENTURY)

STAINED IVORY; H. 1⅜ IN. (3.5 CM)

SIGNED: *OKATOMO*

PRIVATE COLLECTION

A stag crouching on its haunches, its forelegs supporting its long neck as it looks directly upward with its mouth slightly open, the fur rendered by fine, lightly stained striations, the pupils inlaid in dark horn, the himotōshi *formed by a large and a slightly smaller hole in the right side, signed with incised and stained characters on a rectangular reserve underneath the right hind leg.*

This posture is strikingly similar to that of the imaginary *kirin* (see cats. 73–82), which often is described as having a body like a deer's. As with the previous netsuke, despite this figure's excellent technical quality, the quieter style of carving is suggestive of a transition from an individual, experimental stage to a more commercial, mass-produced phase of netsuke production; even Okatomo's signature seems less assertive than that of Tomotada or Masanao.

OKATOMO OF KYOTO (LATE 18TH–EARLY 19TH CENTURY)
STAINED IVORY AND HORN; H. 2¹¹⁄₁₆ IN. (6.8 CM)
SIGNED: *OKATOMO*
PRIVATE COLLECTION

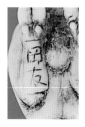

A wolf crouching over a crab, which lies at its feet, the crab's claws drawn in underneath its body, the wolf's mouth open revealing its sharp teeth, its tail curled between its legs, the backbone and ribs visible under its coat, the fur indicated by delicately incised and stained striations that are much worn through repeated use, the wolf's eyes inlaid in brown horn, the crab's single eye inlaid in black horn, the himotōshi *formed by the wolf's legs, signed with incised and stained characters on a rectangular reserve underneath the wolf's left hind leg.*

The unusual subject gave Tomotada the opportunity to carve one of his more inventive bases, the closely observed markings of the crab contrasting with the freer treatment of the wolf's tail and hind legs.

IZUMIYA TOMOTADA OF KYOTO (ACTIVE AROUND 1781)
STAINED IVORY AND HORN; H. 1⅞ IN. (4.7 CM)
SIGNED: *TOMOTADA*
PRIVATE COLLECTION

An emaciated wolf seated with its right front paw on a human skull, its mouth open revealing its sharp teeth, the deep-set eyes inlaid in ivory and horn, the fur boldly scratched and stained, the himotōshi formed by the opening between the body and the forelegs, signed with deeply incised and stained characters on an irregular reserve on the left haunch.

In *Netsuke no kenkyū*, Ueda Reikichi claims that most of Tomochika's netsuke were carved during the Bunsei and Tenpō eras (1818–1844). Tomochika and his two recorded followers are known today mainly for a large number of detailed figural netsuke that are described politely by Ueda as "laying stress on subject matter rather than fine craftsmanship." This powerful figure, an interesting example of what may be considered the early Tomochika style, is much closer to the miniature animal sculptures of Kyoto and Osaka than to the fussy storytelling netsuke more usually associated with his name.

YAMAGUCHI TOMOCHIKA I OF EDO (1800–1873)
STAINED BOXWOOD, IVORY, AND HORN;
H. 2½ IN. (6.4 CM)
SIGNED: *TOMOCHIKA*
MUSEUM OF FINE ARTS, BOSTON RES. 18.161

229 | SEATED CAT AND KITTEN

A large adult cat, with a collar around its neck and a tiny kitten climbing on its back, the original hairwork rubbed away through prolonged use, the himotōshi *formed by two very large holes in the underside.*

The pleasing simplicity of this carving owes something to its graphic origin, which is probably one of the rather unsophisticated depictions of cats in early encyclopedias such as *Kinmō zui* (1666). These often show an adult cat with a diminutive kitten climbing on its back; the fact that the kitten's paws are so small in relation to its body is proof enough that carvings such as this owe little or nothing to direct observation.

ATTRIBUTED TO GARAKU RISUKE OF OSAKA
(EARLY–MID-18TH CENTURY)
STAINED IVORY; H. 1⁵⁄₁₆ IN. (3.3 CM)
UNSIGNED
PRIVATE COLLECTION

230 | KITTEN LICKING ITS HIND PAW

A simple carving of a recumbent kitten, its large front paws spread out, twisting around to lick its right hind paw, the details very lightly incised and stained, the body of polished ivory with no incised and stained hairwork, the himotōshi *formed by a very large hole in the stylized left haunch and a smaller hole in the center of the underside.*

This more lifelike study may have been based partly on direct observation, unlike the preceding example.

EARLY–MID-18TH CENTURY
STAINED IVORY; L. 2¹⁄₁₆ IN. (5.2 CM)
UNSIGNED
PRIVATE COLLECTION

231 | RESTING CAT

A resting cat, crouching with its four paws close together, looking straight ahead, its tail curled up against its right side, the delicately incised and stained fur much worn through prolonged use, the himotōshi *formed by the gaps between the hind paws and the underside of the cat, signed with very worn incised and stained characters on an oval reserve between the hind legs.*

Masanao's skillful combination of compact form and appealing facial characterization caused this netsuke to be much loved and fondled by its previous owners, so much so that the hairwork has been worn away from all of the most exposed surfaces, and the signature is barely visible.

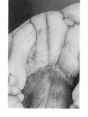

MASANAO OF KYOTO (ACTIVE AROUND 1781)
STAINED IVORY; H. 1¼ IN. (3.2 CM)
SIGNED: *MASANAO*
PRIVATE COLLECTION

232 | CAT AND MOUSE

An elongated, seated cat with a dead rat in its jaws, leaning over so that the rat's tail rests on the ground, both animals with finely incised and stained hairwork, the eyes inlaid in dark horn, the himotōshi *formed by a hole in one side emerging at the base, signed with rather small incised and stained characters in a rectangular reserve on the back.*

The unusual elongated form of the cat and the rather small signature have led some commentators to suggest that this striking piece is not from the hand of Tomotada or his immediate circle of craftsmen, but there are many similarities in detail between this and other Tomotada animals.

IZUMIYA TOMOTADA OF KYOTO (ACTIVE AROUND 1781)
STAINED IVORY; H. 2³⁄₁₆ IN. (5.6 CM)
SIGNED: *TOMOTADA*
PRIVATE COLLECTION

A standing cat in the dress of a human prostitute, taking leave of a yawning cat client, the eyes of both inlaid in horn, the himotōshi formed by the large fold of material at the back of the obi.

This is a variation on a common netsuke type (derived from woodblock prints) depicting a standing prostitute about to take her leave of a sleepy client, who attempts to restrain her. Scenes involving cats playing human roles are common in mid-nineteenth-century prints, particularly those by Utagawa Kuniyoshi.

MID–LATE 19TH CENTURY
STAINED BOXWOOD AND HORN; H. 2¹⁄₁₆ IN. (5.3 CM)
UNSIGNED
MUSEUM OF FINE ARTS, BOSTON 47.681

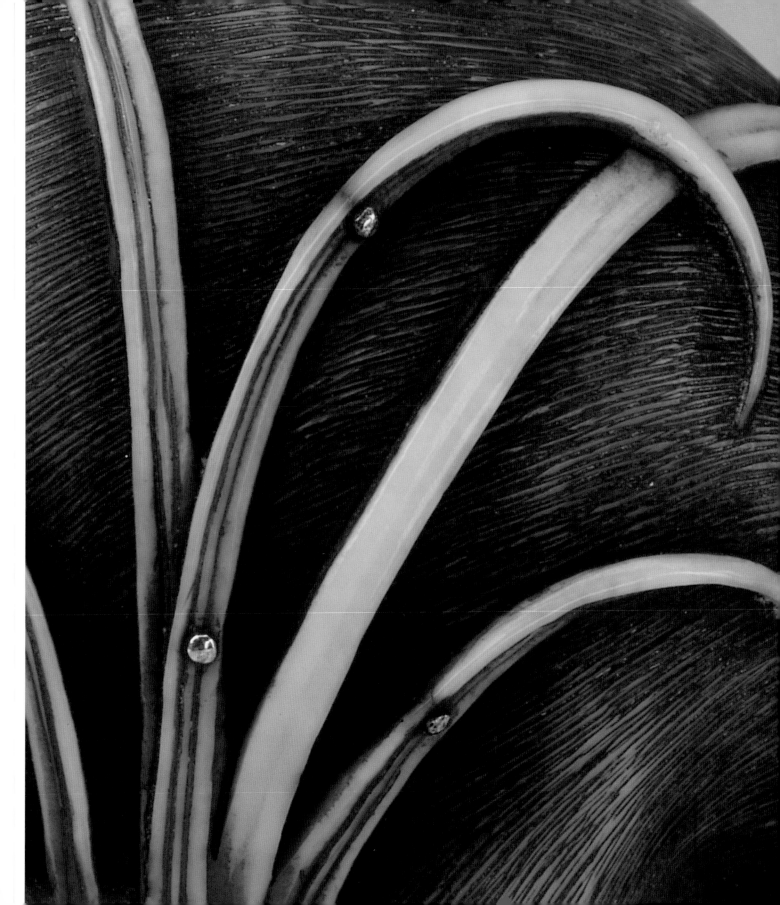

A tsukinowaguma (Japanese bear) walking past a rock, with its muzzle close to the ground, grasses growing up from the rock curling around its right side, its eyes inlaid in horn, the dewdrops on the grasses in silver and those on the rock in horn and amber, its entire body (except for the marking under the neck) covered in very minutely incised and heavily stained hairwork, signed with incised and stained characters on a polished background underneath the rock.

This very rare carving is essentially an adaptation of the boar and autumn grasses motif (see cat. 300), one of Masatsugu's favorite types toward the end of his long career. Although there is the possibility of a *himotōshi* between the animal's right hind leg and the rock, these very delicate, late animal figures make no serious attempt to pass themselves off as netsuke, and should be regarded really as miniature *okimono*. Rarely depicted in Japanese art, the *tsukinowaguma* (literally, "moon-disk bear") is about five feet in length and has a glossy black coat, with a patch of white fur shaped like a crescent moon on the underside of its neck. It lives in the mountains throughout Japan and formerly was hunted for its gall bladder, which was valued for medicinal purposes.

KAIGYOKUSAI MASATSUGU OF OSAKA (1813–1892)
ABOUT 1860–1892
STAINED IVORY, SILVER, HORN, AND AMBER; L. 1⅝ IN.
(4.2 CM)
SIGNED: *KAIGYOKUSAI MASATSUGU*
PRIVATE COLLECTION

Zodiac Animals

THIS LARGEST AND FINAL SECTION IS DEVOTED TO THE ANIMALS OF THE East Asian zodiac, a grouping with its origins in early Chinese cosmology. The *jūnishi* (twelve zodiac animal "stems;" see cat. 239), in their traditional order of Rat, Buffalo, Tiger, Hare, Dragon, Snake, Horse, Goat, Monkey, Cock, Dog, and Boar, have been known in Japan ever since the introduction of the Chinese writing system nearly two thousand years ago. They were used on their own to count the years and the twelve hours of the Japanese day, and in combination with the *jikkan* (ten branches), they formed a sequence of sixty years that was the standard method of dating (for an example of such a date, see the signature to catalogue number 182).

The *jūnishi* played an increasingly important part in everyday life during the early Edo period, and it is no surprise to find that a large proportion of all surviving netsuke depict the twelve zodiac animals. Such netsuke would have made ideal New Year gifts, were suitable for wear throughout the following twelve months, and could, of course, be recycled every twelve years. However, the vogue for zodiac figures seems to have taken hold a little later than the custom of wearing carved netsuke, since most of the oldest animal carvings depict nonzodiac animals such as elephants, cats, *shishi*, and *kirin*, and only rarely does one come across an early tiger (cat. 247) or boar (cat. 295).

Although this section includes a few netsuke by the Tanba Province master Toyomasa (cats. 258, 264, 282, and 298), and by others from the provinces of Chikuzen (cats. 257 and 267), Hida (cats. 272 and 273), Ise (cat. 256), and Echigo (cat.

254), and from the cities of Nagoya (cat. 271) and Edo (cat. 280), more than three-quarters of these netsuke were carved in the Kamigata cities of Osaka and Kyoto. The animal carvings by the two Kyoto masters Masanao and Tomotada are regarded rightly by today's connoisseurs as among the pinnacles of netsuke art, combining the inherited traditions of skillful carving and staining, as well as compact form, with a new naturalism that reflects the influence of the Kyoto-based Maruyama and Shijō schools of painting.

A ryūsa manjū *netsuke, intricately carved with the twelve animals of the East Asian zodiac, some of them shown singly and others in groups, one of the monkeys standing on the back of another, dressed as a New Year dancer carrying an elaborate* gohei, *the eyes of several of the animals inlaid in horn, the dragon's head on one side and its tail on the other, where it curls around to form the* himotōshi, *signed with incised and stained characters within an irregular reserve on a* daikon *(radish) at the side of the netsuke.*

According to Ueda Reikichi, the signature Masatsugu, without the names Kaigyoku, Kaigyokusai, or Kaigyokudō, was used by Masatsugu only until he was about twenty years old. Even if this information is not accepted as being strictly verifiable, it does seem reasonable to assign this complex and yet not wholly original carving to the early part of the artist's career. It is significant that monkeys are singled out for special treatment here. Performing monkeys in human dress played an important role in New Year entertainments, and often held *gohei*, Shinto ritual wands with pendant paper strips. This netsuke thus would have made a perfect New Year gift.

KAIGYOKUSAI MASATSUGU OF OSAKA (1813–1892)
MID-19TH CENTURY
RYŪSA MANJŪ NETSUKE
STAINED IVORY AND HORN; D. 1½ IN. (3.8 CM)
SIGNED: *MASATSUGU*
MUSEUM OF FINE ARTS, BOSTON 11.23376

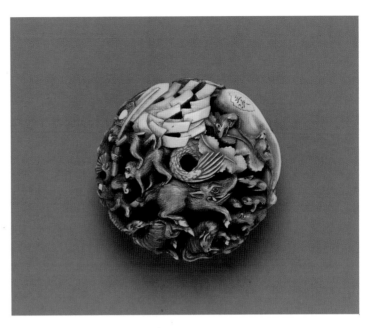

A male rat scratching his left ear with his left hind leg, his other three limbs holding his tail to his mouth, the large eyes inlaid in horn, the fur rendered in delicately incised and stained hairwork, the himotōshi *formed by a gap between the tail and the body, signed with incised and stained characters on an oval reserve by the right hind leg.*

Matsura Seizan (1760–1841), Lord of Hirado, surely was thinking of a piece like this when he mentioned an ivory netsuke of a rat from his lost collection, describing it as *shashin* ("drawn from real life").

MASANAO OF KYOTO (ACTIVE AROUND 1781)

STAINED IVORY; H. 1⁷⁄₁₆ IN. (3.7 CM)

SIGNED: *MASANAO*

PRIVATE COLLECTION

A sleeping male rat lying on his side, his head to the right, his front feet holding his tail, which curls around his muzzle, the underside almost perfectly flat, the fur rendered in delicately incised and stained hairwork with darker staining between the legs and underneath the neck, the himotōshi *formed by a very large, almost oval hole and a much smaller round hole in the underside, signed with incised and stained characters on an oval reserve next to the larger hole.*

Although the tail could have been used to form a *himo-tōshi*, as in the previous example, here Masanao cut two very carefully sized and positioned holes, which ensured that the rat lay snugly on the wearer's side – the hindquarters on the *obi*, and the head, facing upward, held close to the body.

MASANAO OF KYOTO (ACTIVE AROUND 1781)
STAINED IVORY; L. 2⅛ IN. (5.4 CM)
SIGNED: *MASANAO*
PRIVATE COLLECTION

242 | RECUMBENT RAT

A male rat lying on his side, his head to the right, his tail passing over his hind feet and under his muzzle, where it is held by his front feet, the almost perfectly flat underside formed by the base of the tail, the hind feet, and left haunch, the eyes inlaid in horn, the fur rendered in delicately incised and stained hairwork, the ears unstained, the himotōshi *formed by a large round hole in the left haunch and a smaller hole in the left side, signed with incised and stained characters on an oval reserve between the larger hole and the tail.*

MASANAO OF KYOTO (ACTIVE AROUND 1781)
STAINED IVORY AND HORN; L. 1¹³⁄₁₆ IN. (4.6 CM)
SIGNED: *MASANAO*
PRIVATE COLLECTION

A male rat about to bite a chili pod, which he holds down with his front feet, the chili curving over his back, his tail curling under his body, the large eyes inlaid in dark horn, the fur and other details very finely incised and stained, the himotōshi *formed by the chili and the tail.*

This unsigned netsuke, which can be attributed with a fair degree of confidence to Masanao, is another example of the ingenious variations that could be achieved within the same basic type. Here the chili pod takes the place of the tail, which itself is less prominent, but which forms a *himotōshi* in conjunction with the chili. The introduction of the chili also gave the carver an opportunity to contrast its polished surface with the intricate hairwork on the rat, a contrast that still may be appreciated today thanks to the netsuke's excellent condition.

ATTRIBUTED TO MASANAO OF KYOTO (ACTIVE AROUND 1781)
STAINED IVORY AND HORN; H. 1½ IN. (3.9 CM)
UNSIGNED
PRIVATE COLLECTION

A male rat licking the tip of his tail, which passes over his back feet, curls along his left side, and is held by his front feet, the fur and other details finely incised and stained, the eyes inlaid in dark horn, the himotōshi *formed by a large hole in the right haunch and a smaller hole behind the right foreleg, signed underneath with incised and stained characters on a rectangular reserve next to the larger hole.*

Okatori is said by Ueda Reikichi to have been the younger brother and pupil of Okatomo, an artist Ueda describes as being "like Masanao." These later Kyoto rats, while still very finely carved, lack some of the sculptural dynamism of Masanao's masterpieces.

OKATORI OF KYOTO (LATE 18TH–EARLY 19TH CENTURY)
STAINED IVORY; L. 2 1/16 IN. (5.2 CM)
SIGNED: *OKATORI*
PRIVATE COLLECTION

A recumbent female water buffalo, her neck turned to the right, her head and right hind leg protecting a male calf that lies by her side, a halter around the adult's nose passing between her ears and trailing loose over her back, the eyes inlaid in horn, the hides rendered in finely incised and stained hairwork, the flat underside incorporating the eight legs in a complex composition, the himotōshi *formed by a large, almost oval hole in front of the adult animal's left haunch and a smaller round hole by its right foreleg, signed with incised and stained characters on an oval reserve on the adult animal's left haunch.*

Thanks to the existence of a large number of low-quality, almost mass-produced examples bearing the signature of Tomotada, buffalo and calf netsuke are not always as highly regarded as they should be. In this masterly treatment by Masanao, parent and offspring are fused into an effective and lively composition that is also a highly practical netsuke. Like the Masanao rat (cat. 241), this carving has a large oval *himotōshi* that would have accommodated the knot in the hanging cord comfortably, ensuring that the netsuke lay securely against the wearer's clothing, with its upper two-thirds above the top edge of the *obi*.

MASANAO OF KYOTO (ACTIVE AROUND 1781)

STAINED IVORY; L. 2½ IN. (6.4 CM)

SIGNED: *MASANAO*

PRIVATE COLLECTION

A recumbent water buffalo with a halter through its nose, its long horns curling back to touch its neck, the halter of ivory, the eyes inlaid in pale and dark horn, the himotōshi *formed by two equal holes in the underside, signed with incised characters on a polished reserve underneath the right haunch.*

Here the Osaka artist Mitsuhiro reinterprets a model that first came into fashion some thirty years before his birth. Although this is something of a revival piece, the *himotōshi* are fairly large by comparison with those on netsuke of tea bowls and serving dishes by the same artist (see cats. 175 and 211), suggesting that this carving might have been intended for actual use.

ŌHARA MITSUHIRO OF OSAKA (1810–1875)
EBONY AND IVORY; L. 2⅜ IN. (6.1 CM)
SIGNED: *MITSUHIRO*
PRIVATE COLLECTION

247 | TIGRESS AND CUB

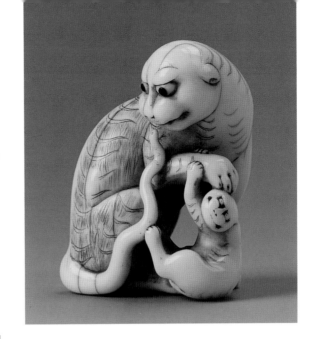

A powerfully carved tigress and cub, the tigress resting her weight on her haunches and left foreleg, the cub on its back, reaching up and clasping the adult's foreleg in its own forelegs, the adult looking down while the cub looks out playfully toward the viewer, the adult's tail curling up over its right haunch toward its face, the markings simply incised and stained, the adult's large eyes with pupils inlaid in dark horn, the himotōshi *formed by a hole drilled vertically upward underneath the parent's tail connecting with a hole in its left side, signed with incised and stained characters on a rectangular reserve underneath the adult's left hind leg.*

Like the *shishi* and cub by Garaku (cat. 92), this powerful early carving is quite distinct from the more standardized treatments that would emerge during the second half of the eighteenth century. In addition to the obvious iconographic differences, the inner surfaces are not given the same degree of finish as on later tigers, and the rather undignified *himotōshi* would not have enabled the netsuke to hang very neatly at the owner's waist.

GECHŪ (EARLY–MID-18TH CENTURY)
STAINED IVORY AND HORN; H. 2 IN. (5.1 CM)
SIGNED: *GECHŪ*
PRIVATE COLLECTION

A male tiger licking his left hind paw, his left front paw held slightly off the ground, his tail curving up the side of his body, the eyes inlaid with dark horn pupils underneath his huge eyebrows, the markings incised and stained in minute detail, his genitals carefully delineated, the himotōshi *formed by a small hole between the right haunch and the right foreleg.*

Matsura Seizan (1760–1841), Lord of Hirado, owned an ivory netsuke of a tiger licking its paw that he used with an *inrō* depicting bamboo – like the tiger, a symbol of strength.

EARLY–MID-18TH CENTURY

STAINED IVORY AND HORN; H. 1⁹⁄₁₆ IN. (4 CM)

UNSIGNED

PRIVATE COLLECTION

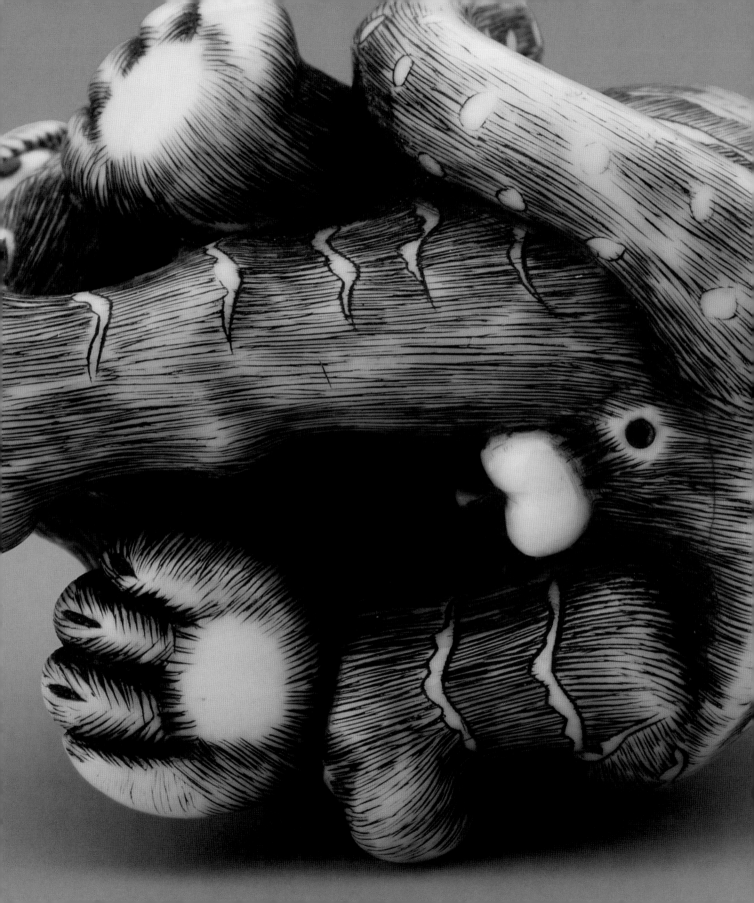

249 | TIGRESS AND CUBS

A complex model of a tigress and two cubs, the adult resting her weight on her haunches and right foreleg, raising her left forepaw protectively over one of the cubs, the other sheltering underneath her body, the eyes with large eyebrows, the pupils inlaid in dark horn, the markings delicately incised and stained, the long himotōshi formed by a hole under the adult's tail connecting with one in her side, signed with incised and stained characters on a rectangular reserve underneath her right hind leg.

This rare example of a Tomotada tigress with two cubs, instead of the more usual one, provides an opportunity to study the ways in which this artist and his contemporaries modified the visual resources at their disposal in order to create compact netsuke that are also powerful miniature sculptures. In the illustration by the netsuke carver and book illustrator Yoshimura Shūzan (see page 21), the adult's tail trails some distance away from its body, the bamboo plants partially frame the family group, and one of the cubs is, in visual terms, almost independent of its parent. The netsuke version of the subject eliminates the bamboo, draws the adult's tail near to her side, and places both cubs underneath her body, but the overall similarities, in particular the modeling of the adult, outweigh these differences. By contrast with early tigers such as those by Gechū (see cat. 247), the complex inner surfaces between the parent and the cubs are finished almost as carefully as the more visible outer surfaces.

IZUMIYA TOMOTADA OF KYOTO (ACTIVE AROUND 1781)
STAINED IVORY AND HORN; H. 1⁷⁄₁₆ IN. (3.6 CM)
SIGNED: *TOMOTADA*
PRIVATE COLLECTION

TIGRESS AND CUBS,
FROM YOSHIMURA
SHŪZAN (ILLUSTRATOR),
WAKAN MEIHITSU ZUHŌ
[1767], VOLUME 1, PP.
2–3. MUSEUM OF FINE
ARTS, BOSTON

250 | TIGRESS AND CUB

*A tigress and cub, the adult resting her weight on all four paws,
turning her head and body sharply to the right to protect her
cub, which leans up playfully against her right side, both
animals facing at different angles toward the viewer, the
adult's pupils inlaid in dark horn, the markings delicately
incised and stained and much worn through prolonged use, the
long* himotōshi *formed by a hole under the adult's tail
connecting with one underneath her chest, signed with incised
and stained characters on a rectangular reserve underneath the
adult's right hind paw.*

IZUMIYA TOMOTADA OF KYOTO (ACTIVE AROUND 1781)
STAINED IVORY; H. 1⁵⁄₁₆ IN. (3.4 CM)
SIGNED: *TOMOTADA*
PRIVATE COLLECTION

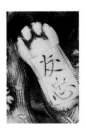

251 | SEATED TIGER

A tiger seated on his haunches, raised on his front legs, his tail curling up his back, the pupils inlaid in dark horn, the markings delicately incised and heavily stained, the haunches and hind paws forming an almost completely flat base, the himotōshi *probably formed by the junction of the left paws, signed with incised and stained characters on an oval reserve underneath the left haunch.*

MASANAO OF KYOTO (ACTIVE AROUND 1781)
STAINED IVORY AND HORN; H. 1½ IN. (3.9 CM)
SIGNED: *MASANAO*
PRIVATE COLLECTION

252 | CROUCHING TIGER

A tiger seated with his right front paw resting on his tail, which curves around to the right of his body and over his back legs, the head turned slightly to the right with a watchful expression, the eyes inlaid in dark horn, the markings minutely incised and stained, the himotōshi *formed by the junction of the paws and tail, signed with incised and stained characters on an oval reserve underneath the left haunch.*

Despite the fact that tigers were imaginary creatures in premodern Japan, both this and the preceding netsuke by Masanao seem more naturalistic and less exaggerated than the Tomotada tigers or the example by Hakuryū (cat. 253). A similar distinction could be made between the anonymous, fantasy Dutchmen (cats. 55–57) and the two examples signed by Masanao (cats. 58 and 59), which, although not based on actual observation, are models of believable human beings.

MASANAO OF KYOTO (ACTIVE AROUND 1781)
STAINED BOXWOOD AND HORN; L. 2$\frac{1}{16}$ IN. (5.3 CM)
SIGNED: *MASANAO*
PRIVATE COLLECTION

253 | SEATED TIGER

A tiger seated on his haunches, his weight supported on his left foreleg, his head turned fully to the right, his right forepaw resting on the end of his tail, which curves around to the right of his body, the markings incised and stained in wavy lines, much worn from handling, the eyes inlaid in gilt metal with black pupils, the himotōshi *formed by the junction of the tail and forelegs, signed with very worn incised and stained characters on an irregular reserve underneath the left haunch.*

Both the outer surface of the tail and the left side of the body are very worn, suggesting that the netsuke was hung through the opening behind the right foreleg, and was fondled constantly by its owner while it was being worn. Although Ueda Reikichi claims that Hakuryū worked during the Ansei era (1854–1860), this and other examples of his work seem so close in style to earlier Kyoto animals that this date is probably too late. The chief difference between Hakuryū's tiger and those by Masanao and Tomotada is in the markings of the animals' coats, which Hakuryū depicts with characteristic wavy lines. The eye inlays are probably later replacements.

MIYASAKA HAKURYŪ OF KYOTO (EARLY 19TH CENTURY)
STAINED IVORY AND GILT METAL; H. 1⅜ IN. (3.5 CM)
SIGNED: *HAKURYŪ*
MUSEUM OF FINE ARTS, BOSTON 11.23665

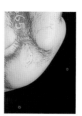

254 | SEATED TIGER

A seated tiger with his forequarters resting on a rock, his head turned fully to the left, his tail against the left side of his body, the markings rendered by areas of intricate incising and staining, contrasting with areas of polished wood, each eye inlaid with a ring of gilt metal around a horn pupil, the himo-tōshi *formed by a transverse hole through the rock, signed with incised and stained characters underneath the rock.*

Ueda Reikichi records that this little-known artist lived in the region of Echigo Province and specialized in wood zodiac animals, human figures, and masks. According to Ueda, his work "is somewhat lacking in refinement," a judgment that is not supported by this well-finished and dramatic sculpture.

SHŪZAN OF ECHIGO PROVINCE (EARLY 19TH CENTURY)

STAINED BOXWOOD, HORN, AND GILT METAL;

H. 2¹⁄₁₆ IN. (5.3 CM)

SIGNED: *SHŪZAN*

PRIVATE COLLECTION

255 | STANDING TIGER

A standing tiger, his head held high, his mouth wide open revealing his sharp teeth, the inside of the mouth with red pigment, the eyes inlaid in pale horn with dark horn pupils, the markings rendered in black staining and the fur in incised and stained lines, the himotōshi *formed by the junction of the tail and the body, signed with incised and red-stained characters on a rectangular reserve on the animal's left flank.*

This netsuke is very worn, and the red staining of the signature is apparently a later restoration added to enhance its legibility and visibility. The artist is probably Chingendō Hidemasa, the earlier of the two artists called Hidemasa featured in this catalogue (see cats. 33 and 43).

CHINGENDŌ HIDEMASA (LATE 18TH–EARLY 19TH CENTURY)

STAINED IVORY AND HORN; H. 1¹³⁄₁₆ IN. (4.6 CM)

SIGNED: *HIDEMASA*, WITH A *KAŌ*

PRIVATE COLLECTION

A tiger and dragon locked in combat, the tiger biting the dragon's body, the dragon biting the tiger's right hind leg, the dragon's eyes inlaid in dark horn, the tiger's eyes inlaid in pale and dark horn, the himotōshi *probably formed by the curve of the dragon's body above the tiger's head, signed with three incised and stained characters on a polished reserve on the tiger's left haunch.*

This wonderfully compact model, carved out of a piece of ivory from near the tip of the tusk, bears Otoman's three-character signature O-to-man (see also cat. 143). Since the tiger and dragon are the third and fifth, respectively, of the twelve "stems," there may be no special calendrical significance to this particular conjunction, unlike the dragon and puppy in the following example.

MATSUSHITA OTOMAN OF CHIKUZEN PROVINCE
(EARLY–MID-19TH CENTURY)
STAINED IVORY AND HORN; H. 1⅜ IN. (3.5 CM)
SIGNED: *OTOMAN*
PRIVATE COLLECTION

A flaming, horned dragon entwined around a puppy, the puppy's fur depicted by fine, unstained incised lines, the dragon with extensive staining, the puppy's eyes inlaid in translucent horn with dark horn pupils, the dragon's eyes inlaid in dark horn, the himotōshi *formed by the junction of the puppy's left legs, signed with incised and stained characters on a rounded rectangular reserve underneath the puppy's right hind leg.*

There are several possible interpretations of this particular pairing of animals. Since the dragon represents, roughly speaking, the hours from 7 to 9 a.m., and the dog the hours from 7 to 9 p.m., the netsuke may encapsulate the idea of pleasurable recreation constrained by unremitting toil, but the antiquarian Takeuchi Kyūichi, writing in 1914, also mentioned a custom whereby people would acquire netsuke for both their birth years and the seventh year after their births. On a more straightforward and craftsmanly level, the conjunction of dragon and dog enabled Rantei to show off two different styles of netsuke: the refined white ivory and careful naturalism that would become the hallmark of Kaigyokusai Masatsugu (see cat. 203), alongside the more established combination of inherited imaginary motifs with mannered carving and an incised and stained finish.

NAGAI RANTEI I OF KYOTO (LATE 18TH–EARLY 19TH
CENTURY)
STAINED IVORY AND HORN; H. 1⅜ IN. (3.5 CM)
SIGNED: *RANTEI*
PRIVATE COLLECTION

272 | COILED SNAKE

A coiled snake, the scales deeply carved and with variegated staining, the eyes inlaid with dark horn, several himotōshi *formed by the coils of the body, signed with incised and stained characters in a rectangular reserve on the side near the base.*

MATSUDA SUKENAGA OF TAKAYAMA, HIDA PROVINCE
(1800–1871)
STAINED BOXWOOD AND HORN; H. 1¼ IN. (3.1 CM)
SIGNED: *SUKENAGA*
PRIVATE COLLECTION

273 | COILED SNAKE

A coiled snake, the scales carved out and stained to contrast with the polished wood between them, the eyes inlaid with dark horn, several himotōshi *formed by the coils of the body, signed underneath with incised and stained characters in a rounded rectangular reserve on the thickest part of the body.*

Although Shōko has occasionally been identified with Suketada (see cat. 104), it seems likely that they were two separate artists; the scales on this snake are carved in a particularly realistic and distinctive manner.

SUGAYA SHŌKO OF HIDA PROVINCE (MID–LATE 19TH
CENTURY)
STAINED BOXWOOD AND HORN; L. 1⅝ IN. (4.2 CM)
SIGNED: *SHŌKO*
PRIVATE COLLECTION

A compact model of a grazing horse, three legs placed together, the right foreleg slightly raised, the details incised and heavily stained, especially the mane and tail, the eyes inlaid in horn, the himotōshi *probably formed by the right hind leg, signed with incised and stained characters on a rectangular reserve near the top of the left foreleg.*

This is an unusual subject for Tomotada; the majority of early Kyoto examples of this model are unsigned.

IZUMIYA TOMOTADA OF KYOTO (ACTIVE AROUND 1781)
STAINED IVORY AND HORN; H. 3¼ IN. (8.3 CM)
SIGNED: *TOMOTADA*
PRIVATE COLLECTION

A compact model of a grazing horse, the legs placed together, the muzzle just above the ground, the mane and tail incised and heavily stained, the himotōshi *probably formed by one of the right hind legs.*

MID–LATE 18TH CENTURY
STAINED BOXWOOD; H. 3¼ IN. (8.2 CM)
UNSIGNED
PRIVATE COLLECTION

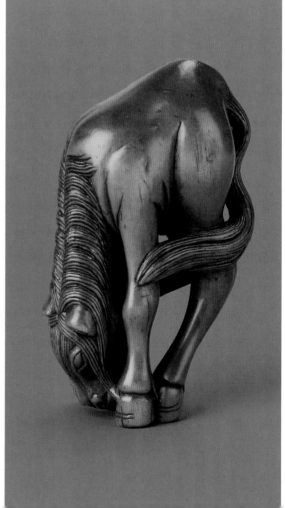

276 | RECUMBENT GOAT

A reclining goat, his head turned slightly to the left, the eyes inlaid in dark horn, the intricately incised and stained hairwork contrasting with the polished, raised backbone, the himotōshi *formed by a large hole in the center of the base and a smaller one nearer the head, signed underneath with incised and stained characters on an oval reserve by the larger hole.*

MASANAO OF KYOTO (ACTIVE AROUND 1781)
STAINED IVORY AND HORN; L. 2¹⁄₁₆ IN. (5.3 CM)
SIGNED: *MASANAO*
PRIVATE COLLECTION

277 | RECUMBENT GOAT

A reclining goat, his head turned back to the right, the eyes inlaid in dark horn, the carved and incised hairwork with contrasted areas of polished wood and heavy staining, the himotōshi *formed by large and small holes in the base, signed with incised and stained characters on an oval reserve next to one of the holes.*

MASANAO OF KYOTO (ACTIVE AROUND 1781)
STAINED BOXWOOD; L. 1¹⁵⁄₁₆ IN. (5 CM)
SIGNED: *MASANAO*
PRIVATE COLLECTION

278 | GOAT AND *BIWA*

A goat squatting on his hindquarters and left foreleg, his right foreleg on two biwa *(loquat) fruits, the pupils and the calyxes of the fruit inlaid in horn, the hairwork finely incised and stained, the* himotōshi *formed by a hole between the hind paws and the branch to which the* biwa *are still attached, signed with incised and stained characters on a rectangular reserve underneath the left hind leg.*

Netsuke by Tomotada and his contemporaries often are praised for their "realism," perceived as the result of painstaking observation in the field; indeed, they are sometimes catalogued as "studies." This might be reasonable in a very few instances and it certainly parallels what we know of some contemporary Kyoto-based painters, but in the case of these goat studies, it must be remembered that, although goats and sheep were important as animals of the Chinese Zodiac, they were not seen commonly in Japan. It is also worth noting that these would be giant *biwa*, since they are the same size, relative to the animal, as those in the hare and *biwa* netsuke (cat. 260). Clearly, then, most of these animal netsuke should be admired properly as sculptural fantasies rather than as naturalistic representations.

IZUMIYA TOMOTADA OF KYOTO (ACTIVE AROUND 1781)
STAINED IVORY AND HORN; L. 2 IN. (5.1 CM)
SIGNED: *TOMOTADA*
PRIVATE COLLECTION

A very small model of a goat, squatting on his hindquarters and left foreleg, his right foreleg on three biwa *(loquat) fruits, the pupils and the calyxes of the fruit inlaid in horn, the hairwork finely incised and heavily stained, the* himotōshi *integrated into the design and formed by a larger hole between one of the* biwa *leaves and the left foreleg, connecting with a smaller hole by the right hind leg, signed with incised and stained characters on a rectangular reserve underneath the right hind leg.*

Later versions of well-established Kyoto models by second-generation carvers, such as Okakoto and Okatomo, are often (though by no means always) considerably smaller than the originals by Tomotada, Masanao, and their contemporaries.

OKAKOTO OF KYOTO (LATE 18TH–EARLY 19TH CENTURY)
STAINED IVORY AND HORN; H. 1¼ IN. (3.2 CM)
SIGNED: *OKAKOTO*
PRIVATE COLLECTION

A very tall figure of a monkey, reaching up with its arms outstretched, its head turned to the left, the eyes inlaid in ivory or stag antler with horn pupils, the himotōshi *formed by the monkey's clenched paws, signed with incised and stained characters on the belly.*

This monkey has the distinctive facial features and very short tail that are among the distinguishing characteristics of the Japanese macaque, *Macacus fuscatus*. When worn, this macaque would have appeared to be clinging onto the hanging cord, as if trying to climb up its owner's *obi*.

UEDA JUGYOKU OF EDO (MID–LATE 19TH CENTURY)
STAINED BOXWOOD, IVORY OR STAG ANTLER, AND
HORN; H. 6⁵⁄₁₆ IN. (16.1 CM)
SIGNED: *JUGYOKU*
PRIVATE COLLECTION

281 | MONKEY SCRATCHING HIS EAR

A male monkey lying down, his front paws held together, scratching his left ear with his left hind paw, the details naturalistically rendered with very fine incised and stained hairwork, the eyes inlaid in pale horn, the himotōshi *formed by large and small holes in the base, signed underneath with incised and stained characters on an oval reserve.*

It is interesting to note that the wear on this netsuke was caused by handling rather than through practical use as a toggle, since it is on the right side, rather than the base, that the highly finished hairwork has been rubbed away. Although we are apt to regard netsuke primarily as practical items, it should be remembered that this monkey, for example, normally would have been suitable for public use only in one year out of twelve, leaving plenty of time for its owner to appreciate its tactile qualities in private.

MASANAO OF KYOTO (ACTIVE AROUND 1781)
STAINED IVORY AND HORN; L. 1¹⁵/₁₆ IN. (5 CM)
SIGNED: *MASANAO*
PRIVATE COLLECTION

282 | MONKEY CLIMBING OVER A HUGE PEACH

A monkey climbing on the branch attached to an enormous peach, the eyes inlaid in pale translucent horn, the himotōshi *formed by a very large hole in the base connecting with a smaller hole in the side, signed with incised and stained characters on the peach.*

Although apparently skilled in naturalistic depiction of animals, and clearly influenced by contemporary developments in painting, Toyomasa delighted in exaggeration, and this freakishly large peach is paralleled by the oversized toad seen in his figures of Kō Sensei (see cats. 18 and 19).

NAITŌ TOYOMASA OF TANBA PROVINCE (1773–1856)
STAINED BOXWOOD AND HORN; H. 1⅝ IN. (4.1 CM)
SIGNED: *TOYOMASA*
PRIVATE COLLECTION

A very compact, almost spherical figure of a single monkey, playing the role of the Mizaru (Three Monkeys), using its paws to cover its eyes, ears, and mouth, the himotōshi *formed by two tiny holes, signed and sealed with incised and stained characters, the seal on a rectangular reserve with a double outline.*

The monkey deity Saruta Biko (or Sarugami) has played an important part in Japanese religious belief since early times, because of his healing power (see cat. 159) and his function as an intermediary between other gods, especially the mountain deity Sannō, and humans. The Mizaru were already popular in the thirteenth century, in part because of the imaginative opportunities offered by the homophonic *mizaru* ("three monkeys") and *mizaru* ("do not see"), later extended to the "three nots" – *mizaru*, *kikazaru* (do not hear), and *iwazaru* (do not speak). The best-known monkey image in Japan is the Mizaru sculpture attributed to Hidari Jingorō (1594–1634) on the mausoleum of Tokugawa Ieyasu (1542–1616), the unifier of Japan, at Nikkō, where its presence is alleged to be an ironic comment on the unwilling acquiescence of the Japanese people to Tokugawa rule. It is not clear when the Mizaru entered the mainstream of Western popular culture as the "Three Mystic Apes," which "Hear no evil, see no evil and speak no evil," but it is likely that Masatsugu played a part in the process, since this combined design was one of the first netsuke models to be copied widely in the West – in particular by the Russian jeweler Carl Fabergé, whose workshop created versions in several materials including amazonite, obsidian, chalcedony, and bowenite.

KAIGYOKUSAI MASATSUGU OF OSAKA (1813–1892)

STAINED IVORY; H. 1³/₁₆ IN. (3 CM)

SIGNED: *KAIGYOKU*

SEALED: *MASATSUGU*

PRIVATE COLLECTION

284 | COCKEREL

A cockerel with its legs folded underneath its body, the darker stippling and staining on its elaborately carved tail contrasting with the lighter staining on the rest of its body, the eyes inlaid in dark horn, the himotōshi *formed by a large hole in the base connecting with a smaller hole at the right, signed with incised characters on an oval reserve behind the right wing.*

MASANAO OF KYOTO (ACTIVE AROUND 1781)
STAINED IVORY AND HORN; H. 2$\frac{1}{16}$ IN. (5.2 CM)
SIGNED: *MASANAO*
PRIVATE COLLECTION

285 | HEN AND CHICKS

A seated hen and two chicks, one climbing on the hen's back and the other partially sheltered by its tail, the eyes of the parent inlaid in pale horn with dark horn pupils and those of the chicks in dark horn, the himotōshi *formed by large and small holes in the flat base, signed underneath with incised and stained characters on an oval reserve next to the larger hole.*

MASANAO OF KYOTO (ACTIVE AROUND 1781)
STAINED BOXWOOD AND HORN; L. 2$\frac{3}{16}$ IN. (5.5 CM)
SIGNED: *MASANAO*
PRIVATE COLLECTION

286 | *MUKUGE-INU* AND PUPPY

A long-haired dog seated with its left foreleg resting on the back of a male puppy, the adult's eyes inlaid in dark horn, the long himotōshi formed by a large hole between the adult's hind legs connecting with a smaller hole in the right side of its chest, signed with incised and stained characters on a rectangular reserve underneath the adult animal's right hind leg.

These dogs are *mukuge-inu*, a long-haired breed said to be fond of swimming, depicted frequently in picture books by Tachibana Morikuni and his contemporaries. The adult's pose, sitting on its haunches with one foreleg down and the other raised, is seen in a wide variety of Kyoto animal subjects: the raised paw is sometimes held over a young animal, but also often over a toy or a piece

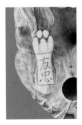

of food (see cats. 291 and 294). The long *himotōshi*, a Tomotada specialty, was designed to ensure that the adult dog would be upright when the netsuke was worn.

IZUMIYA TOMOTADA OF KYOTO (ACTIVE AROUND 1781)

STAINED IVORY AND HORN; H. 1¹⁵⁄₁₆ IN. (4.9 CM)

SIGNED: *TOMOTADA*

PRIVATE COLLECTION

MUKUGE-INU, FROM TACHIBANA MORIKUNI (ILLUSTRATOR), *EHON SHAHŌ BUKURO* [1720; THIS EDITION 1770], VOLUME 9, PP. 20–21. MUSEUM OF FINE ARTS, BOSTON

A whippet or greyhoundlike dog, probably a puppy, seated upright on its hind legs with its forelegs resting on a ball, its tail curled at its side, its ribs and backbone visible under its coat, the eyes inlaid in dark horn, the hairwork rendered by long incised and stained lines, the himotōshi *probably formed by the right foreleg.*

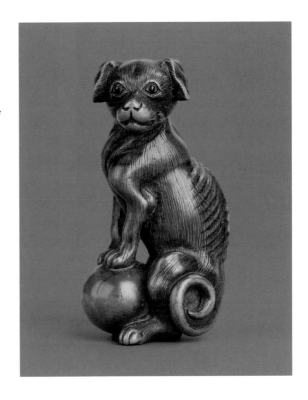

Like the *mukuge-inu* seen in the preceding example, the thinner and more greyhoundlike *kōken* (more accurately, *gōken*) is illustrated frequently in picture books and encyclopedias of the Edo period. *Wakan meihitsu ehon tekagami* (1720) includes a design, attributed there to no less an artist than the great Kanō school painter Eitoku (1543–1590), depicting one black and one white *gōken* with a litter of puppies. Netsuke depictions of *kōken* normally tone down their rangy features in the interests of compactness and durability, making their muzzles shorter and giving them a less keen, more playful expression.

LATE 18TH CENTURY
STAINED BOXWOOD AND HORN; H. 2³⁄₁₆ IN. (5.6 CM)
UNSIGNED
MUSEUM OF FINE ARTS, BOSTON 47.555

292 | PUPPY AND BALL

A male puppy with a bell tied around its neck in an elaborate bow, seated on his hindquarters with his right foreleg on a ball, his ribs clearly visible under his incised and stained coat, the eyes inlaid in dark horn, the himotōshi *formed by two holes on the body between the left legs, signed with incised and stained characters on a rectangular reserve underneath the left hind leg.*

The dog probably is playing with a silk ball, the incised band around its equator representing embroidered decoration.

IZUMIYA TOMOTADA OF KYOTO (ACTIVE AROUND 1781)
STAINED IVORY AND HORN
H. 1⅝ IN. (4.2 CM)
SIGNED: *TOMOTADA*
PRIVATE COLLECTION

293 | BITCH AND PUPPY

A bitch seated protectively over her puppy, her head turned sharply to the left, her left foreleg resting on the puppy's back, the bitch's eyes inlaid in pale horn with dark horn pupils, the puppy's eyes inlaid in dark horn, the bitch with delicately incised and stained hairwork, the puppy almost without staining, several himotōshi *formed by the animals' legs, signed with incised and stained characters on a rounded rectangular reserve on the bitch's right haunch.*

Rantei here adds his unmistakable touch to a well-tried Kyoto formula. The pose is different from that seen in dog netsuke by Tomotada and his pupils, while points of detail such as the way in which the ribs protrude on the right (where the skin is stretched) and not on the left, unlike in most earlier dog netsuke, may be the result of more observation and less copying, or at least of increased influence from later generations of Kyoto painters working in a broadly Maruyama-Shijō manner.

NAGAI RANTEI I OF KYOTO
(LATE 18TH–EARLY 19TH CENTURY)
STAINED IVORY AND HORN
H. 1⅝ IN. (4.2 CM)
SIGNED: *RANTEI*
PRIVATE COLLECTION

*An emaciated dog seated on its haunches in a patch of grass,
gnawing the end of a human arm and hand, which it holds
with its right hind foot and right forepaw, its eyes inlaid in pale
horn with dark horn pupils, its bones visible through its incised
and heavily stained coat, its tail curled between its legs, the
himotōshi probably formed by the left hind leg, signed with
incised and heavily stained characters on a rounded
rectangular reserve between the hind legs.*

This grotesque subject normally features a wolf rather
than a dog, but the grass perhaps is intended to indicate
that this is a wild rather than a domesticated animal.

NAGAI RANTEI I OF KYOTO
(LATE 18TH–EARLY 19TH CENTURY)
STAINED IVORY AND HORN
H. 1⅝ IN. (4.1 CM)
SIGNED: *RANTEI*
PRIVATE COLLECTION

295 | BOAR SLEEPING ON DEAD LEAVES

A boar sleeping on a broken branch and a pile of autumn leaves, the delicate hairwork almost completely worn away through years of handling, the himotōshi *formed by a small hole in the center of the base, connecting with a larger one between the hind legs.*

The arrangement of the large and small *himotōshi* holes indicates that this netsuke would have been worn with the animal's snout uppermost. As with many early netsuke, the greatest wear is not on the side carried against the body but on the outside, suggesting that the netsuke was handled lovingly over a period of many years.

EARLY–MID-18TH CENTURY
STAINED IVORY; L. 2³⁄₁₆ IN. (5.6 CM)
UNSIGNED
PRIVATE COLLECTION

A female boar and one of her adolescent male offspring, lying with their left sides together, their legs folded underneath their bodies, the adult's head over the younger animal's hindquarters, the fur depicted by very fine incised and stained lines, both on top of and underneath the animals, the prominent areas of the carving slightly worn, the eyes of the adult inlaid in dark horn and those of the younger animal in pale horn, the himotōshi *formed by a very large oval hole underneath the adult, connecting with a smaller hole in the center of the base, signed with incised and stained characters in an oval reserve on the adult's right haunch.*

Only one other example of this highly original and very compact Masanao composition is known, with the animals' right rather than left sides touching. The very large *himotōshi* hole clearly was intended to be uppermost when the netsuke was worn, in contrast to earlier figural netsuke and other long, thin pieces in which the larger hole is always below the smaller.

MASANAO OF KYOTO (ACTIVE AROUND 1781)
STAINED IVORY AND HORN; L. 2 IN. (5.1 CM)
SIGNED: *MASANAO*
PRIVATE COLLECTION

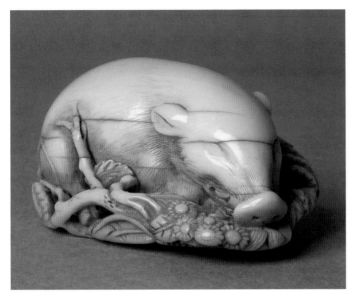

297 | BOAR SLEEPING ON AUTUMN PLANTS

A boar sleeping on a broken branch and a pile of autumn leaves and flowers, the delicate hairwork almost completely worn away through years of handling, the himotōshi *formed by large and small holes in the center of the base, signed next to the larger hole with incised and stained characters on a slightly raised rectangular reserve.*

By comparison with the earlier, unsigned example (cat. 295), the underside of this netsuke features a much wider variety of leaves and plants, carved in greater detail, including ferns, maple, bamboo, daisies, and *hagi* ("bush clover"), one of the canonical *Aki no nanakusa*, or Seven Autumn Plants. Tomotada was probably influenced by pictorial versions of this theme, and unlike Masatsugu (see cat. 300), chose to include the *hagi* and daisies shown by Tachibana Morikuni rather than eliminating them altogether, but hid them underneath the boar so as not to interfere with the compact shape.

IZUMIYA TOMOTADA OF KYOTO
(ACTIVE AROUND 1781)
STAINED IVORY; L. 2⁷⁄₁₆ IN. (6.2 CM)
SIGNED: *TOMOTADA*
PRIVATE COLLECTION

298 | BOAR RAISED ON ITS FORELEGS

A boar squatting on its haunches, its head turned to the left, its jaws slightly open revealing its teeth and tusks, its forelegs half folded, the eyes inlaid in pale horn, the fur indicated by fine incised and stained lines, the himotōshi *formed by large and small holes in the base, signed with incised and stained characters on an elongated rectangular reserve between the holes.*

In addition to very elaborate, heavily undercut carvings such as the figure of Chinnan Sennin, Toyomasa also specialized in animal carvings that develop the simplicity and compactness of earlier Kyoto models by showing the animals in a range of naturalistic poses.

NAITŌ TOYOMASA OF TANBA PROVINCE (1773–1856)
PROBABLY ABOUT 1854
STAINED BOXWOOD AND HORN
H. 1⅝ IN. (4.1 CM)
SIGNED: *HACHIJŪNISAI TOYOMASA*
(TOYOMASA, AGED EIGHTY-TWO)
PRIVATE COLLECTION

299 | RECUMBENT BOAR

A boar squatting on its haunches, its forelegs very slightly raised and supporting its head, the eyes inlaid in pale horn with dark horn pupils, the tusks of ivory, the fur indicated by minutely variegated carved and stained lines, the himotōshi *formed by a large hole in the base connecting with a smaller hole in the side, signed with incised and stained characters on a rounded rectangular reserve between the forelegs.*

No other wood boar by Mitsuhiro appears to be recorded.

ŌHARA MITSUHIRO OF OSAKA (1810–1875)
STAINED BOXWOOD, IVORY, AND HORN;
L. 2⅜ IN. (6.1 CM)
SIGNED: *MITSUHIRO*
PRIVATE COLLECTION

300 | **BOAR SLEEPING ON AUTUMN PLANTS**

A sleeping wild boar, lying on a pile of dead leaves next to a rock, wet grasses adhering to its left side, the dewdrops inlaid in pale and dark horn, the fur depicted by extremely fine incised and stained lines, a possible himotōshi *formed by the left foreleg, signed with incised and heavily stained characters on a polished background underneath the rock.*

In this outstanding example of one of Masatsugu's best-known models, the artist follows iconographic convention in his choice of the plant, visible when the netsuke is placed on a flat surface: the grass gracefully arranged over the animal's left side is *susuki* or pampas grass, one of the autumn plants from a canonical list of seven established by a poem in the eighth-century poetry anthology *Man'yōshū*. Such grasses, alongside a boar in a pose similar to this one, are shown in a version of the painterly theme of *Akikusa ni fusuru inoshishi* (A Wild Boar Lying Amidst Autumn Plants) that was published in 1720 in an instructional picture book by Tachibana Morikuni. However, in keeping with the netsuke artist's concern for compactness and durability (even where the carving has no real *himotōshi*, as here, and almost certainly is not intended for use), the grasses lie close to the animal's body, while other autumn plants such as *hagi* ("bush clover") and daisies are eliminated in the interests of simplicity. Underneath the carving, on the secret surface seen only by the owner, Masatsugu has developed the arrangement of overlapping fallen leaves already established in anonymous netsuke carved more than a century earlier (see cat. 295). A study of the interplay between observation, copying of earlier netsuke, and both direct and indirect borrowing from pictorial sources may hold the key to our further understanding of the art of netsuke carving.

KAIGYOKUSAI MASATSUGU OF OSAKA (1813–1892)

AFTER 1863

STAINED IVORY, HORN, AND SILVER; H. 1 IN. (2.6 CM)

SIGNED: *KAIGYOKUSAI MASATSUGU*

MUSEUM OF FINE ARTS, BOSTON 11.23373

BOAR SLEEPING ON AUTUMN PLANTS, FROM TACHIBANA MORIKUNI (ILLUSTRATOR), *EHON SHAHŌ BUKURO* [1720; THIS EDITION 1770], VOLUME 9, PP. 19–20. MUSEUM OF FINE ARTS, BOSTON

ACKNOWLEDGMENTS

It was a great pleasure to work with the many individuals whose enthusiastic support and cooperation have contributed to this exhibition and catalogue. I am indebted to the private collectors and their associates who generously lent their netsuke as well as their time and acumen to the project. In Miami, Dr. Joseph Kurstin allowed me unrestricted access to his treasures as well as offering not only his hospitality but also many valuable insights into netsuke connoisseurship and history. By freely sharing his unrivaled practical knowledge and unique stock of materials, Clive Hallam made it possible for the exhibition to include a highly instructive display on the techniques of netsuke carving. Keiko Thayer kindly loaned a man's kimono, thereby enabling us to show visitors how a netsuke is worn. Calvin Stillman, son of Museum benefactor Ernest G. Stillman, provided important information used in preparing the introduction to the Museum's collection. Thanks are also due to Barry Davies for sharing his expertise with the Museum in the recataloguing of the netsuke collection.

At the Museum of Fine Arts, Boston, Katie Getchell, Deputy Director for Curatorial Administration, helped set the entire operation in motion, while my colleagues Anne Nishimura Morse and Louise Virgin have offered every assistance despite the pressures of their own professional commitments. A special word of gratitude is due to Ann B. Simonds, who served as curatorial liaison from the outset. Angie's hard work and painstaking attention to detail ensured the smooth progress of the project despite the fact that the curator was several thousand miles away in London for much of the time.

Jennifer Bose, director of exhibitions and design, has coordinated the efforts of the large team that brought the exhibition into being. In the exhibition design department Susan Wong, Susan Tomasian, and Andi Cocito conceived and executed a highly original setting for the netsuke. Gilian Shallcross of the department of Education and Public Programs helped prepare the exhibition texts, while in the conservation department Susanne Gänsicke, Karen Gausch, Jacki Elgar, Tanya Uyeda, and Joan Wright ensured that the Museum's netsuke, paintings, and prints were in the best possible condition for display.

Thanks are due to Mark Polizzotti and Dacey Sartor for their patient planning and execution of this catalogue, as well as to Masami Sugimoto, Gary Ruuska, and Dave Matthews for their outstanding photography, Melanie Drogin for her knowledgeable editorial work, and Lucinda Hitchcock for her sensitive and imaginative design.

– Joe Earle

BIBLIOGRAPHY

In order to make this catalogue more user-friendly for the nonspecialist, no endnotes have been included, but the list below gives details of all publications consulted in the course of the preparation of this volume. Pages from many of the ehon *(picture books) listed in Section 1 are reproduced in the body of the catalogue, while most of the other* ehon *and primary sources are referenced at one or more points in the text. Section 2 lists relevant reference works in all languages, in some cases including a brief note with regard to the utility and reliability of the source. Section 3 lists secondary sources mainly in Western languages.*

1.

PRIMARY SOURCES IN JAPANESE
OR CHINESE

Anon. *Ehon shoshin hashiradate* (An illustrated primer for beginners). 1715; later edition 1761.

Anon. *Yūshō ressen zenden* (Complete illustrated stories of immortals). Wang Shizhen, ed. Kyoto, 1650.

Enbaiken, pub. *Bankoku jinbutsu zu* (Illustrated peoples of the world). 1714.

Inaba Tsūryū Shin'emon. *Sōken kishō* (Strange and wonderful sword-fittings). Vol. 7, *Furoku netsuke-shi meifu narabi ni zu* (Supplement with illustrations and a list of netsuke artists). Osaka, 1781.

Katsushika Hokusai, illustrator. *Manga*. 1814–78.

Katsushika Isai, illustrator. *Kachō sansui zushiki* (Designs for birds, flowers, and landscapes). 1847–65; later edition 1881.

Katsushika Taitō, illustrator. *Banshoku zukō* (Pictures and designs for all crafts). 1835–50.

Kitao Masayoshi, illustrator. *Shoshoku ekagami* (A pictorial reference book for all crafts). 1794.

Matsura Seizan. *Kasshi yawa* (Night chats started on the first day of the rat). Nakamura Yukihiko and Nakano Mitsutoshi, ed. 1821–41. Modern edition, Tokyo: Heibonsha, 1978, Vol. 5, pp. 76–83.

Nakamura Tekisai, ed. *Kinmō zui* (An illustrated encyclopedia). 1666.

——. Shimokawabe Jūsui, illustrator. *Zōho tōsho kinmō zui taisei* (An annotated and illustrated compendium, improved and expanded). Kyoto, 1789.

Ōoka Shunboku, illustrator. *Gashi kaiyō* (Essentials of the history of painting). 1753.

——. *Wakan meigaen* (A garden of masterpieces of Japanese and Chinese painting). 1739.

——. *Wakan meihitsu ehon tekagami* (An illustrated handbook of masterpieces of Japanese and Chinese painting). 1720.

Tachibana Morikuni, illustrator. *Ehon kojidan* (A picture book of historical events). 1715.

——. *Ehon nezashitakara* (A treasury of historical examples). Osaka, 1744.

——. *Ehon shahō bukuro* (An illustrated treasure sack of pictures for copying). 1770.

——. *Ehon tsūhōshi* (A treasury of instructional illustrations). 1729–30.

——. *Morokoshi kinmō zui* (An illustrated encyclopedia of China). Osaka, 1719

Terashima Ryōan. *Wakan sansai zue* (Illustrated Japanese-Chinese encyclopedia of the three powers). Osaka, 1716. Modern facsimile edition, Tokyo: Tōkyō Bijutsu, 1970.

Yang Shen, ed. Guo Pu, commentary. *Shanhaijing tu* (The illustrated book of hills and seas). China, about 1524–59. Reprinted, Nagoya: Bunkōdō, 1902.

Yoshimura Shūzan, illustrator. *Wakan meihitsu gaei* (Glories of Japanese and Chinese painting). 1750; later edition 1807.

———. *Wakan meihitsu zuhō* (An illustrated treasury of Japanese and Chinese painting). 1767.

2.

REFERENCE WORKS AND COMPILATIONS

Arakawa Hirokazu. *The Gō Collection of Netsuke* (in Tokyo National Museum). Tokyo, New York, and San Francisco: Kodansha International, 1983. Conveniently assembles the surviving pictorial and literary evidence for the early use of netsuke.

Cihai Editorial Committee, ed. *Cihai* (Chinese dictionary). Shanghai: Shanghai Cishu Chubanshe, 1979. Later, more Marxist-oriented edition of the work edited by Shu Xincheng, listed below.

Lazarnick, George. *Netsuke and Inrō Artists and How to Read Their Signatures.* Honolulu: Privately Printed, 1982. A vast, if sometimes uncritical and haphazard, collection of photographs of signatures from netsuke in private and public collections.

Leiter, Samuel E. *New Kabuki Encyclopedia (A Revised Adaptation of Kabuki jiten).* Westport, Conn.: Greenwood Press, 1997.

Makino Tomitarō. *Makino shin Nihon shokubutsu zukan* (Makino's new illustrated flora of Japan). Tokyo: Hokuryūkan, 1961.

Ōsumi Kazuo et al., ed. *Nihon kakū denshō jinmei jiten* (A dictionary of Japanese imaginary and traditional personalities). Tokyo: Heibonsha, 1986. Guide to the evolution of legends surrounding leading historical personalities, with useful direct quotations from literary sources.

Sandfield, Norman L. *The Ultimate Netsuke Bibliography: An Annotated Guide to Japanese Miniature Carvings.* Chicago: Art Media Resources and Norman L. Sandfield, 1999. Exhaustive, very well organized listing of works on netsuke.

Satō Takahira et al., ed. *Genshoku gyorui zukan* (An illustrated guide to fish). Kesennuma, Miyagi Pref.: Kesennuma Shiyakusho, 1987.

Shibuya Kuritsu Shōtō Bijutsukan (The Shōtō Museum of Art). *Nihon no zōge bijutsu: Meiji no zōge chōkoku o chūshin ni* (History of Japanese ivory carving: Gebori okimono and Shibayama of Meiji Period). Tokyo: Shibuya Kuritsu Shōtō Bijutsukan, 1996.

Shinmura Izuru Kinen Zaidan (Shinmura Izuru Memorial Foundation). *Kōjien* (Japanese encyclopedia). CD-ROM edition. Tokyo: Iwanami Shoten, 1998.

Shu Xincheng, ed. *Cihai* (Chinese dictionary). Shanghai: Zhonghua Shuju, 1947. Provides useful early literary references for many of the Chinese personalities represented in netsuke carvings.

Tazawa, Yutaka, ed. *Biographical Dictionary of Japanese Art.* Tokyo: Kodansha International, 1981.

Tōkyō Kokuritsu Bunkazai Kenkyūjo (Tokyo National Research Institution of Cultural Properties). *Naikoku kangyō hakurankai bijutsuhin shuppin mokuroku* (Catalogs of objects exhibited at the National Industrial Expositions). Tokyo: Chūōkōron Bijutsu Shuppan, 1996. Useful source of information regarding netsuke carvers who also exhibited larger works at the late-nineteenth-century expositions.

Ueda Reikichi. *Netsuke no kenkyū* (A study of netsuke). Osaka: Bun'endō, 1943. Pioneering, primarily biographical study of netsuke; the information must be treated with caution, as virtually no sources are listed.

Wakayama Homatsu (Takeshi), ed. *Kinkō jiten* (A dictionary of metalworkers). Tokyo: Yūzankaku, 1972. Provides information on the metalworkers involved in the manufacture of catalogue numbers 3–4.

Weber, V.F. *Koji Hōten, Dictionnaire à l'usage des amateurs et collectionneurs d'objets d'art japonais et chinois*. Paris: Privately Printed, 1923. Vast compilation of information concerning the subject matter of the art of the Edo period (chiefly), marred by a complete absence of supporting references, but invaluable as a primary means of identifying less well known myths and legends.

3.
SECONDARY SOURCES

Akatsu, Kentaro. "Ikkan and His Family." *International Netsuke Society Journal* 16, no. 2 (Summer 1996), pp. 25–29.

———. "Nagoya School Carvers: Genealogical Update." *International Netsuke Society Journal* 17, no. 2 (Summer 1997), pp. 30–32.

Asano, Shugo, and Timothy Clark. *The Passionate Art of Kitagawa Utamaro*. London: British Museum, 1995.

Baten, Lea. *Playthings and Pastimes in Japanese Prints*. New York: Weatherhill; Tokyo: Shufunotomo, 1995.

Camman, Schuyler. *Substance and Symbol in Chinese Toggles: Chinese Belt Toggles from the C.F. Bieber Collection*. Philadelphia: University of Pennsylvania Press, 1962.

Chappell, Sharen Thane. "The Proud Tradition of Hida-Takayama Wood Carvers." *Netsuke Kenkyukai Study Journal* 9, no. 4 (Winter 1989), pp. 17–27.

Clunas, Craig. *Pictures and Visuality in Early Modern China*. London: Reaktion Books, 1997.

Ducros, Alain. "In Search of Tametaka." *Netsuke Kenkyukai Study Journal* 6, no. 4 (Winter 1986), pp. 15–17.

———. "Tametaka." *Bulletin Association Franco-Japonaise*, no. 24 (April 1989), pp. 19–24.

———. "Toyomasa." *Bulletin Association Franco-Japonaise*, no. 41 (July 1993), pp. 15–22.

Earle, Joe. *The Robert S. Huthart Collection of Iwami Netsuke*. Hong Kong: Privately Printed, 2000.

Forrer, Matthi. *Hokusai: Prints and Drawings*. London: Royal Academy of Arts; Munich: Prestel, 1991.

———. "Netsuke: A Historical Approach." *Apollo* 149, no. 445 (March 1999), pp. 54–58.

Jansen, Marius B. *China in the Tokugawa World*. Cambridge, Mass.: Harvard University Press, 1992.

Jirka-Schmidt, Patrizia. *Netsuke: 112 Meisterwerke: The Trumpf Collection* (in German and English). Vol. 1; Vollstündiger Bestandskatalog der Sammlung Trumpf. Vol 2. Stuttgart: Staatliches Museum für Völkerkunde and Arndolsche Art Publishers, 2000.

Joly, H. L., and K. Tomita. *Japanese Art and Handicraft, An Illustrated Record of the Loan Exhibition Held in Aid of the British Red Cross in October–November 1915*. London: Yamanaka, 1916.

Kyōto Kokuritsu Hakubutsukan (Kyoto National Museum). *Shiboruto to Nihon* (Von Siebold and Japan). Tokyo: Asahi Shinbunsha, 1988.

Mayer, Fanny H. *Ancient Tales in Modern Japan*. Bloomington: Indiana University Press, 1984.

Meech, Julia. *Rain and Snow: The Umbrella in Japanese Art*. New York: Japan Society, 1993.

Noma, Seiroku. *The Arts of Japan*. Tokyo, New York, and San Francisco: Kodansha International, 1996.

Ohnuki-Tierney, Emiko. *The Monkey As Mirror: Symbolic Transformations in Japanese History and Ritual*. Princeton: Princeton University Press, 1987.

Okuno, Hidekazu. "Tanaka Minko, Retained Carver for the Todo Clan of Tsu." Nori Watanabe, trans. *International Netsuke Society Journal* 16, no. 3 (Fall 1996), pp. 16–22.

Oriental Ceramic Society. *Chinese Ivories from the Shang to the Qing*. London: British Museum Publications for the Oriental Ceramic Society, 1984.

Schiffeler, John William. *The Legendary Creatures of the Shan Hai Ching*. San Francisco: Privately Printed, 1978 (with illustrations based on Anon., *Shanhaijing tushuo* [An illustrated commentary on Shanhaijing], Shanghai: Huiwentang, 1917).

Screech, Timon. *Ō-Edo ijin ōrai* (Foreigners in the Edo period). Takayama Hiroshi, trans. Tokyo: Maruzen, 1995.

——. *Sex and the Floating World: Erotic Images in Japan 1700–1820.* London: Reaktion Books, 1999.

——. *The Western Scientific Gaze and Popular Imagery in Later Edo Japan.* Cambridge, England: Cambridge University Press, 1996.

Sekido, Kengo. "About Tokoku." Nori Watanabe, trans. *International Netsuke Society Journal* 16, no. 3 (Fall 1996), pp. 16–22.

——. "Morita Sōko to sono ippa (Morita Sōko and the Sō school)." *Rokushō*, no. 27 (July 1998), pp. 34–35.

——. "Ohara Mitsuhiro." Nori Watanabe, trans. *International Netsuke Society Journal* 17, no. 1 (Spring 1997), pp. 26–31.

Shimatani, Yoichi. "Matsuda Sukenaga: His Legend and Mystery." *International Netsuke Society Journal* 16, no. 2 (Summer 1996), pp. 30–37.

——. "Red Robe Kokusai." Parts 1 and 2. Nori Watanabe, trans. and ed. *International Netsuke Society Journal* 19, no. 2 (Summer 1999), pp. 29–45; 20, no. 3 (Fall 2000), pp. 28–41.

Tabako to Shio no Hakubutsukan (Tobacco and Salt Museum). *Netsuke: te no hira no naka no geijutsu* (Netsuke: Art in the palm of the hand). Tokyo: Tabako to Shio no Hakubutsukan, 1995.

Takeuichi, Kyūichi. "Netsuke no kenkyū (A study of netsuke)." *Shoga kottō zasshi*, no. 68 (February 1914); no. 69 (March 1914); no. 70 (April 1914). Translated and adapted by Misao Mikoshiba and Raymond Bushell as "Study of Netsuke," parts I, II, and III, *Journal of the International Netsuke Collectors Society* 7, no. 3 (December 1979), pp. 49–51; no. 4 (March 1980), pp. 52–54; 8, no. 1 (June 1980), pp. 44–47.

Tsuji Nobuo, ed. *Nikuhitsu ukiyo-e* 1 (Ukiyo-e Paintings in the Museum of Fine Arts, Boston). Vol. 1. Tokyo: Kōdansha, 2000.

Waley, Paul. *Tokyo Now and Then.* New York and Tokyo: Weatherhill, 1984.

Watanabe, Nori. "News from Japan: Kano Tomokazu." *International Netsuke Society Journal* 20, no. 2 (Summer 2000), pp. 18–21.

——. "News from Japan: Yoshimura Shuzan." *International Netsuke Society Journal* 19, no. 4 (Winter 1999), pp. 19–21.

Welch, Matthew, and Sharen Chappell. *Netsuke: The Japanese Art of Miniature Carving.* Minneapolis: Minneapolis Institute of Art, 1999.

Wu Ch'eng-en. *Monkey.* Arthur Waley, trans. London: George Allen & Unwin, 1942.

Yoshida, Yukari, and Joseph Kurstin. "Questions and Answers." *International Netsuke Society Journal* 19, no. 1 (Summer 1999), pp. 26–27.

——. "Questions and Answers." *International Netsuke Society Journal* 20, no. 1 (Spring 2000), p. 9.

SUGGESTIONS FOR FURTHER READING

The bibliography by Norman Sandfield listed in Section 2 above gives a full listing of Western books and articles on netsuke up to 1999. Of the many general works published over the last forty years or so, the recent studies by Patrizia Jirka-Schmidt (especially Volume 1) and Matthew Welch, both detailed in Section 3 above, are especially recommended. These works break significant new ground by attempting, like this catalogue, to set netsuke in the context of East Asian culture instead of Western collecting.

GLOSSARY

This short list is confined to words that occur frequently in the catalogue text but are not defined on each appearance.

amaryō Smooth-skinned rain dragon, in China traditionally said to be yellow, without horns, and similar to a sea horse

ashinaga Imaginary humanoid with long legs, often seen in the company of *tenaga*

bakemono Generic term for freakish imaginary beings and ghosts

baku Imaginary being of Chinese origin, with an elephant's trunk, rhinoceros's eyes, ox's tail, and tiger's feet

biwa Loquat or Japanese medlar, *Eribotrya japonica*

geta Traditional wooden clog with high supports

gohei Ritual staff with pendant paper strips used in the Shinto religion

hakutaku Imaginary being of Chinese origin, capable of human speech and typically with a human face, two horns, and several eyes and horns on either side of its body

himotōshi Channel drilled through a netsuke, allowing it to be threaded onto a carrying cord

hōgen The middle of three priestly ranks often awarded to Japanese artists

hokkyō The lowest of three priestly ranks often awarded to Japanese artists

hō-ō A Chinese fabulous bird that appears only during the reigns of virtuous monarchs

hossu Ritual whisk carried by Buddhist priests and monks

ijin "Different person" or "person of difference," a term used during the Edo period to describe foreign beings of all kinds

inrō Small container, usually lacquered, made up of several interlocking sections and sometimes intended for carrying medicines

kaō Cursive monogram used by Japanese artists

kappa Imaginary Japanese being, river-dwelling and fishy-smelling, with a depression in its head to hold water

kirin Imaginary Chinese being with a deer's body, a horse's hooves, an ox's tail, and a single horn on its head

manjū Flat circular netsuke

mokugyo Wooden gong used in Buddhist ritual

nue Nocturnal monster with a monkey's head, tiger's paws, the body of a badger or tiger, and a snake for a tail

obi Sash worn around the waist in traditional Japanese dress

ojime Bead for tightening the cord of an *inrō* or other item hanging from the *obi*

okimono An ornamental object with no practical function, usually of late Edo or Meiji period date

oni Small horned demon

rakan Disciple of the Buddha, typically depicted with noble, craggy features

rokurokubi Bakemono with an enormously long neck

Ryūsa Manjū netsuke with openwork carving

sashi Type of long netsuke that fits behind the wearer's *obi*

sennin Perfected, semidivine human being associated with the Chinese Daoist religion *shakudō* Blue-black patinated alloy of copper with a small quantity of gold

shibuichi Gray-green patinated alloy of copper with varying quantities of silver

shishi Lionlike imaginary creature of Chinese origin

shōjō Imaginary Japanese being, usually female, with a fondness for drinking sake (rice wine)

sōsho Cursive script

tanuki Brown and black raccoon dog about two feet long, similar to the European badger

tenaga Imaginary humanoid with long arms, often seen in the company of *ashinaga*

tengu Imaginary mountain-dwelling bird-deity with either a crow-like beak or a long nose

tonkotsu Rigid tobacco pouch

ukibori Special technique of low-relief carving, see catalogue number 187

umimatsu Type of marine fossilized wood

APPENDIX: *Japanese titles and artists' names*

1 |
印籠、根付、緒締
印籠銘：尾山作

2 |
印籠、根付、緒締
印籠銘：梶川文龍斎（花押）
根付銘：岡佳　緒締銘：（花押）

3 |
胴卵、煙管筒、鏡根付、緒締
金具銘：於東京音無川辺応需
貞幹生　鏡根付銘：盛寿　緒締銘：
一寿

4 |
胴卵、煙管筒、鏡根付、緒締
鏡根付銘：みつよし

5 |
仙人、雨龍、魚
無銘

6 |
漁師仙人
無銘

7 |
張果老仙人
無銘

8 |
鐵枴先生
無銘

9 |
鐵枴先生
無銘

10 |
一角仙人
銘：宜光（花押）

11 |
琴高仙人
無銘

12 |
琴高仙人
無銘

13 |
象に乗る老子
無銘

14 |
西王母仙人
無銘

15 |
刀を背負った仙人
無銘（吉村周山とされる）

16 |
候先生
銘：吉長

17 |
候先生
銘：民谷

18 |
候先生
銘：豊昌

19 |
候先生
銘：豊昌

20 |
候先生
銘：豊昌

21 |
陳楠仙人
銘：六拾二才豊昌（花押）

22 |
陳楠仙人
銘：正香

23 |
聖母子
銘：浅井翁依好藻水作
箱書：
聖母子像　木彫根付
浅井翁依好
想起禁制時代和様式
藻水刻　印：藻水

24 |
手長を背負った脚長
無銘

25 |
手長を背負った脚長
銘：菊川

26 |
鼓を持つ脚長
銘：舟月

27 |
鼓を持つ異人
銘：舟月

28 |
樹幹に抱きつく脚長（差根付）
無銘

29|
崑崙
無銘

30|
崑崙
銘：幻良斎

31|
女人魚
無銘

32|
男人魚
無銘

33|
女人魚を抱く蛸
銘：秀正

34|
女怪鳥（精衛とされる）
無銘

35|
水虎
無銘

36|
龍神
無銘（吉村周山とされる）

37|
曽祖母に乳を与える崔山南
銘：正廣

38|
高位の唐人(おそらく諸葛亮、又は
呉猛とされる
無銘

39|
関羽
無銘

40|
関羽
無銘

41|
関羽
銘：後釜

42|
関羽
無銘

43|
馬に乗る関羽
銘：珍元堂秀正

44|
唐子を持つ異人
無銘

45|
猿を持つ異人
無銘

46|
虎を持つ異人
無銘

47|
獅子を持つ異人
無銘

48|
獅子を持つ異人
無銘

49|
鶴を持つ異人（小刀根付）
無銘

50|
刀を背負った異人
銘：六甲

51|
唐人の商人
無銘

52|
壺を持つ清人
銘：如文

53|
韃靼人
無銘

54|
楽器を吹く異人
無銘

55|
唐子を抱える和蘭陀人
無銘

56|
鶏を抱える和蘭陀人
無銘

57|
楽器を持つ和蘭陀人
無銘

58|
野兎を背負った和蘭陀人
銘：正直

59|
鹿を背負った和蘭陀人
銘：正直

60|
天虞山神
無銘（河井頼武とされる）

61|
雨龍
無銘

62|
雨龍
無銘（おそらく谷斎とされる）

63|
怪鳥
無銘

64|
鉢を頭上に持ち上げる雨龍
無銘

65|
飛龍
無銘

66|
飛龍
無銘

67|
飛龍
無銘

68｜
飛龍
無銘

69｜
白澤
無銘

70｜
白澤
無銘

71｜
漆呉山神
無銘（吉村周山とされる）

72｜
漆呉山神
銘：一山

73｜
雲に乗る麒麟
銘：正直

74｜
麒麟
銘：友忠

75｜
鳴く麒麟
銘：友忠

76｜
鳴く麒麟
銘：友忠

77｜
鳴く麒麟
銘：友忠

78｜
鳴く麒麟
銘：友忠

79｜
鳴く麒麟
銘：吉正

80｜
鳴く麒麟
銘：吉正

81｜
麒麟
銘：一貫

82｜
麒麟
銘：豊昌

83｜
獏
銘：牙虫

84｜
獏
無銘

85｜
獏
無銘

86｜
獏
銘：夢亭

87｜
獏
無銘

88｜
獏
無銘

89｜
獏鸚鵡
銘：金玉、友

90｜
獏王
銘：玉民（花押）

91｜
怪獣
無銘

92｜
獅子の親子
銘：我楽

93｜
球に後足を乗せた飛猊
無銘

94｜
前足を嘗める獅子
無銘（花押）

95｜
頭を掻く獅子
無銘

96｜
狂獅子
銘：友忠

97｜
獅子の座像
銘：友忠

98｜
獅子の立像
無銘

99｜
獅子の座像
銘：豊昌

100｜
牡丹に獅子（柳左饅頭根付）
印：連

101｜
獅子の頭（差根付）
印：谷

102｜
亀に乗る河童
銘：正一

103｜
亀に乗る河童
銘：忠一

104｜
指を嘗める河童
銘：亮忠

105｜
魚を抱える河童
無銘

106｜
舌を出す河童（差根付）
印：谷

107
眠る猩々
銘：忠利

108
眠る猩々
銘：一雲

109
天狗の巣立ち
銘：頼竹

110
天狗の親子
銘：一虎

111
龍灯鬼
無銘（吉村周山とされる）

112
鍾馗と鬼
無銘

113
綱を持つ鬼
無銘

114
鍾馗の面を付けた鬼
銘：月生

115
鬼の念仏
銘：三小

116
鍾馗と鬼（饅頭根付）
銘：玉光斎守正（花押）

117
鍾馗と鬼
銘：東谷　印：楳立

118
雷神と風神
銘：正香

119
鯉を手に持つ恵比寿
無銘

120
驢馬に乗る布袋
無銘

121
水牛に乗る布袋
無銘

122
布袋と大黒の相撲
無銘

123
布袋と大黒の相撲
無銘

124
福禄寿の額に登る床屋
銘：雪斎刀

125
亀に姿を変えた福禄寿
銘：亀玉

126
孫悟空
銘：遊藻刀

127
獅子を持つ羅漢
無銘

128
達磨の幽霊
銘：奉真

129
払子を持つ達磨人形
銘：嘉永三年吉日安楽造之

130
仁王の腕相撲
銘：肥後大掾作

131
道成寺
印：雪川

132
羅漢
銘：玉真斎　印：定

133
化する傘
無銘

134
三つ目小僧
無銘

135
男に迫る見越し入道（山都）
銘：一虎

136
轆轤首
無銘

137
轆轤首
銘：舟月

138
髑髏、蛇、蛙、晒し首（置物）
銘：東京旭玉山作之

139
小野道風の姿を変えた蛙
銘：我楽

140
鵺
無銘（友忠とされる）

141
鵺を殺す猪の早太
銘：岡言

142
猪を殺す仁田忠常（四郎）
銘：岡言

143
大蛇を殺す漢高祖
銘：於兎満

144
牛の腹に隠れる鬼同丸（鬼童丸）
無銘

145
碁盤に乗る小栗判官
銘：一重

146｜
蛤の中の草紙洗小町
銘：秀翁斎秀正（花押）

147｜
関寺小町
無銘

148｜
文福茶釜
銘：光廣（花押）

149｜
舌切雀
印：空哉

150｜
新田義貞の晒し首
銘：大江春造

151｜
籠脱
無銘

152｜
曲芸師
銘：月生

153｜
鶴舞
銘：民谷

154｜
鶴舞
銘：舟月作

155｜
浪人の役を演ずる俳優
銘：五瀬岷江図（花押）

156｜
扇を持つ落語家
銘：豊昌

157｜
力持
銘：龍珪（花押）
石に「さし石百貫目」の記

158｜
卵を見る人
銘：舟月

159｜
猿回
無銘

160｜
おかめの仮面を背負った男
銘：三笑（花押）

161｜
力士
無銘

162｜
相撲を取る老人
無銘

163｜
相撲を取る川津三郎と俣野五郎
銘：正利刀

164｜
風呂あがり
銘：我楽

165｜
褌結
無銘

166｜
ひょっとこ顔の浴客
無銘

167｜
性器に赤ちゃん
無銘

168｜
遊女の役をするおかめ
無銘

169｜
盲人と犬
無銘

170｜
縁起屋
銘：為隆

171｜
草紙を被る小僧（喜多川歌麿
「当世子供六歌仙」より）
銘：涼

172｜
渡舟に乗る旅人
銘：玉藻　印：治

173｜
樹下の旅人
銘：藻水

174｜
玩具の虎（印根付）
印：谷斎

175｜
茶碗に茶筅
銘：光廣

176｜
箒
無銘

177｜
御物産
銘：東谷　印：楳立

178｜
化け物の木魚
印：谷

179｜
大黒占地茸
無銘

180｜
万年茸に乗る蝸牛
銘：東谷　印：楳立

181｜
月に朴の木（柳左饅頭根付）
印：普随

182｜
芋の葉に乗る蜈蚣
銘：石見州可愛河青陽堂文章女
彫刻于時天保丁酉春也

183｜
河骨の根に乗る蛙
銘：亮長

184｜
蛇、蝸牛、蛙の三踞み
銘：亮長

185｜
蝦蟇
銘：光廣

186｜
茸に乗る蜥蜴
銘：日東阿岐五鳳道人文化六年刀

187｜
蓮の葉に乗る蛙
銘：石州石河西青陽堂富春彫刻

188｜
蝸牛
銘：石見州可愛河青陽堂文章女
彫刻

189｜
蝙蝠と蜘蛛
無銘

190｜
亀
銘：光廣（花押）

191｜
雀蜂の巣
銘：豊昌

192｜
胡瓜に雀蜂
銘：一得斎

193｜
竹の節に乗る蜻蛉
銘：光廣

194｜
流木に乗る蟹
銘：青陽堂富春

195｜
馬に乗る蛸
無銘

196｜
海女を抱える甲烏賊
無銘

197｜
蛸と猿
銘：岷江（花押）

198｜
蛸に捕えられた猿
銘：友一

199｜
甲烏賊
銘：正勝

200｜
蛸
銘：寿玉

201｜
蛸壺に捕えられた蛸
印：楳立
蛸壺に「蛸壺やはかなき夢を
夏の月」の記

202｜
蛸（差根付）
印：谷

203｜
蛸（とんこつ）
銘：懐玉斎 印：正次

204｜
烏賊の親子
銘：松雲

205｜
鯰
銘：正民刀

206｜
白魚
銘：寿玉

207｜
白魚
銘：明恵

208｜
干物
銘：懐玉斎

209｜
干物
銘：公鳳斎

210｜
擂り鉢に魚の頭
銘：光廣（花押）

211｜
鉢に石鯛
銘：丁酉季冬光廣 印：逍

212｜
干鮭
銘：鉄斎刀（花押）

213｜
龍門の滝鯉
無銘

214｜
鸚鵡
無銘

215｜
羽を繕う鳳凰
無銘

216｜
松に鸚鵡
銘：草臣

217｜
松に輪頭鳥の親子
無銘

218｜
鴛
銘：正直

219｜
鳩
銘：青陽堂富春彫刻

220｜
鷲に捕えられた猿
銘：蘭亭

221｜
粟を啣る鶉
銘：光定

222｜
象の立像（印根付け）
無銘

223|
横たわる象
無銘（牙虫の形式）

224|
横たわる鹿
銘：我楽

225|
横たわる鹿
銘：岡友

226|
鳴く鹿
銘：岡友

227|
蟹を捕らえた狼
銘：友忠

228|
狼と髑髏
銘：友親

229|
猫の親子の座像
無銘（我楽とされる）

230|
後足を嘗める子猫
無銘

231|
横たわる猫
銘：正直

232|
鼠を捕らえた猫
銘：友忠

233|
猫の遊女
無銘

234|
蓮の葉に隠れる狸
銘：豊一

235|
狐踊
無銘

236|
狐の親子
無銘

237|
白蔵主
無銘

238|
月の輪熊
銘：懐玉斎正次

239|
十二支（柳左饅頭根付）
銘：正次

240|
尻尾を嘗める鼠
銘：正直

241|
眠る鼠
銘：正直

242|
横たわる鼠
銘：正直

243|
唐辛子を持つ鼠
無銘（正直とされる）

244|
尻尾を嘗める鼠
銘：岡佳

245|
横たわる牛の親子
銘：正直

246|
横たわる水牛
銘：光廣

247|
虎の親子
銘：牙虫

248|
後足を嘗める虎
無銘（我楽の形式）

249|
虎の親子
銘：友忠

250|
虎の親子
銘：友忠

251|
虎の座像
銘：正直

252|
身を屈める虎
銘：正直

253|
虎の座像
銘：白龍

254|
虎の座像
銘：秋山

255|
虎の立像
銘：秀正（花押）

256|
虎の座像
銘：岷江（花押）

257|
虎の立像
銘：音満

258|
虎
銘：豊昌

259|
毛繕いする野兎
銘：正直

260|
野兎と枇杷
銘：岡友

261|
身を屈める野兎
銘：岡友